F.W. Woolworth and the American Five and Dime

F.W. Woolworth and the American Five and Dime

A Social History

by JEAN MADDERN PITRONE

McFarland & Company, Inc., Publishers
Jefferson, North Carolina, and London

Library of Congress Cataloguing-in-Publication Data

Pitrone, Jean Maddern, 1920–
F.W. Woolworth and the American five and dime :
a social history / by Jean Maddern Pitrone.
p.   cm.
Includes bibliographical references and index.

ISBN 0-7864-1433-2 (illustrated case binding : 50# alkaline paper)

1. F.W. Woolworth Company—History.   I. Title: FW Woolworth
and the American five and dime.   II. Title.
HF5465.U64 W667   2003   381'12'0973—dc21   2002153996

British Library cataloguing data are available

Foreground cover image: Woolworth store, Public Square, Watertown, N.Y.
(author's postcard collection)
Background cover images: The Woolworth Building, New York City, N.Y., 1913 *(Art Today)*;
portrait painting of founder Frank Winfield Woolworth; and Ronald Martin, Robert Patterson,
and Mark Martin in a sit-in at an F.W. Woolworth luncheon counter,
Greensboro, N.C., 1960 *(Library of Congress)*

Manufactured in the United States of America

McFarland & Company, Inc., Publishers
Box 611, Jefferson, North Carolina 28640
www.mcfarlandpub.com

To my daughter, Julie Anne Williamson,
for her invaluable and continuing help
with photos and the collecting of memorabilia;

to John Compton, former Woolworth employee,
for assistance from his fine collection
of Woolworth information and photos;

and to Lori Hawkins, Joyce Hawkins, Jane Rossi and Janet Kasic
for their unstinting help along the way.

Contents

Preface

For more than a century, Americans shopped at Woolworth's Five and Tens. These stores were as American as apple pie, baseball and Norman Rockwell paintings. The struggles of Frank Winston Woolworth, a poor farmer's son who borrowed enough money to set up his first rudimentary store ("The Great Five Cent Store," which promptly failed) are typical of the Horatio Alger and rags-to-riches stories in which a protagonist of humble background rises, if not always to fortune, at least to great achievement.

Woolworth Five and Tens proliferated quickly and became strongly identified as the epitome of Americana. This image positioned them as a prime target for those who advocated societal changes: better working conditions, child labor restrictions, Civil Rights and other causes. I began working on this book to bring into focus these aspects of the many problems that the Woolworth Company faced in wartime, economic depression, and political upheaval. At the same time, I was fascinated with the story of Frank W. Woolworth, his fortune and his family.

As happens in many "new money" families of great wealth, tragedies abounded for the Woolworths. While the family patriarch quickly learned to enjoy his multi-millions, his loyal wife began to crumble when she could not adapt to living in mansions where servants took her place as caretaker for her husband, children and home. Most of the Woolworth descendants lived idle and unfulfilled lives of conspicuous consumption and broken marriages. Some of them found relief only in suicide.

Multi-millionaire F. W. Woolworth died in 1919, just before the dawning of the prosperous 1920s and at a time when his forty-year-old stores were rapidly expanding. He never had to cope with the Great Depression of the 1930s and its series of strikes, including the first sit-down strike ever to bring the business of a department store to a halt. The store was Woolworth's in Detroit, and this precedent-setting strike was followed by others at Woolworth stores in New York City.

The sit-down strikes were only the beginning of a series of problems including ongoing disputes between the Woolworth Company and the newly created National Labor Relations Board; harassment by Nazis in Germany, who accused Woolworth's of being a Jewish-owned enterprise and closed down the stores; bombings of stores by political dissidents; and, with the arrival of the 1960s, sit-ins at Woolworth's lunch counters in the south. The first such sit-in, in Greensboro, North Carolina, set off an entirely new and contagious method of protest at bus stations and other build-ings containing lunch counters that had been reserved solely for white customers.

My search for Woolworth materials took me, first, to Watertown, New York, where I was given access to the Historical Department and the Genealogical Department of the Flower Memorial Library; then to the Jefferson County Historical Society Museum in Watertown. I owe a very special thank you to David L. Poremba, manager of the wonderful Burton Historical Collection of the Detroit Public Library, who was extremely helpful in searching out useful materials both in Burton and in the Arts and Entertainment section of the library. Another thank you must go to Thomas Featherstone, Audio Visual Archivist, Walter P. Reuther Library, Wayne State University. A thank you, also, to John Compton, long-time manager of Woolworth stores, who has come to my aid with phone calls and mailings from his personal collection of Woolworth materials.

1

The Worst Time of His Life

"Meet you at the dime store," we'd say to our teenage girl friends. Located at a busy corner of Main Street in our little upper–Michigan mining town, the red-fronted "dime store" (Woolworth's) was a favorite meeting place. There I could browse among the counters while waiting for my friends and wishing I had enough money in my pocket to buy a thin little tube of orange Tangee lipstick and a pancake-type makeup called Hide-It. Those of us who did not suffer the embarrassments of acne liked to use Hide-It, nonetheless, to match the very tan complexions (tan even in mid-winter of upper–Michigan's notoriously cold, snowy and long-lasting frigid season) of those who smeared the makeup on thickly to cover facial blemishes.

The dime store reigned grandly over the heart of our prime two-block shopping area fronting on Main Street. For expanded shopping, we could move on to the "Penny Store" (as the townspeople called JCPenney) and, a little more than a decade later, to the recently opened Newberry variety store that was challenging Woolworth's for supremacy.

Young lads customarily hung out on Main, lolling against the pool-hall facade and leaving oily imprints (from Brilliantine bought at Woolworth's and slicked onto their hair for a glistening effect) on the pool-hall windows. Older balding men were thwarted in their inclinations to lean, half sitting, in the window bases of the building at the corner of Main and Cleveland Avenue because, protruding from the stone bases, were iron barbs (an inch long and installed there in 1884 by orders of the builder so "there won't be any room for loafers to sit").[1] Instead, the "loafers"— hands clasped behind their backs and eyes following pretty females as they moved in and out of the leased dime store quarters— stood, clustered together, on the corner curbing.

Political correctness was totally unknown in those days. Ethnic jokes were the preferred humor in our little town. Rarely did they arouse anger. Nicknames were attached to most males, usually without rancor. To paraphrase Walter Cronkite, that's the way it was. Pride could be taken in names such as "Ace" or "Speed," attached to good athletes; less pride, surely, in the names "Fats" or "Skinny." "Blackie" for a dark-complexioned fellow. "Hollywood Jim" for a guy who dressed in a snazzy fashion. "Gimpy Joe" for a lame man.

F. W. (Frank Winfield) Woolworth, the dime store magnate, apparently never really acquired a lasting nickname. But when the multi-millionaire died suddenly in 1919, a bold-faced *New York Times* newspaper caption exposed the secret, senile frailties of his shy, withdrawn widow, Jennie Woolworth, who always had chosen to avoid publicity. "DEMENTED WIFE GETS ALL,"[2] the caption read. There was no intentional cruelty in it. The political niceties of euphemisms simply had not yet become public policy.

At the death of the chief of the Woolworth empire, his 1,081 stores did not languish. Despite the hands-on leadership that Frank Winfield Woolworth had provided for his business affairs through the years, he also had built up a reliable board of directors consisting of lifelong friends and relatives ("my boys," he called them) who could be trusted to continue his policies. And the "Five and Tens" red awnings continued to front an increasing number of Woolworth stores on the Main Streets of America. ("Our goal is to have a Woolworth store in every town of 10,000 or more inhabitants," F.W. stated confidently.[3])

In our town (population 10,000) my mother liked to have my dad wrestle our second-hand Buick into a Main Street parking spot (somewhere between the dime store and the penny store) on busy Saturday nights. From one of those choice spots she could observe friends and neighbors crowding the sidewalks as they shopped.

We bought the sheet music for "I Found a Million Dollar Baby in the Five-and-Ten-Cent Store" and played it on our upright piano where a fringed paisley scarf was carefully arranged on top to dip down in just the right sort of swag for dramatic effect. My mom played the catchy melody over and over. The Woolworth stores had become an American icon — and more. By 1954, considered a peak year for the Woolworth Company, there would be 2,850 of its five and tens around the world.[4]

During his lifetime, Frank W. Woolworth had learned to love Main Street, USA, because he made the discovery, in his earliest experimentations with setting up his stores, that the enterprises worked out better when located on bustling streets such as Main. This was fine with Frank because the further he was removed from the isolation of rural areas, such as the farm on which the Woolworth family lived during Frank's youth, the better he liked it.

Born on April 13, 1852, at his grandfather's farm on which his father worked near the tiny village of Rodman, New York,[5] the child Frank was taken to the nearby Great Bend area (close to the Canadian border) by his parents, John and Fanny Woolworth, when the grandfather sold his farm in 1859. If, in later years, young Frank could remember little of the birth of his only brother in 1856, he soon would be old enough, at almost seven years, to have clear recollections of his family moving to Great Bend — of riding in a wagon with[6] high sides as his father lightly slapped the reins over the horse's rump to encourage the animal to trot briskly along the road leading to the newly mortgaged farmhouse and acreage that John and Fanny recently had acquired.

The boy would remember, too, the September morning when his mother walked with him to the little limestone Great Bend district schoolhouse, a half-mile down the dusty road. After that first day, he walked alone until his brother also was old enough to begin mastering the "three R's" — reading, writing, and 'rithmetic.[7]

By this time, 10-year-old Frank was old enough to be responsible for an ever-growing number of farm chores, so his attendance at school was restricted to the winter months. There was simply too much to be done on a farm in the spring and fall to allow for schooling. In later years, he would clearly remember being roused, groaning, from his bed in the very early morning hours to go out to the barn and help with the milking and afterwards to shovel manure from the horse's stall or to take care of one of the other myriad tasks that awaited him.

His father, the slow-spoken, taciturn John Hubbell Woolworth, who worked "from sunup till sundown" in the tradition of his small-farmer English ancestors, seemed to the boy to be satisfied with his lot in life. At least, he was not a complainer as long as his milk cows were healthy, his potato crop was a plentiful one, and he was able to sell the wood that he cut from his own timberlands so that

Frank Winfield Woolworth as a young man. (Courtesy of Detroit Public Library)

he could look forward to paying off the farm mortgage before he died. And yet, young Frank surmised that his Woolworth ancestors surely must have had dreams (similar to his own) of improving their lives when they left England as early as 1665 and sailed for New England. On arrival, they settled in the Massachusetts area and set up their own little farms. Frank's great-great grandfather, Phineas Woolworth, became a Revolutionary War soldier who lost his right arm in the service of his country.[8] With an influx of immigrants from various nations into Massachusetts and because of increasing industrialization of the area, Frank Winfield Woolworth's paternal grandfather, Jasper, was among the many Yankees who moved westward. Jasper had settled on acreage near the village of Rodman in northern New York, where fertile land could be bought cheaply, and retained his independence as a farmer. Some of the westward-shifting Yankees, more daring perhaps, went farther — to more rugged Illinois or Ohio territories to set up homesteads. Few, if any, pushed on west of the Mississippi into what was known only as the "great American desert" until after the Civil War.[9]

"Farmers," President Thomas Jefferson stated, "are the true representatives of the great American interest and are alone to be relied upon for expressing the proper American sentiments."[10] Neither Jasper nor his son, John Woolworth, had the ability to speak eloquently as had Jefferson, but both knew that they were secure in their individuality — that their free and independent spirits would have been crushed had they remained in Massachusetts, taken work in the mills at low wages and long hours, and lived in one of the grubby, over-crowded towns that were springing up there.

John expected that first-born son Frank and the boy's younger brother would follow Woolworth family traditions. Someday his farm would be free of mortgage payments and could be passed on to his boys, both of whom had to be trained for the hard work demanded of independent farmers. Even though the older son was not a strong child (the father must have been bewildered by Frank's paleness and susceptibility to sniffles), John expected the boy to lead the way for his brother to follow — pitching hay up to the loft, digging potatoes, rounding up the cows, and always, everlastingly it seemed to Frank, shoveling manure.

To pamper a sickly child would be tantamount to fostering a weakling, unfit for the hard labor required of a farmer, unable to wrest his livelihood from the soil. And the thought of committing the boy to a life of working in a mill, without the healing benefits of sunlight and fresh air, had to have been unthinkable to the father.

Young Frank did not appreciate the benefits of fresh air and sunlight or the manual labor that was strengthening his muscles. He hated the blisters and calluses on his hands; he hated the shovels, the pitchforks, rakes, spades and hoes. Hated going barefoot, sometimes in cold weather, to save wear and tear on boots that absolutely had to last as long as possible before a new pair could be bought.

"My youth," he would tell a reporter in 1911, "was the worst time of my life."[11] Still, there were rare, lighter moments for the boy. Some of these occurred when a peddler, who might be on foot with a pack on his back or might travel by horse and buggy from one farmhouse to another, arrived at the Woolworths' home. Frank was fascinated by the tin pots and pans and perfumed soaps and gewgaws that emerged from the peddler's pack. But Fanny Woolworth, eminently practical and mindful of Methodist strict decrees against vanity, surely was not tempted by the colorful gewgaws. Instead, her son would remember her trading old iron and brass, produce from her garden, and even rags for a new tin basin, perhaps, or a tea kettle from the peddler's pack.

When his father was otherwise occupied, possibly hitching the horse to the wagon to deliver a load of firewood to a buyer, Frank liked to set up a board for a counter and play store with his brother.[12] The boy was fascinated, too, by his mother's piano. Guided by Fanny, he would pick out tunes on the instrument. Likely they were tunes to some of their favorite Methodist hymns, sung by the congregation, including the Woolworths, at Sunday morning services. "Abide With Me." "The Old Rugged Cross."

Fanny, whose parents — the Scotch-Irish McBriers — had come from Ulster to America in 1827, was a woman of strong convictions.[13] Unlike her reticent husband, she was quick to express her opinions, especially so when she talked about the abolitionist movement and the right of every man and woman, black or white, to be free. She had named her second son Charles Sumner Woolworth in tribute to the Massachusetts senator (Charles Sumner) who gave "a violent speech" in Washington, D.C., "on the 'Crime against Kansas'," wrote James Truslow Adams, and was thereupon "beaten into insensibility by Preston Brooks of South Carolina."[14] The passionate abolitionist speech and the resulting savage beating had taken place in 1854, two years before the Woolworths' younger son was born. The boy always used his second name, Sumner, and was known to the family and close friends as "Sum."

It can only be surmised how much Fanny Woolworth's ardently expressed abolitionist views could have influenced the future behavior of her son Frank had he lived

to see his Woolworth chain of stores snared in the Civil Rights struggles of the tur-
bulent 1960s. But Fanny's sons were too young to become Union soldiers when the
Civil War began in 1861, and she was spared the pain of seeing either Frank or Sum
go off to fight for the cause in which she so firmly believed. Still, boys as young as
14 — some even younger — went along with the armies as drummer boys. And many
poor farm boys, older than Frank Woolworth, were paid a small amount of money
to serve in the army in place of wealthier fellows in the North who chose not to serve.

At age 16, when he finished his schooling in Great Bend, Frank did not look forward to a lifetime of working on his father's farm, although he knew John Woolworth expected him to do exactly that; he knew, too, that his father needed the help.
Once again, Fanny Woolworth proved her independence of spirit when she declared
that she'd been putting away a few pennies and nickels for a period of time and, well
aware that her son wanted to work in a store, she now had enough savings to pay for
the boy to take some commercial classes in nearby Watertown,[15] a flourishing town
edged by the Adirondacks, with abundant water power from the Black River.

The lanky, blond-haired Frank completed a semester of bookkeeping in Watertown; then, with high hopes, he looked for a job in a store. His hopes lagged and
died as, he would say later, when Watertown merchants, one after the other, told
him he was a "greenhorn" and they needed someone with experience. So it was back
to milking cows and pitching hay with Sum at his side. Still, dreams die hard. Soon,
Frank took on occasional jobs at neighboring farms — a day's work here and a day's
work there — to collect a little cash for his labors. By his twenty-first birthday, he had
accumulated $50 from the extra farm work, and had gained a little clerical experi-
ence by working for two winter seasons, without payment, at a small grocery store
in Great Bend.

With his $50 stake, he returned to Watertown to apply for a job at a dry-goods
store where he'd been told there was an opening. He got the job, without pay, at the
Corner Store — so-called because it was located on a prime corner overlooking Watertown's Public Square. The job would be an apprenticeship, a learning experience, he
was told by the man who hired him, William H. Moore of Augsbury & Moore. Still,
Frank was grateful to Mr. Moore for giving him the opportunity to work and learn,
even though he worried about his cash dwindling away when he was also told that
appearances were important and he'd need a new shirt, collar and tie. For now though,
he was put right to work on the day he was hired, "unpacking dry goods boxes on
the sidewalk," Frank would recall.[16]

He found a place to live with a Mrs. Kinney, board and room for $3.50 a week.
The next morning, a blustery February day in 1873, he came to work riding on a load
of logs that his father was delivering to Watertown. The following morning he had
to rise from his bed at Mrs. Kinney's and begin work very early to take care of his
daily chores at the store, where he was expected to sweep wet sawdust from the back
of the building to the front door, wash the windows, straighten the stock and dust
the counters before anyone else arrived. After a full day of delivering packages, running errands, cleaning spittoons and keeping the shelves and their contents in perfect order, he returned to his boarding house in the February darkness of evening
with the realization that his hours were, indeed, very similar to those of farmers. He

The Watertown, New York, Public Square pictured around the time young Frank Woolworth served as an unpaid store apprentice. (Jefferson County Historical Society)

could console himself, however, with the thought that the work was much tidier. To young Frank, even cleaning spittoons was preferable to shoveling manure.

Mrs. Kinney was a motherly person who kept the boy's supper in the warming oven when he worked late. Frank, in turn, was very kind to the invalid Kinney daughter, Frances. On weekends (likely late on Saturday until Sunday evening) Frank often went home to the Woolworth farm and returned with provisions that he gave to his landlady.[17] So, things worked out well at the boarding house for three months until Frank began to worry about his carefully hoarded cash running low and realized that he must talk to Mr. Moore about payment.

Evidently Moore was satisfied with Frank's work because he agreed to begin paying his employee. "Enough to cover my board," Frank would say in later years.[18] Mrs. Kinney, owner of the boarding house, was not the only motherly person to take an interest in Frank. Mrs. A. C. Coons, Moore's senior clerk, also became a mentor to the new employee, going out of her way to instruct the eager young man in his duties. At this point, though, Frank was not expected to wait on customers except during the noon hour if everyone else had gone home for noontime dinner.

At his first opportunity (outside the noon hour) to wait on a customer at the dry-goods counter, the event turned into a near disaster when the customer, who had come into town from a tiny village on the other side of Great Bend, walked into the store and asked for "the young clerk." Flattered by the attention, the "young clerk" listened to his customer's instructions as the man said he wanted to buy calico yardage for a dress for his wife. Frank took a bolt of calico from a shelf and began to unroll the material and to measure off the requested ten yards. Somehow, the bolt flipped away from him and yard after yard of cloth ballooned high on the counter and swelled to the floor. By this time, Mr. Moore, who had returned from his dinner and didn't miss much from his raised seat and desk at the back of the store where he could survey workers, shouted at the clerk and hurried up front to retrieve the excess yardage from the floor and to bring order out of chaos.[19]

It was a deflating experience for Frank, but he continued working 12-hour, sometimes 14-hour, days for Moore until after a couple of years he was earning one dollar a day. When a dry-goods competitor offered him $10 a week, Frank switched jobs. He could save his boarding-house expenses because his new boss wanted him to sleep in the basement of the store and guard the place against thieves.[20]

After a short while, the boss, while voicing no complaints about the guard job, said he was not satisfied with his employee's salesmanship. He cut the young man's pay to eight dollars, explaining that Frank was not sufficiently enterprising in pressing the employer's wares on a reluctant or undecided customer.[21]

The cut in pay and the criticism must have been like stabs of a knife to the ambitious Frank, who was willing to work hard as long as he felt he was advancing and saving a little money. But to go backwards— he surely felt his ambition, his strength, his dreams draining away from him.

He had worked at his latest job less than a year when he told his boss he could work no longer, that he was sick. The boss nodded. He had noticed the pallid complexion, the bad cold that hung on and on. It was true; Frank was sick. His health had failed after less than four years of hard work in Watertown. A younger fellow, Carson Peck, took over the job that Frank left. Overwhelmed by discouragement, Frank returned to the only place he could go— back to the Great Bend farm and the waiting chores that he had hated so much.[22]

2

"The Great Five" Acquires a Family

In later years after Frank had become a multi-millionaire, he talked freely about his boyhood experiences, the farm and his struggles to go into business for himself, but rarely mentioned the months he spent at his parents' farmhouse, confined to bed much of the time after he left Watertown. "His health broke," his former employer had said to explain Frank's absence from the store. But the illness, or weakness, appeared to have been rooted in a depression caused by discouragement and disappointment.

In the 1870s, this type of illness was referred to as "nervous exhaustion" if it was referred to at all. For the most part a breakdown of this sort was kept secret, especially in the case of an ailing man; if the sufferer was a woman, the illness might be termed "a case of the vapors." But if possible, a male victim of depression remained almost as secluded as were mentally or physically defective children who, in that era, often were concealed in locked rooms of their parents' homes.

Fanny Woolworth waited on her bedridden son as much as she could, but she also had to help her husband and son Sumner with farm chores. According to a Woolworth scrapbook at the historical archives of the Flower Memorial Library, Fanny was surprised when a blonde, blue-eyed young lady appeared at the door of the farmhouse one day and politely asked if she might visit Frank.[1] Fanny soon learned that the visitor, Jennie Creighton, had left her father's home in Ontario, Canada, a couple of years earlier to cross the border into Watertown where she rented a room from a cousin living there. She hoped to earn a better living by working as a seamstress in Watertown, and had met Frank when she went into the dry-goods store for a spool of thread and other sewing supplies. The two had talked, and talked again on other occasions when Jennie came into the store, although Frank kept a wary eye on Mr. Moore seated at his desk on the elevated platform. He knew that Mr. Moore did not approve of clerks wasting time chatting with pretty young ladies.

Fanny learned more about Jennie Creighton from her son after the visitor left and, later, according to a scrapbook, was inspired to ask the girl if she would consider moving in with the Woolworths to take care of Frank. There could be no salary paid; just free room and board. The shy, introverted Jennie, who, nonetheless, had mustered the courage to find someone to give her a ride via horse and wagon out to the Woolworth farm, had found, by this time, that the seamstress work that came to her in Watertown was sporadic. Moving to the Woolworth farmhouse would solve her financial problems, at least temporarily. She accepted Fanny's offer.[2] She had no idea that the move would solve her financial problems permanently in the not-too-distant future.

It was not long before Frank Woolworth had fallen deeply in love with pretty Jennie Creighton. Jennie — so sympathetic and patient when he complained of the slightest discomfort; so soothing, her hands soft and tender as she brought him a pitcher of warm water from the cook-stove reservoir and gave him a soapy washcloth and a towel; Jennie — so sweetly encouraging when she coaxed him to eat a little more after he had pushed away his food.

Frank, 24, and Jennie, 23, were married at the farmhouse in June 1876.[3] In his book *The Woolworths*, James Brough informs readers that Jennie's father turned over a little house with six acres, in Great Bend, to the young couple. Frank signed a $300 note and the rest was covered by a bank mortgage.[4]

Frank put up with the payments and the work on the very small farm — raising chickens, a garden, and potatoes—for approximately one year when William Moore, his first Watertown employer, got in touch with him and offered him a $10-dollar-a-week job as senior clerk at his store. Nothing suited Frank better than shaking the soil of the little farm from his feet. Unfortunately he could not simply abandon the place. Jennie had to stay on and do the best she could with farm chores while Frank boarded again with Mrs. Kinney and visited his uncomplaining wife every other weekend from Saturday night through Sunday.[5]

Things changed, though, when Jennie found out she was pregnant. They leased the farm to a tenant and the couple moved into a small extension built onto a Franklin Street house in Watertown. (The extension has been referred to as a "wing" but actually was too small to fit the usual description of a wing.) The young Woolworths were renting three tiny rooms there when, during the blustery cold of a Watertown February, Frank learned that his mother was very ill. He rented a horse and sleigh and he and Jennie set out for Great Bend. Fanny Woolworth died shortly after their arrival and was laid to rest in Sunnyside Cemetery.[6]

Soon after Fanny's death, Sumner announced his intention to leave the farm and go to Watertown, hoping to get work, also, at Moore's store — now known as Moore & Smith.[7] Although another young fellow, Fred Kirby, was already employed by Moore to take care of errands and deliveries, as well as cleaning chores, Kirby moved up a notch and Sumner Woolworth took over the sweeping of floors and tending the fires. Left alone at the Great Bend farm, the widower John Woolworth would soon find it necessary to hire a woman as housekeeper to keep the farmhouse functioning.

Winter moved into spring when, to Frank's dismay, his weekly salary was cut from $10.00 to $8.50[8] because, as William Moore carefully explained, his store was undergoing difficult times. Sales had slowed and were not recovering in those early months of 1878. The salary cut disheartened Frank. The baby was expected in July and he and Jennie had been building a bank account by scrimping so that they could save a small amount of money from each of his pay envelopes. Now, the reduced salary would make it nearly impossible to save anything at all.

Soon after the birth of Helena (called "Lena" by her parents), Jennie came in to help out at the store on Saturday evenings and to earn a little extra cash, bringing the baby with her.[9] She set the infant in a packing box lined with blankets, and concealed the box under the counter while she waited on customers, the Flower Memorial Library Woolworth scrapbook reveals.

By this time, Frank was turning over another idea in his mind. A traveling salesman who frequently visited the dry-goods store had told Frank about several stores in Michigan that had set up five-cent counters (everything selling for a nickel) and were doing well with them. Frank talked excitedly to his employer, Moore, trying to convince the older man to allow him to try out a similar counter.[10] When Moore went on a buying trip, he returned with a hundred dollars' worth of pins, pens and tin pans plus an assortment of other goods, including a variety of brightly colored jewelry.

Frank set out the items on a long table covered with a red cloth, and attached a sign reading "Any Article 5c." By the end of the day, every five-cent bargain had been sold and Moore quickly sent a second order for the same type of goods to his supplier.

The success of the five-cent counter fired Frank with a desire to set up his own store selling five-cent articles. The profit on each item was small, true, but the secret of success, he felt, was in selling large numbers of each article to make a tidy total profit. He talked to William Moore and persuaded his employer to give him $300 credit in stock,[11] then boarded a train to Utica where he planned to find a site to rent for his own five-cent store.

Paying rent would be a problem for him at this point, so when he found a site that rented for $30 a month, he made his decision as soon as he talked the owner of the building into waiting until the end of the month to collect the rent. The Utica store (with 13-feet frontage on Bleeker Street) opened late in February 1879 as "The Great Five-Cent Store."[12] Frank was elated when, after the first customer bought a tin fire-shovel, sales of his five-cent items continued to be consistent enough, if not exactly brisk, to offer hope that business would improve as word-of-mouth publicity spread.

By May, he had to concede that the only thing he had gained in Utica was some experience as a storeowner and a very small profit after expenses and repaying Moore. He worried about Jennie and the baby and how Jennie would continue to pay her rent and bills at the tiny house in Watertown if he remained in Utica, with little hope of improved sales. He made his decision to return home, sent the remainder of his stock to Watertown and, with his account books in his suitcase, boarded a train, planning to do a better study of possible cities and store-sites before repeating his experiment.

"Wrong location," Frank explained the failure of his store to Jennie. It took him a month to decide that Lancaster, Pennsylvania, could be a wise choice for his next store. Again, he asked Moore for additional credit in stock and boarded a train for Lancaster to select a site. He knew that the population of the prosperous Pennsylvania town was made up largely of old Anglo-Saxon stock and Germans, or "Pennsylvania Dutch," farming people. In Lancaster, he looked forward to dealing with people very much like himself—thrifty, conservative, and eager for a bargain.[13] His window displays would lure customers, he thought, to shop at "The Great Five-Cent Store" he planned to open.

Frank stayed at a Lancaster boarding house where there were several other young boarders, including Robert E. Diefenderfer.[14] Both Frank and Diefenderfer were ambitious fellows (Diefenderfer would, in later life, become a congressman) but Frank talked very little about his plans for a store; in fact, he looked worried. When the landlady asked him what was the matter, Frank replied: "If I had an additional $200 my fortune would be made."

There must have been something about young Woolworth's attitude that impressed the landlady. According to Diefenderfer, she offered to lend Frank the money he needed.[15] He soon found a site not much bigger (14 feet of frontage and 35 feet in depth) than the site of the failed store in Utica. The North Queen Street building was old and the show windows not as large as he would have liked, but he could put up with those disadvantages. The furnishings—display tables and shelving—cost him less than $20.00.

He opened his business ("The Great Five Cent Store") on June 21—only a month after the Utica store had closed and as soon as the stock arrived from Watertown. For the rest of the stock, Frank had watched for an excursion fare to Philadelphia and then had gone by train to that larger city to select more supplies with money supplied by his landlady.

The Saturday of the opening was a busy day, which became even busier that evening as farming families did their shopping. Frank had as many as seven quickly recruited clerks working in the store on that Saturday, and was elated when he found that 30 percent of the stock was sold by closing time. Some of the fellows at his boarding house began to call him "The Great Five," but Frank remained unruffled by the teasing.[16] He had no time to think about trifling matters. He was already planning another store in Harrisburg, Pennsylvania.

He rented a small house in Lancaster and sent for Jennie and the baby to come, urging his brother Sum to come also.[17] Jennie could supervise the Lancaster store while he and Sum went on to Harrisburg, after which Sum could manage the proposed Harrisburg store. Things were moving along according to plan, and the little Harrisburg store opened on July 19, not quite one month after the Lancaster opening. They couldn't expect to get rich on the meager profits from selling five-cent merchandise in just one store, he explained to Jennie, but they might get rich by opening a number of stores in different cities, selling the same kinds of merchandise. The more stores he had, the more clout he would have in bargaining with suppliers for lower prices.

The payroll at the Harrisburg store totaled $11 a week. Cash receipts at the end of the first Saturday night of business were $85.41. Not too bad, Frank thought. The trouble was that the receipts went downhill after that first Saturday. Frank learned, then, not to waste time with false hopes or regrets. Facts were facts, and wishful thinking would not change them. He closed the Harrisburg store and moved the

This was Frank Woolworth's first successful, but primitive, store. It opened in the summer of 1879 in Lancaster, Pennsylvania. (John Compton Collection)

stock to York, Pennsylvania, where he and Sum opened another store in March 1880, with Sumner as partner-manager. The York store closed after three months with a profit of only $36.00. A dejected Sumner returned to the still thriving Lancaster store to help out there, temporarily.[18]

There was little doubt that Frank felt something like an old-time peddler, moving his tin-whistle goods around from one place to another. Still, the Lancaster store was doing nicely and he was certain there had to be other cities where "The Great Five Cent Store" could succeed as well.

He soon sent Sumner to the industrial town of Scranton, Pennsylvania, to make another try for success. By this time, they were calling the businesses "5 and 10 Cent Stores" after the Lancaster store had begun successfully to sell ten-cent articles. The Scranton store did well and, in 1883, the younger brother bought Frank's interest and became sole owner.[19]

This Scranton, Pennsylvania, "Woolworth Bro's." store opened November 6, 1880, advertising the "Great Five Cent Store" in front. The younger brother, Charles Sumner Woolworth, became the sole owner of this store in 1883. (John Crompton Collection)

In that same year, Frank and Jennie's second daughter, Edna, was born.[20] As his family expanded, Frank pushed harder for expansion of his stores. He began making plans for a store in Wilkes-Barre, Pennsylvania, and got in touch with Fred Kirby — the young fellow who had been working for William Moore in Watertown when Sumner Woolworth had started to work in the same Watertown store. Would Kirby like to come to Wilkes-Barre and manage a "Five and Ten" that Frank was going to open in that city, Frank wanted to know. If Kirby didn't want to do it, Frank had a list of suitable prospects — young fellows who were relatives or friends (all from within the Jefferson County, New York, area) who, Frank knew, were dependable and industrious workers.[21] But as Frank had anticipated, Kirby definitely wanted to take on the assignment. The store in Wilkes-Barre was opened and Kirby officiated as manager and later as partner-manager. At that point, it is likely that Fred Kirby never imagined that, within the next 24 years, he would control a chain of 96 Five and Tens.

With the Wilkes-Barre store flourishing, Frank learned that William Moore's store in Watertown was facing bankruptcy. Frank took action immediately; he provided Moore with a loan to straighten out his financial affairs and then converted

Seymour Knox (left) and cousin Frank Woolworth stand in front of a Woolworth & Knox store they opened October 13, 1888, in Buffalo, New York. (John Compton Collection)

the store into another Woolworth enterprise. Arranging for Moore to continue as owner of the store, Frank took over only the buying operations. His wholesale buying expanded as he established two more stores; one was in Easton, Pennsylvania, and then he moved on into Elmira, New York.

Frank's next recruit from Jefferson County was a cousin, Seymour Knox. The two went into partnership and opened a Woolworth & Knox store in Reading, Pennsylvania, in 1884.[22] This venture turned out to be an unlucky one from its beginning. Frank came into the store one day and found Knox crying, with a letter in his hand. The letter, with $40 inside, was from his mother. Frank must have given his younger cousin a pep talk, likely reminding him of his own misadventures with some of his failing stores, because the two agreed to close the Reading store and move on to a new location in Erie, Pennsylvania. Location was everything, Frank reminded his cousin. In Erie, they had a very successful opening day and the continuing profits from the Erie store would impel Knox to expand his operations until, in 1911, he would control 112 Five and Tens.[23]

Frank imported still another younger friend from Watertown in 1888, when he invited Carson Peck (the young fellow who had taken Frank's place when Frank had become ill in Watertown and returned to the farm) to become a partner-manager in one of the Woolworth enterprises by managing another new store Frank wanted to open.[24] Despite the earlier failure of a Woolworth store in Utica, Frank still felt it would be possible to succeed with a Five and Ten in that city. He felt comfortable with Carson Peck managing the Utica store because he liked to work with young men

The Woolworth pioneers posed for this photograph at the 1888 group meeting in the back yard of Frank Woolworth's Brooklyn home. Standing, left to right: S.H. Knox, B.W. Gage, C.S. Woolworth, F.M. Kirby, A.H. Satterthwait, Oscar Woolworth and W.D. Rock. Seated: H.H. Hesslet, F.W. Woolworth, Mary A. Creighton and W.H. Moore. (Courtesy of Detroit Public Library)

who had backgrounds similar to his own. All were farm "boys," accustomed to the rigors of agricultural life; none had extensive educations but were honest fellows and quick learners (as Frank had evaluated them) who were eager to put in long hours and hard work to advance themselves in the competitive retail business. Peck had another important asset; Frank had noticed how quick and accurate the fellow was with figures. And, as this second try to set up a store in Utica became successful under Peck's management, the Utica establishment took its place in the burgeoning chain of Woolworth stores as Frank did the mass buying for the chain, paying cash for all his purchases.

By 1889, with new stores in Pennsylvania, New Jersey, New York, Delaware and Connecticut, he had opened two more stores in Syracuse and Poughkeepsie, New York, and hired his first female managers.[25] Mrs. Coons (his former mentor from Watertown) was to manage the Syracuse store; his wife's sister, Mary Ann Creighton (who was as outgoing as Jennie Woolworth was timorous) was to manage the store at Poughkeepsie.

By this time, Frank had determined that he wanted no more partner-managers for his stores. His former choices of partner-managers and his new and ongoing choices of managers (not partners) would evolve into his frequently expressed "my boys" philosophy. "I pick out boys of the right sort," F. W. Woolworth would expound to a reporter in 1911, by which time his empire consisted of 286 stores and 9,000 employees. "I guess I have the knack of knowing the right sort of man when I see him."[26]

Frank's loyalty, not only to William Moore but also to all the people who had befriended him as a youth, was proved again (as his old friend, Diefenderfer, would tell the story, later, to an audience) when Frank discovered that his former landlady in Pennsylvania, who had loaned him $200 in his time of need (and had been repaid) became impoverished in her late years. Frank Woolworth, Diefenderfer said (and his statements were picked up by a reporter on May 13,1913), provided the aging woman with a "substantial" monthly pension for the rest of her life.

While Frank worked long hours at building his chain of stores, Jennie occupied herself with the care of their family. There were no sons born to Jennie to carry on the heritage that her husband was forging and constantly expanding. But there were three daughters now, with the birth of Jessie in 1886.[27]

Despite her husband's frequent absences from home, Jennie Woolworth was quite content in her Lancaster home with her daughters. But Jessie was still an infant when Frank decided that, since he was doing most of his wholesale buying in New York City, the family should move to Brooklyn where he had found a house for them to rent.[28]

Jennie was not the type to take pleasurable anticipation in moving to another city when she was very satisfied with Lancaster. But neither was she the type to deliberately set out to thwart her ambitious husband's wishes and choices. She was still slowly adjusting to her new Brooklyn neighborhood when her husband suddenly announced his plans to move his family again — this time into a brownstone that was for sale. Certainly the house was roomier and more comfortable than the rented place in Brooklyn, so Jennie had plenty of space to set out her yard goods and sewing machine as she happily sewed dainty dresses for her Lena, Edna and little Jessie — each blonde and blue-eyed — whom she enjoyed dressing like princesses.

It seemed that Frank, after all, was more unsettled after the move to New York than was Jennie. He moved his rented office (the Woolworth administration headquarters) from one tiny loft in a building to another loft, not much larger, and finally to a small office at Chambers and Broadway where he had the Woolworth trademark (a diamond symbol centered with a W) painted on the door.[29]

At home, Jennie noticed how tired he looked, and she worried about his growing nervousness and restlessness. His business was doing so well that she had to have wondered what the reasons might be for his hypersensitivity, which must have reminded her of his illness at the farm, years earlier, when she had taken care of him. Was it overwork causing the problem? She wondered about that. But her suggestions that he should take things easier were ignored. He was, she realized, driven by ambition and by his need to keep expanding his business and to retain control of everything in his own two hands.

Actually, Frank Winfield already had begun to concede, in his own mind, that his business was expanding too rapidly for any one-man executive-controller to handle efficiently. It took him only a short time to decide that he would call upon Carson Peck (the young man who had proved his mathematical precision in Watertown and, later, in his efficient management of the Woolworth store in Utica) to become his management-aide.[30]

On New Year's Eve of 1889, Carson Peck arrived in New York to assist in Woolworth's administration office as "manager-buyer." If Peck was surprised (as he surely

must have been) to find that the "administration" consisted of only Frank Woolworth, plus a 16-year-old boy assistant (a
relative of Jennie's), and a stenographer —
all crowded together in a paper-littered
office, he would have been too gentlemanly
to give any indication of his wonderment.
He was astonished, too, at Frank Woolworth's penchant for paying cash for all his
purchases and supplies, and at his continuing refusal to do any advertising. The
Woolworth stores' show-windows were the
only necessary advertising, Frank insisted,
pointing out that his stores had grossed
more than $246,000 in sales for 1889.[31]
Many figures such as these were stored away
only in Woolworth's ledger-type mind,
Peck discovered.

Carson Peck, Woolworth's "right hand
man" in the early years of the company.
(John Compton Collection)

Before Peck's arrival, Frank had bought
the younger man's interest in the Utica store,
and now, in Peck's new position as "manager-buyer" in administration, he would be
working under a profit-sharing agreement. His duties would include the major job of
helping to organize finances, assisting with wholesale buying, and assuming responsibility for training the "learners."

The "learners'" programming was an important and basic factor in the success
of the entire Woolworth enterprise, especially so because Frank was pushing harder,
now, to open stores in other states.[32] In the 1800s, employers who hired young boys
generally were of the opinion that the younger the boy, the more tractable. At Woolworth stores, 12-year-old boys could start working as cheaply paid janitors and stock-
boys and, if industrious, could advance through the ranks to assistant managers and,
finally, to managers. For the "girls" (Frank had advised managers not to employ girls
younger than 15) there was little opportunity for advancement. They would get a
very nice wedding present from Woolworth, though, when they left the stores to get
married. It was largely unheard of for women to work after marriage. Not much
more was expected of Woolworth "girls" (usually paid between $2.00 and $3.00 a
week) except a willingness to work long hours, to be neat and have a pleasant
demeanor, and to take care, uncomplainingly, of extra clean-up chores when they
were not busy at the counters.

With Carson Peck quickly absorbing the methods of buying mass merchandise
and shaping up the "learners' programming," Frank Woolworth finally looked forward to having some time to relax. Ocean voyages were physicians' widely prescribed
remedy for overworked or ailing men who could afford such voyages. Within a couple of months of Carson Peck's arrival in New York, Frank had gained faith in Peck's
abilities to handle all administration duties. Accordingly, he planned a trip to Europe.

He wanted to purchase merchandise directly from European suppliers, without going through a New York middleman. He could visit some of these suppliers and acquaint himself with their wares, and possibly place substantial orders. A work-vacation of this sort was, very likely, the only kind of relaxing that Frank Woolworth could have accommodated at this point in his life.

3

Luxury in the Gay Nineties

The arrival of Carson Peck in New York City had coincided with the arrival of the "Gay Nineties" decade. But many people saw nothing gay or favorable about the increasing influx of Southern and Eastern European immigrants into the United States that began at this time. Most Americans viewed the newcomers as intruders ... as uneducated peasants who, in this country, congregated in masses of racial groups in or near cities and provided cheap labor in factories and mines. This was to the advantage of industrial corporations that wanted laborers who could be cowed into submission and would not be influenced by American workers who were demanding union representation to acquire shorter hours, higher wages and less dangerous working conditions.[1]

Frank Woolworth saw things differently. Immigrants could mean many new customers for his stores, even though great numbers of them did not plan to stay in this country. For the most part, these new arrivals wanted to work at any kind of job, keep their low standard of living, and save as much money as they possibly could to take back to their native lands in the future.[2] Nonetheless, there were inexpensive items that immigrants would need or want — things they could find at Woolworth stores. Hair pins, hat pins, and feathers (plumes were too expensive for a Five and Ten) and ornaments for a Sunday-go-to-church hat for a woman with a bit of vanity. Shoelaces. Shoe and boot polish. Stove polish (called "stove-black"). Knitting needles and yarn. Combs and brushes. Dishpans.

And then there was candy. In the same year that Frank's youngest daughter, Jessie, was born (and a couple of years before Carson Peck arrived in New York to become a part of administration) Frank had sired a new concept for his Woolworth enterprise — to sell candy on a trial basis in several stores. He personally haggled with reliable candy-makers (confectioneries were considered to be expensive treats at that early date) until he ordered enough pounds of candies to get a cut rate from one candy-wholesaler, making it possible for his Five and Tens to sell sweets. The candies were tempting to customers — fresh mints, lemon drops, and a variety of other kinds (chocolate kisses would be highly favored) along with peanuts, scooped from behind gleaming glass panels, weighed into quarter-pound amounts and sold, for five cents, in small bags. As candy sales boomed, other Woolworth store-managers clamored to become a part of the candy bonanza, following Frank's instructions to locate their candy counters as close to store entrances as possible. Soon, candy sales would sweeten Woolworth's sales totals to the jingle of cash registers (installed in 1900) metering millions of pounds of candy sold annually. [3]

Less than two months after Peck had come into the administration office, Frank Woolworth, who now leaned on Peck to assume many responsibilities never before trusted to anyone but the Chief himself, departed on his first trip to Europe. Before he sailed, in the company of an experienced traveler who worked for an import firm, he wrote a simple will on a single sheet of paper, expressing his wish that at his death, everything he owned should become the property of his wife, Jennie. [4]

Aboard ship, it was difficult for him to concentrate on descriptions of the countries and cities his companion told him they would visit because Frank became miserably seasick as the liner tossed up and down in the great swells of the ocean. He began to wish he never had undertaken such a trip in February when weather could be so treacherous day after day. But with arrival in England, Frank's spirits lifted and his appetite returned as the two men visited English potteries and left their orders, then went on to Germany where Frank placed large orders for small wax dolls, painted and dressed, that would sell for ten cents in Woolworth stores. Even larger orders were placed for hand-painted tree ornaments for Christmas. [5]

By the time he returned to New York in May, Frank had established strong, direct relationships with European suppliers and was enthusiastic about expanding his chain of stores, with Carson Peck's help, to blanket the eastern states and to spread west and south. In 1892, he hired 20-year-old Hubert T. Parson as his first bookkeeper.

That same year (though it was a part of the so-called "Gay nineties"), the country was having severe financial problems that would slow, if not stifle, the inclinations of retail businessmen to make heavy investments. A major strike at Carnegie Steel Works at Homestead, Pennsylvania, helped to slow the economy, as Carnegie employees demanded higher wages and a recognition of a workers' union. Three hundred Pinkerton detectives began guarding the steel works, resulting in a clash with angry workers. Ten strikers were killed and 60 wounded before 8,000 state troops appeared on the scene to help the company win the strike. There were other problems for the country to deal with as well, including declining gold production, depreciation of the silver dollar to sixty cents in value, and diminishing prices for farm produce, which brought disaster to farmers. [6]

Frank Woolworth found that his stores remained largely untouched by the country's problems, which resulted in the Panic of 1893. In fact, even greater numbers of customers trekked to the Five and Tens to shop for bargains they hoped to find there. Bargains could be found at the Five and Tens because manufacturers and suppliers had lowered their prices during the panic and bank-closings, to get rid of a surplus of unordered goods. Frank also learned that his cousin Seymour Knox (one-time partner in the failed store in Reading, Pennsylvania) was far removed from crying into his handkerchief these days when, in 1894, he opened what he called a "de luxe" store in Detroit — S.H. Knox and Co., 5 and 10 Cent Store. [7] It was apparent to Frank that Seymour was a serious competitor from his Buffalo, New York, headquarters. Frank was determined to stay out front.

Since Woolworth stores were debt-free, Frank inaugurated a one-week paid vacation for every employee who had worked at least six months, plus a cash Christmas gift that could be as large as $25.00 if an employee had worked for the company for at least five years.[8] Such benevolence could pay off in employee loyalty to the company, Frank felt. It can be assumed that Frank Woolworth believed, as did most American business men, that there was virtue in making money and successfully managing one's profits to benefit employees (as a benevolent employer — not any union — saw fit) and to expand the growth and development of the country. "God gave me my money,"[9] John D. Rockefeller would say, out of his firm belief that great wealth accruing to victors in cut-throat business competition was the victors' just reward and carried the blessings of God.

Seymour Knox, a Woolworth cousin and early partner of Frank Woolworth. (John Compton Collection)

By 1895, as Frank prepared for a second trip to Europe, he had sufficient trust in Carson Peck's ability to rely on his aide not only to oversee the 28 stores in the Woolworth chain but also to take care of the planning for new stores in the owner's absence. This time, Frank's wife and three daughters would go with him. They sailed from New York on the steamship *Teutonic* in May 1895. Daughter Helena was almost 17 years old, Edna was 12, and Jessie was 9.

Greatly invigorated by the excitement and eager to show his family the sights of Europe, Frank still found time to write long, handwritten and enthusiastic letters about the trip and sent them to his New York office, where he had left instructions for the letters to be typed and for copies to be sent on to friends and business acquaintances. Mrs. Kinney, his former landlady in Watertown, was one of the recipients of his letters.[10]

The earliest letter told of all of his party being seasick during the Atlantic crossing except Frank himself and 12-year-old Edna. After they had enjoyed sight seeing in London, Frank left his family in their London hotel while he went on a business trip to Stokes-on-Trent. Afterwards, when the family crossed the English Channel to head for the Continent, a different sort of delineation of Frank Woolworth emerged from the letter he wrote after the crossing — quite different from that of the successful business man who worked long hours every day and saw little of his family. He wrote that all three girls became violently ill during the choppy crossing of the Channel and his was the task of nursemaid as he cleaned up after them with mop and bucket.

Frank's second letter, found among the many descriptive missives written to friends and preserved in the Watertown library, told of the family's Cologne, Germany, hotel room, draped in red silk, where they paid only $3.75 a day. In Baden Baden he was impressed, he wrote, by orchestral music emanating from the courtyard each evening. Many of the refrains were familiar American ones such as "After the Ball Is Over," featured to please the hotel's wealthy American tourists. From Munich, he wrote of his awe at the great quantities of beer consumed by Germans.

Letter-writing (almost a lost art in current American society) was engaged in by most literate people in the 1890s. Frank's letters kept coming—a very long one arriving from Lucerne where he was greatly impressed by the picturesque scenery. The letter was "thirty-five pages long, when typed," a library report claimed. By this time, the Woolworths had moved on to Paris and then back to London. They returned to New York in early October, bedazzled by their European experiences.

While the family was in Europe, the Woolworth chain had expanded into Washington, D.C., and then into Brooklyn with an elegant three-story, plus basement, Five and Ten. When the company's sales were tallied for 1895, they amounted to more than a million dollars.[11] The following year, Frank opened his first store in Boston (although he already had Five and Tens in Springfield and Worcester, Massachusetts, and two in Virginia) and then announced the opening of his first New York City store in Manhattan on Sixth Avenue between 16th and 17th streets.

On opening day for the Manhattan store, as elevated railroad-trains rumbled above Sixth Avenue, hundreds of women charged into the new F.W. Woolworth 5 and 10 Cent Store in a frenzied search for bargains.[12] However, extra salespeople, trained for crowd control and quick rearrangement of shelves and counters, were on hand to retain a semblance of order among throngs of customers. Every newly leased, or constructed, F. W. Woolworth 5 and 10 Cent Store was fitted, now, with highly polished floors, oaken or cherry-wood counters and expanses of clear-paned glass and mirrors—an elegance planned to subdue the baser instincts of bargain-hunters.

Since the original Woolworth store was opened in Lancaster, Frank's company had advanced light-years from its primitive beginnings. With the arrival of the 20th century, Frank was having a new 6-story (including an attractive roof garden) Five and Ten built, close to the original store's location. Equipped with every refinement—carved mahogany counters, marble floors and ornamental lighting fixtures—the new store would be known as Woolworth's Flagship Store.[13] There were plans already formulating in the fertile minds of Woolworth and Peck to move even faster to lease or build more and bigger Five and Tens. If Frank had hopes to double, or even triple, Woolworth sales in another four or five years (by the turn of the century) his hopes would succeed beyond his wildest dreams when sales would balloon to $5 million by 1900.

By 1900, Frank Woolworth was learning slowly to enjoy luxury. Although he persisted in small economies and conservations (turning off lights when not in use and reminding his daughters to do the same) such frugalities seemed merely to be sops to his conscience when money was flowing freely into his coffers and as he planned to build a luxurious home for his family within the exclusive sphere of Fifth Avenue multimillionaires. After all, there were no taxes on income and what else was he to do with his money except spend and enjoy it? If his mother had lived to see his success, he would have taken great pleasure to surround her with some of the luxuries of which she had never dreamed. He continued to look after the needs of his

austere father but John Woolworth's needs were few and he
wanted nothing beyond the kind of
life with which he was familiar.

Frank bought a piece of property fronting on Fifth Avenue,
installed his sister-in-law Mary
Anne in the Woolworths' brownstone, and moved his family into
plush quarters of the prestigious
Savoy Hotel while a new 30-room
mansion was being completed for
the Woolworth family.[14] Frank continued to settle each bill, paying by
cash, as promptly as it arrived from
the architect, builders, or land-
scapers.

Frank may have thought that
living in a Savoy suite would accus-
tom his wife to a way of life that he
felt she should have — a life of luxury and freedom from any kind of
household chores. He was mistaken, however. Jennie sat in
enforced and bored idleness,
intimidated by hotel employees
who tried their best to be polite
and solicitous, but whose atten-
tiveness made Jennie uneasy. She
felt out of place and unneeded in

This postcard photograph shows the company's flagship store" in 1900 near the site of Frank Woolworth's
first successful store in Lancaster, Pennsylvania. The
new store was Lancaster's first "skyscraper" and featured two gold-domed towers and a roof garden
where food was served. (Author's Collection)

the comfort of the suite; she felt as awkward, surely, as Frank would have felt had he
been compelled to write checks instead of comfortably carrying wads of cash with
him.

Her three daughters were Jennie's only ties, now, to the life to which she was
accustomed; the three girls still needed her in some respects. There was, perhaps, a
hem to "put up" on a skirt. Buttons to be replaced. A braid to be brushed out and
re-plaited. A curling iron to be heated and applied to the back of a daughter's long
hair. A mustard plaster to be affixed to the chest of a family member (Frank, for one)
to help cure a cold and cough. The youngest daughter, Jessie, was 14 now and still
young enough to frequently require attention and reassurances from her mother. But
Edna was 17 and rapidly developing the independence of a young lady. And Lena was
22. She'd had no higher education; that was something her parents likely had never
even considered five years previously.

Jennie was not satisfied to sit all day while she crocheted or embroidered doilies,
or runners for the tops of dressers and long tables. She wanted — needed — to be use-

ful. Frank, however, scarcely could find enough time for the hobby that he enjoyed. He could sit, enthralled, for hours at the piano he'd had installed in the Savoy suite; a mechanized piano that, as he pumped the pedals, would pour forth music of the great composers that he liked. If he wanted to satisfy the tastes of his daughters for more up-to-date music, he might have purchased a cylindrical roll that would bring forth the very popular melody, complete with brilliant arpeggios, of "She's Only a Bird in a Gilded Cage." Jennie could have appreciated that one.

In November 1900, under the slogan of "a full dinner pail," the popular Republican William McKinley had been re-elected to the presidency of the United States. Times were prosperous and inventions were bringing electricity and telephones into homes. The president, a kindly and gracious man, was so well liked that a crowd turned out to see him on the afternoon of September 6, 1901, when he appeared at a hand-shaking reception at the Pan-American Exposition in Buffalo, New York. The reception had nearly ended when a 28-year-old Polish-American, Leon Czolgosz, approached, his right hand, apparently injured, wrapped in a white handkerchief and held at his side. As he faced the president, Czolgosz pushed aside McKinley's arm and quickly pressed his bandaged hand against the president's vest. Two successive shots were heard before Secret Service agents and soldiers leaped at the assassin and took him to the floor. There were angry cries of "lynch him" as the assassin was whisked away into protective custody and the wounded president was rushed to a hospital.[15]

When the president died on September 14 from gangrene that had spread through his vital organs, Vice President Theodore Roosevelt was on his way back to Washington after climbing the Adirondacks' Mount Marcy. A stunned nation, thought by its citizens to be so blessed by God and far-removed from the troubles of what Americans thought of as less civilized countries, was shaken from its complacency. The new President Roosevelt had many admirers, but others were wary of the 43-year-old Roosevelt and referred to him disparagingly as a young "cowboy."

Justice was swift in the early 1900s, and Czolgosz was found guilty on September 24 after a two-day trial. The assassin was electrocuted one month later, still claiming he killed the president because McKinley was the enemy "of the good working people."[16] Angered by the murder of their president, Americans began ranting about "anarchists" in their midst. Carry Nation, who had nothing to do with anarchism but everything to do with the temperance movement as she went about with a hatchet and broke open barrels of beer in saloons, was surrounded by a threatening mob in Rochester, New York, because she had called McKinley a friend of the brewers.[17]

Frank Woolworth, who had little to say about politics but was a supporter of the Republicans, was unsympathetic toward the contentious Carry Nation. But S. S. Kresge (a Detroiter who had opened his first store of the nickel-and-dime type in 1897) was an outspoken supporter of the temperance movement.[18] Frank, who enjoyed a drink or two on occasion, might have attributed his dislike of Kresge to the man's temperance views, but it was more likely that Frank's animosity was triggered by his fear of competition from the growing numbers, and popularity, of Kresge stores.

Since Frank knew that the best way to keep ahead of any competition was to purchase new merchandise to display in his stores, he began stocking books of the youth-inspirational type such as the Horatio Alger series. Aware of the popularity of various lodges such as the Odd Fellows, Sons of St. George, Eagles, Elks, Masons, National Grange and a variety of others, plus religious societies, Frank stocked his stores with pins and emblems that were in demand by lodge and religious society members. For many men of the Gay Nineties and early 1900s, lodges filled a void in their lives as they sought companionship, possibly financial assistance in times of serious illness, and insurance (a relatively small amount) in death, during an era when no insurance was available from most employers of average workers. Frank Winfield, a fervent music lover, also found great satisfaction in adding sheet music to his wares at the Five and Tens.

His Sixth Avenue Five and Ten in Manhattan was doing such good business in its first few years of existence that, by 1900, Frank had decided to build an even larger and more luxurious store right across the street. The night before this super-sized Five and Ten opened for business, the usual reception (hosted as each new store in the fleet was christened) was made distinctive by music emanating from the store's own pipe-organ as visitors made their way up and down the aisles.

At the turn of the century, it was an accepted way of advertising for great department stores to sponsor uniformed brass bands, orchestras and, even, singing groups—trios, quartets, and chorales. These groups performed not only at the openings of stores but also for special events and to represent the particular stores in parades and civic celebrations. For Frank Woolworth, to whom the pealing of a pipe organ—from chimes to triumphal trumpeting—offered unmatched magnificence, it must have seemed fitting to select the organ for his store, even though it could not be transported for parades and celebrations.

By the time Theodore Roosevelt became president, the Woolworths had moved into their spacious Fifth Avenue home and hired enough servants to take care of both the house and grounds. Frank made it clear to Jennie that she must not try to help the housekeeper or the cook. It was not appropriate, he answered any protests she might have uttered. He could not understand why a woman ensconced in such a magnificent home—amid her thick oriental rugs, parquet floors, elaborately carved plaster ceilings and golden wall paneling—would prefer to clean her own floors and cook her family's meals. Instead, he wanted her to shop at exclusive clothing stores and purchase a new wardrobe so that she could mingle with other society women who lived on Fifth Avenue. She could have her own dainty calling cards, embossed with her name, to deposit on the silver trays of her neighbors who would be "at home" to their friends at certain hours of certain days. It took just a little effort, after all. And she could entertain at home; could start perhaps with a tea. But Jennie could not make the effort. The thought was terrifying to her.

Frank was disappointed that there were few visitors to come and admire his home, so he invited old friends from Watertown to visit. Mrs. Kinney came on one such occasion. Her visit gave him the happy opportunity to display the great organ that he'd had installed in the drawing room. Like the piano at the hotel, the organ had a mechanical device to play the symphonies and nocturnes of various composers while Frank sat at the keyboard. But there was more—a row of buttons that, when one or the other was pressed, would display a portrait of the selected composer on the ceiling. Other buttons would cast different hues on the portrait while Frank could choose from a variety of sound effects using other devices.[19]

When the aging John H. Woolworth was invited to visit his son's new home, the old man displayed no enthusiasm for the splendid Fifth Avenue mansion and its crystal chandeliers. The father remained largely silent, clearly unimpressed, and seemed eager to return to his farm.[20]

A heatless winter faced Americans in the fall of 1903 when an anthracite coal strike, that had begun almost a year earlier, threatened to continue through the winter of 1903–1904.[21] Almost everyone depended on coal for heat. And most people realized, by now, that miners worked under oppressive conditions. In his book, *The Good Years*, Walter Lord writes that coal miners earned, on average, $560 a year — other mine workers were paid less. Hours were long, the work dirty and dangerous. Miners' wives, buying food and necessities at inflated prices at the company store, had to take in unmarried miners as boarders. Worse, they sent their young sons into the dark underground passages of the mines to follow the same perilous jobs held by their fathers.

Frank Woolworth's concerns centered around getting enough coal to keep heat circulating throughout his new steam-heated stores. He did not relish closing off unnecessary rooms in his 30-room house to conserve heat, as the government was advising. The price of coal soared from $5 to $20 a ton. Woolworth could afford it, but most people could not. People chopped down telephone poles for firewood in Rochester, New York. Riots broke out. Still, John Mitchell, leader of the United Mine Workers, remained firm in his demand for higher pay, shorter hours and union recognition.

President Roosevelt stepped into the dispute to try to resolve the strike, putting pressure on the owners to at least talk with union leader Mitchell. The owners refused. One mine owner pointed out to Roosevelt that he had a lot of children working for him and he was concerned about having the minds of these innocent youngsters dangerously exposed to radicals like John Mitchell. (There had been desultory talk, from time to time, about the need for child-labor laws, but nothing was being done to prevent very young boys from working in stores, and what was much worse, little was being done to prevent other boys from working in mines and, along with young girls, in mills.)

The coal strike continued as National Guardsmen moved into Pennsylvania when a bridge was blown up and two trains were wrecked by strikers. Before taking the final step of requesting federal troops and seizing the mines, Roosevelt conferred with financier J. Pierpont Morgan, then summoned a number of people to Washington to become what the President referred to as an "impartial commission" to work at quickly settling the strike. The strike was soon ended and, within months, many of the union's demands were met. Most Americans credited President Roosevelt for arousing the conscience of the nation.[22]

Woolworth stores numbered 76 by the end of the year of the great coal strike, and 44 more stores were added the following year, proliferating Frank's Five and Tens to 120 in 1904.[23] Droves of customers stopped by just to pick up five- or 10-cent bags of chocolate kisses or peppermints, and went on through the aisles to the notions counters to select their choices from an array of colorful ribbons and laces or perhaps to the toy counter to buy a wind-up trinket for a child — possibly a tiny tin bird that, when wound with a key, would turn in a circle and peck at pretend seeds on the floor.

Something for everyone, and all under one roof — that was Woolworth's Five and Tens at the turn of the century. Wireless messages were being transmitted across the English Channel, and there was the promise of many innovations and labor saving devices to come in the twentieth century. The one-cylinder gasoline-powered Oldsmobile had wobbled about city streets as early as 1901, and by 1903 Henry Ford's two-cylinder, eight-horsepower Model A was snorting about as well, startling bicyclists, horses and teamsters. Before long, Frank Winfield Woolworth would own an automobile, not a so-called "Tin Lizzie" but a luxury model driven by his personal chauffeur and befitting his status as a successful self-made man — a multi-millionaire.

4

The Big Push Overseas

In 1904, a reform movement took hold in America as a National Child Labor Committee began its crusade to prevent exploitation of children in the workplace. The committee pointed out, accusingly, that the census of 1900 had listed 1,750,178 of the country's ten- to 15-year-old children as "gainfully employed."[1]

Because Frank Woolworth already had instructed his managers not to hire girls less than 15 years old as clerks, the reform movement was not threatening to his stores in regard to female employees. But since Woolworth enterprises hired boys as young as twelve years of age to work their way up into the "learners' program" that supplied managers for the stores, there was a threat from the reformers (who were gaining numbers among women's clubs devoted to social-service causes). Now that Frank's stores were spreading south and west, with "area supervisors" needed to oversee new stores in the expanding zones, there was more room for advancement for young men coming out of the "learners' program." Accordingly, there was more need for hiring young boys in the stores. Frank firmly believed in the adage relating idle hands of youth to the devil's workshop.

The reformers harassed states' legislatures relentlessly but it was difficult getting enough support to bring a child-labor reform bill to a vote. When a bill was proposed from time to time, it would exempt stock clerks and delivery boys from its protective provisions.[2] So it appeared that storeowners would have few worries, after all, in regard to child-labor legislation being passed in the near future.

Beginning in early 1904, Woolworth stores were displaying colorful arrangements of mittens, scarves and muffs in their show-windows (muffs possibly covered with pieces of velveteen — certainly not the fur muffs worn by high-fashion ladies of New York's Fifth Avenue) as the Woolworth Company began to celebrate its twenty-fifth anniversary year,[3] highlighted by sales in all of its stores. And with the approach of spring that year, the Frank Woolworth family was in a high state of excitement as preparations were made for an "at home" April wedding for the eldest daughter, 25-year-old Lena, who was three months short of her twenty-sixth birthday and perilously close to being classified as an "old maid."

The solemn strains of the "Wedding March" thundered through the hallways and up the magnificent staircase of the Woolworth mansion, the likeness of composer Felix Mendelssohn lighting up the ceiling of the drawing room as the bride

A "Winter Wonderland" show window is pictured in an early Woolworth anniversary booklet. Mittens and gloves were 49 cents; a plaid scarf was 25 cents. (Jefferson County Historical Society)

came down the curved staircase and took the arm of her proud father, according to a later obituary report in *The New York Times* in March 1938.[4] Frank was not entirely reluctant to welcome the groom, Charles McCann, into the family. Certainly his daughter was of marriageable age, and certainly the young attorney, McCann, who had taken his law degree from Fordham University, was an acceptable son-in-law; acceptable, that is, except for one thing. The McCann family was staunchly Roman Catholic.

Although Frank was not a steady Sunday-go-to-church Methodist, the strict Methodist tenets of his father, John Woolworth, and, particularly, of his beloved mother, Fanny McBrier of Ulster heritage, had been firmly impressed on his character in his youth (even if they were not always adhered to in his adult years). Like many Methodists at the turn of the century, Frank was suspicious and distrustful of Catholics (frequently referred to by Methodists as "papists" while many Catholics labeled all kinds of Protestants as "heathens").

Still, young McCann was well educated and well mannered and was being married to Frank's daughter right there in the Woolworth home. For the curious who had heard of the wedding and wanted to know the details, there was only disappointment when they leafed through the pages of *The New York Times* and found no timely mention of the affair. It was possible, as has been claimed, that either the non-celebrity status of the Woolworths (and possibly the McCanns as well) called for no write-up, or that the *Times* deliberately ignored the wedding because Frank Woolworth never had advertised his stores in the newspaper.

But there could have been another possibility. Perhaps the Woolworths simply kept the wedding as private as they could to avoid speculations by those who might gossip about the Methodist Woolworths' daughter marrying into a Catholic family at a time when the theme of "Abie's Irish Rose" soon would become a popular motif. Still, even gossip was a kind of recognition — a recognition that was not being extended to the Woolworths by families of the prominent banking official, the steel magnate and the other moneyed people who resided in palatial homes on Fifth Avenue.

Jennie Woolworth was unconcerned about this lack of acknowledgement; possibly she was scarcely aware of any social snubbing stemming from their Fifth Avenue neighbors' scorn of the trifling nickel-and-dime business from which the Woolworths' finances had come. However, Frank resented the snubs, but did not have the social skills to push his family into that golden inner circle of the so-called "400 set." Unfortunately, he had inherited a considerable degree of reticence, not easily overcome, from his father, John Woolworth.

As Christmas approached in that year of the 25th anniversary of Woolworth enterprises, a Woolworth Christmas catalog boasted that Woolworths were "America's Christmas Store." The catalog featured beads, sequins, spangles and patterns for "making your own Christmas gifts," listing imported mock pearls at 29 cents a package, sequins at 10 cents a package, spangles in unusual shapes at 15 cents a package, and imported beads encased in a box of 12 glass tubes at 29 cents. Twenty-nine-cent bead-easy patterns were sold — all one had to do was to follow the blue lines on marquisette backing.

Almost as popular as the do-it-yourself kits were canaries (guaranteed to sing) at $5.49 each, and parakeets that would talk and perch on a person's finger — priced "according to size and age."[5]

During that 25th year of business, Frank frequently conferred with Carson C. Peck (recognized as "the able financial organizer" in whose judgment Frank had great faith) about future plans for accommodating the fast-growing number of Woolworth stores. Woolworth Company papers record the incorporation of Frank's enterprises in February of 1905 under the name "F.W. Woolworth & Company." The capital of the newly incorporated company was $10 million with half of that amount in common stock and half in preferred stock at seven percent, the papers reported. Frank chose not to sell stock to the public but to retain total control of his company, pleased to see overall sales growing faster now and reaching nearly $15 million by the end of the first year after incorporation.[6]

It was a memorable year in 1905 for Frank and Jennie for still another reason — the birth of a grandchild, Lena's daughter. Lena named the infant Constance.

By this time, some of the first motion-picture theaters were opening in the larger cities of the country, bringing silent films and cheap entertainment to working-class people who could find relief from their dreary workday lives by watching the jerky movements of heroes and heroines, vamps and villains and a variety of comedians portrayed on the screen. But, for the most part, life for working-people was tough. The average life span was only 49 years; of course, that low average included the many babies and young children who died of various communicable diseases. Typhoid fever and tuberculosis were indiscriminate killers of both young and old. To treat all kinds of minor and major ailments, many people relied upon patent medicines (which, unknown to most consumers, consisted of large percentages of alcohol) advertised in magazines, newspapers and even in some 20 pages of the popular catalog published by Sears Roebuck.

John Woolworth, Frank's father, seemed to have thrived on hard labor however, because, although he no longer lived on the farm, he survived until the early winter of 1906 when he was 80 years old and only a short time after he had married his housekeeper. Years later, Frank confided to a reporter that after he had married Jennie and moved away from the Jefferson County area, he had returned to visit the deserted farm only once, in 1899 when he was 47 years old, and never again went back.[7]

Evidently the reporter and others interpreted Frank's statement as indicating that he never returned to Great Bend after 1899, but that was not so. He returned for his father's funeral, and his burial in the Sunnyside Cemetery where Frank's mother also was buried.

Helen Fargo, current historian and protective custodian of records for the local Methodist church, insists that Frank Woolworth was a benefactor (and an occasional visitor) to Great Bend.[8] Her statements are supported by an October 10, 1997, Associated Press article reporting that Frank Woolworth ordered beautification measures for the little town — new sidewalks and the planting of maple trees to line the streets — as well as personally finding jobs for some of the unemployed young people of the area.[9] At Christmas time (motivated by his own memories of meager childhood Christmases at the farmhouse), historian Ms. Fargo says,[10] he collected a gift list from the children attending the Methodist Sunday School, and filled the list with Woolworth toys.

At this same time, Frank was entertaining much larger visions of expanding his stores. Conferring with Carson Peck, he began to contemplate the idea of setting up a first Woolworth store overseas— in England. The exact location would be decided upon later, after he had taken a trip to England and selected a site that he considered to be the most advantageous for one of his stores.

First, however, there was another family matter to be considered; his second daughter, Edna, was now engaged to Franklyn Laws Hutton (after much delay effected by Frank Winfield) who frequently referred to himself as "a Yale man." Franklyn was indeed a Yale graduate, but the older Hutton brother, Edward, was not even a high-school graduate, but a dropout who had gone to work on one of the lowest rungs of Wall Street's stock brokering business. Through sheer ingenuity and his own high intelligence, Edward finally had established his own brokerage and, later, absorbed his younger brother, Franklyn, into the business (E. F. Hutton) as a partner.

Franklyn Hutton had met the Woolworth daughter seven years previously when Edna was only 17 and the Woolworths were living at the Savoy Hotel.[11] Edna's father never had been comfortable with the stock market or with gambling of any sort for big, or even minor, stakes. Being of a suspicious nature, Woolworth vaguely associated novice stockbrokers with ne'er-do-well bettors on horse races and back-room poker players. He could not easily dismiss his apprehensions that his lovely and delicate Edna might be victimized by a man who possibly would want to marry her for the Woolworth money. Frank was no more impressed by talk of Yale than he had been, previously, by the Harvard credentials of Lena's husband, Charles McCann. By this time, though, Frank Woolworth had found McCann to be a decent, trustworthy and brainy fellow. Frank could only hope that Edna's new husband would turn out the same.

At Edna's April 1907 wedding, her father walked her down the aisle of the Episcopal Church of the Heavenly Rest on Fifth Avenue at 90th Street.[12] The Church of the Heavenly Rest was one of many large and beautiful Episcopal churches in New

York City (the senior Woolworths, by this time, were attending the Episcopal church on occasion, although their church attendance was far from regular anywhere). But the claim to fame attributed to the Church of the Heavenly Rest was because the church was reputed to be, in a New York City guidebook, the largest Gothic building, without steel reinforcement, in the world. Its outstanding features were its magnificent stained glass windows by James H. Hogan. But in his concern for his daughter Edna, it is likely that Frank Woolworth was scarcely aware of the beauty of the church on the wedding day as the ceremony took place, the minister's voice and the organ music reverberating from the vaulted ceiling.

After the newlyweds returned from their honeymoon, they moved into a five-bedroom house, one of three homes that Frank bought and renovated for his daughters and intended to be occupied as each one married. The homes were built on a few lots that he had purchased just around the corner (on 80th Street) from the Woolworths' Fifth Avenue mansion. The compound was, Frank must have thought, a cozy arrangement (if anything so huge could be called cozy) that would keep his daughters near their mother; close to both him and Jennie.

Although Woolworth would launch its first lunchroom in 1910 (in New York at its 14th Street Five and Ten) the company introduced an experimental mini-version of what would eventually become an immensely popular and dominant feature of Woolworth stores when, even earlier, it opened a soda-pop and light-lunch counter in Philadelphia.[13] The year of the opening of the light-lunch counter was 1907 — not a good year for innovations because the Panic of 1907 had struck with a vengeance, a result of bad policies by financiers and of even worse banking practices. Long-standing enmity took fire between President Theodore Roosevelt (hero of the majority of working men and their families) and promoters of big business. Capitalists hurled charges of Roosevelt's interference with business as being the cause of the Panic, while Roosevelt returned fire by calling financiers "malefactors of great wealth."[14]

By the end of October, stocks continued to fall and there were runs on banks in several cities by worried depositors. Through Herculean efforts by financier J. Pierpont Morgan, plus support from the Bank of England (which sent $10 million in gold via the *Lusitania)* and, finally, the reluctant cooperation by Roosevelt with the financiers, disaster was avoided. But the effects of the Panic would linger and fester into a depression extending into 1909.

In March 1909, *New York Times* reporters interviewed a few leading businessmen, including F.W. Woolworth, for their responses to the question: "What is the matter with business, and why is it recovering so slowly from the depression which followed the Panic of 1907?"

Frank Woolworth, now a Director in the Merchants' Association, freely gave his responses, blaming the continuing depression on uncertainty among businessmen because of tariff revisions.[15] "Had not the tariff come up for adjustment, it is likely that business would already have weathered the depression," he said. He spoke of the temporary "good times" right after President Taft was elected (after Theodore Roosevelt had declined to run for a third term)."It was never a real recovery," Frank said. "Only a spasmodic movement, which soon sank back to the condition which existed

A Woolworth lunch counter, location unknown. These were a popular feature of Woolworth stores ever since the first one opened in Philadelphia in 1907. More than five decades later, Woolworth lunch counters would be famed as sites of civil rights sit-ins. (John Compton Collection)

before the election. There will not be much doing in business until the tariff is settled. The manufacturers are waiting," Frank added, concluding the interview.

In fact, the continuing depression did not have great effect on the Woolworth business in the selling of wares considered as necessities. Even the Notions counter, with its frivolous displays of decorative feathers, bird wings, dotted veiling and varieties of ribbons and bows for milady's huge hats or pompadours, frequently had to replenish its supplies.

Jennie Woolworth was not present at the elaborate Saturday afternoon tea given at the Waldorf Astoria by Mrs. William Heynard in March 1909. The hostess, wearing an ornate bird-of-paradise hat, leaned over a candelabra on the table and was stunned when two gentlemen jumped to their feet and began slapping at her huge hat (which a candle had ignited) with their hands. The bewildered Mrs. Heynard, unaware of the flames above her head, stared in amazement and then collapsed, with little more than her pride injured, as she realized her magnificent hat had been afire. A *Times* report of the affair assured its readers that Mrs. Heynard's hair had not been burned or damaged in the incident.[16]

Although invitations to society teas were not a usual part of Jennie's life, she was preparing, in late March, for an early–May trip to England with her husband and youngest daughter, Jessie, when one of the Woolworth Five and Tens made much bigger *New York Times'* headlines than had the unfortunate bird-of-paradise hat. Rivalry between the F.W. Woolworth & Co. store, at 1039 Broadway near the Williamsburg Bridge, and the neighboring Adler department store had escalated into a competitive advertising of 5- and 10-cent bargains, resulting in mobs of people waiting outside the doors of the two stores one hour before the eight a.m. openings. "WOMEN MADLY RIOT AT BARGAIN SALES," the *Times* headline read the next day. "Bonnets and Waists Torn Off During Wild Rushes in Williamsburg Stores." "Police Reserves Called." "Hysterical Women Knock Over Counters, Trample Merchandise, and Beat Each Other."[17]

It was not a pretty picture. About a thousand women (with a few men scattered among them) had stormed inside each store as the doors were opened, pushing aside salespeople and knocking over several counters in the Adler store as even bigger crowds continued to gather outside the buildings. The Adler store, not as commodious as its Woolworth neighbor, phoned for police protection, which promptly arrived. As police tried to clear the stores, six mounted policemen rode through the crowds outside and got them moving.

Three women who fainted were taken away by ambulance. Most of the remaining women, driven out by police to the sidewalk or street, had lost their hats and some of their clothing. As the people were forced out, the Adler manager took down the sales signs in his windows and surveyed the wrecked counters as he tried to estimate the value of stolen merchandise. "I don't want to go up against a crowd like that again; it was the angriest crowd I ever saw," the manager complained.

The Woolworth manager, though, tried to cling to the Woolworth tradition of dignity, continuing its sale despite the clamorous crowds. He later claimed that there was no damage done to his store and that he did not believe that any goods were stolen.

At this same time, reformers had succeeded in arousing the ire of New York City retail merchants as the merchants rallied together to fight a bill that would have barred women from working more than ten hours in a single day in stores. What next would the reformers want? businessmen deplored.

When Frank Winfield, his wife and daughter left for England in May, Frank's third cousin, Fred M. Woolworth, and three other men from F. W. Woolworth & Company accompanied them.[18] The excursion was a family affair because the Woolworth cousin, as well as the additional three men, had been advised by Frank to bring their families along with them.

Regardless of the family-frivolity atmosphere, the business of selecting an English city for the introduction of a first Woolworth store into the British Isles proceeded quickly with the help of an Englishman whom Frank had met on a previous trip to the island country. Before the end of the summer, the thriving seaport of Liverpool, approximately 200 miles northwest of London, was selected and a four-story building was rented and being renovated for the project. The city's shipbuilding and ship-repair business, plus its array of docks (among the busiest and largest in the world) continued to attract a steady stream of immigrants from Ireland seeking jobs in Liverpool. Since Frank Woolworth already had experienced the volume of customers brought into his Five and Tens by immigrants to America, he expected that his Liverpool store and the newly created F. W. Woolworth and Co.,Ltd., could benefit in the same way.

The Liverpool enterprise opened with a band concert on November 5, 1909. The store, with three sales floors (including a restaurant that served free afternoon tea to its customers for a considerable time) was not known as a Five and Ten, but rather as a "Three and Six" ("thruppence and sixpence" in the vernacular, but equaling six and twelve cents, respectively, in American coinage.) [19]

By June 5, 1910, a fifth British Woolworth store was opening in Leeds, England. At that time, United States Consul Benjamin F. Chase commented that the enterprise would change shop-keeping customs in England, making it possible for the public (47,000 people were estimated to have visited the Leeds store on opening day) to enter Three and Sixes and look around without being pressed to buy something by clerks.[20]

Offices for British Woolworth, occupying the fourth floor of the Liverpool store, quickly grew busier as Three and Sixes multiplied within the British Isles—moving into London, Cardiff, Dublin and Glasgow. Though controlled by American Woolworth, which held more than 60 percent of capital stock in its British offspring, the success of the Three and Sixes would soon make Frank Winfield's distant cousin, Fred, a multi-millionaire.

The expansion of his stores into the British Isles was not the only major concept that was stimulating Frank's imagination at this time. He envisioned building a huge skyscraper flaunting the name Woolworth — a gigantic edifice that would tower proudly above the cluster of skyscrapers that loomed into the skyline framing New York City's harbor, the Statue of Liberty and the Atlantic Ocean. The Woolworth Building.

It is quite possible that never before had a businessman's vision of magnificence sprung into life as quickly as the Woolworth Building began to take shape. By July 10, 1910, newspapers were carrying reports that Woolworth would erect a 30-story building at Broadway and Park Place.[21] The 30-story report had grown to 46 stories five months later, which surpassed the Singer structure (previously recognized as the tallest New York City skyscraper) by thirteen feet.

Accidents were common in the workplace in 1910. Every wise merchant, in a building with an elevator serving the public, carried special elevator insurance to settle any claims for injuries or death incurred in an elevator, as frequently happened. In December 1910, work was being done on the foundations for the Woolworth Building when, as people walked along a temporary wooden sidewalk next to a high fence that shut off the view of the foundation work, there was the sudden sound of the snapping of a cable as a fifty-foot boom cut through the fence and crashed to the ground, striking down a man and a boy on the sidewalk. The man, who remained unidentified for a time, was killed instantly by the impact of the boom crushing his skull. The child, a little Italian boy with a fractured skull, was still breathing but dying as he was rushed to St. Gregory Hospital. The engineer of the derrick was arrested on a charge of criminal negligence, although it was soon determined that he was not at fault — the cable (a new one) was suspected to have been defective, it was reported. The company doing the work had put up an $8,000 bond, which would go toward covering any claims for the deaths.[22]

Despite any ominous cloud of foreboding regarding the beginning of the work on the building, Frank Woolworth kept enlarging, expanding and altering his original plans for the grandiose building that would be a monument to his name and success. Although the continuing changes of plans were difficult for well-known architect Cass Gilbert to cope with, Gilbert remained committed to creating the Gothic-styled building originally said to be 30 stories high, but now, in Frank's words, "Above that, will rise a tower about 80 to 85 feet square, containing 25 stories, making 55 stories in all."[23]

The building would, indeed, be the "tallest office building in the world" at a soaring 750 feet and, with the recent purchase by Woolworth of the Barclay Street corner, he intended to enlarge his building to cover the entire block on the westerly side of Lower Broadway between Barclay Street and Park Place. It was expected, he admitted to *The New York Times*, that the cost of the skyscraper would be $12 million or more with an additional cost of $5 million for the land.[24]

He was not worried about expenses. Sales from his 160 flourishing stores had almost reached the $15 million mark at the end of 1906, and sales and the number of stores were increasing each year. He was certain that, once the Woolworth Building reigned proudly over all the New York City skyscrapers, no longer could Frank Woolworth be referred to only as the nickel-and-dime merchant.

5

World's Tallest —
Woolworth Skyscraper

By this time, with Frank Woolworth and his Woolworth Building creating news and *The New York Times* reporting it, the feud between the businessman and the *Times* (if, indeed, there ever was one — supposedly because of the fact that he never had advertised in the newspaper) appeared to be ended. A *Times* reporter interviewed Woolworth at length and the several-pages account of the interview was featured prominently in the newspaper.[1] The interview was complete with illustrations and a photograph of Frank Winfield: a portly man (as a man of wealth and substance was expected to be) with silver-gray hair, a neat silver-gray mustache, and clear blue eyes shadowed by long lashes.

In the early 1900s, a robust appetite, an ample paunch and a waistline of at least 42 inches were considered to be the measure of good health. Frank Woolworth had a hearty appetite; he enjoyed large breakfasts and leisurely roast beef dinners. He also seemed to have enjoyed being interviewed by the newspaper reporter, revealing his pet philosophies as he talked expansively of how he had developed his chain of stores. He spoke of always giving his employees "a square deal," and of refusing to put up with any "graft or hint of it."[2]

As an example, he told of one of his buyers receiving a case of champagne as a gift from an unknown donor. Later, when the buyer visited a wholesale dealer with whom he'd done business, he accidentally discovered that this wholesaler was the man who had sent the champagne. The buyer, Frank said, "did no more buying in that house."

Under these philosophies, his stores had proliferated to a total number of 286, with 9,000 employees, to start the new year of 1911, Frank boasted to the reporter. He pointed out that he employed seven buyers to work in foreign countries, and that three-fourths of all Christmas ornaments made in Germany were sent to Woolworth stores. Since this same reporter had interviewed a reluctant Frank Woolworth several years previously and found the man to be "taciturn and reticent," the reporter had to have been surprised at the change in the well-spoken merchant.

Had success almost beyond his own anticipations changed the man from a skeptic (opposed to personal publicity and suspicious of the interviewer's purpose in posing questions) into an agreeable personality who seemed very open to questions? At one point, Frank confessed to the reporter that some years previously, he had dreaded the thought of venturing into New England territory with his stores; now he had "a half-dozen stores in Boston, alone."[3]

Mention of "my boys" frequently crept into his reminiscences but with no reference to any specific names, although Frank Woolworth leaned heavily on the brilliant, and quietly effective, Carson C. Peck. Caught up in the expansion of British Woolworth (12 stores would be operating there before the end of 1912) and in the creating of the gigantic "tallest in the world" office building that would bear his name, Woolworth surely could not fool himself that his enterprises remained a one-man-operated business—not while many of the burdens of growth and expansion gradually were being relinquished to the able leadership of Peck.[4] And that year, 1911, was one of intense planning and preparation for a tremendous leap forward to expand the corporation.

Frank W. Woolworth, inveterate letter-writer who wrote missives consistently for the Woolworth Company's in-house publication, would write what was termed as a "prophetic" letter, reproduced in his company's Offering Circular in 1912, in which he concluded that "further development of the business (is) independent of the individuality of any one person."

In early August, a newspaper article on the features of the still-in-progress Woolworth Building and its owner vied for reader attention with an even longer article, on the same page, concerning another resident of New York's exclusive Fifth Avenue. The latter article dealt with an announcement of the engagement of the previously married 47-year-old Colonel John Jacob Astor (of considerable social standing and whose town house was located at 840 Fifth Avenue) to 18-year-old Madeleine Force, a recent debutante and "a graduate of Miss Spence's school, having previously studied in Europe and at Miss Ely's school at Greenwich," the news report stated.[5]

The article on the Woolworth Building told of existing conditions—the necessity of digging down to bedrock, 110 to 130 feet below the surface, and to sink caissons, some as large as 19 feet in diameter, for the foundation. With the foundation completed, the construction of the actual building would follow. Readers were informed that a luncheon club, with a gymnasium, would be established in one of the upper floors, and a large swimming pool was to be built in the basement. A huge, square tower, 26 stories high, would be the outstanding feature of the structure, with a powerful electric light beaming from the pinnacle. Completion of the building was set for the fall of 1912.[6]

Three months after the August 1911 publication of the Woolworth Building article, the *Times* announced "A Merger of All Woolworth Stores." Actually, the heading for the article was a bit misleading; the subtitle, though, was accurate in claiming that "About Six hundred 5 and 10 Cent Shops to be run by One Company." Only yesterday, the newspaper reported, had F. W. Woolworth, head of F. W. Woolworth & Co., announced the incorporation of F. W. Woolworth Company. Although the name change was scarcely discernible to the average person (eliminating only the "&" in the former name) the amalgamation of 596 Five-and-Ten-Cent Stores in the United

States, Canada and the British Isles was a tremendous change, bringing the hundreds of stores together under one name. That name was Woolworth.[7]

Although the amalgamation was effected by what was called "the simple exchange of all the capital stock of F. W. Woolworth & Co. for the capital stock" (or assets) "of five other enterprises," there were proud owners and personalities involved. Some of these owners had been reluctant to concede that great benefits could be obtained through the proposed consolidation. But Frank Woolworth, Peck and their backers had carefully prepared solid arguments that eventually convinced the laggards to agree.

Frank Woolworth, owner of 318 stores, owned the largest number included in the consolidation.[8] His cousin Seymour Knox (who had stopped crying into his handkerchief long ago and had presented formidable competition to Frank as Knox joined the ranks of fortunate businessmen who were "laughing all the way to the bank") now owned the second largest number of stores, 112, some of them in Canada.

Frank's old friend F. M. Kirby owned 96 stores. E. P. Charlton & Co. had 53 stores, largely located in the Pacific Coast area and Canada. All surrendered their capital stock for exchange. Brother Charles Sumner Woolworth, who owned 15 stores, exchanged his assets for stock in the new company, as did W. H. Moore (Frank's old Watertown mentor) and W. H. Moore & Son with their two stores.

At the time of the merger, Carson Peck, Frank's trusted subordinate, was named Director, Vice-President, General Manager and Chairman of the Executive Committee. These had been appropriate appointments because President Woolworth was concerned about his health, and Peck frequently served as active president.

Newspapers gave Frank W. Woolworth extensive coverage as he spoke exuberantly of plans for the new company. He, of course, would head the company as president; the other founders would be vice-presidents. He prophesied the expansion of Woolworth Five-and-Ten-Cent Stores into every city of more than 10,000 inhabitants in the United States, Canada and England. And "possibly, some day, in every country on earth," he boasted as he spoke of the previous year's combined sales of the stores now making up the new company.[9] These sales, he said, "amounted to over $50 million." The stores employed some 20,000 people, he added, and the head office would be in the new Woolworth Building presently under construction at 233 Broadway in New York City.

Despite his enthusiastic announcements to the press regarding the merger of Five-and-Ten-Cent Stores, Frank Woolworth had important family matters distracting him from the business deals in which he and Peck were immersed. His youngest daughter, 25-year-old Jessie, was insisting that she was going to marry 25-year-old James Paul Donahue—a young man of Catholic background who was, in Frank's mind, an unemployed playboy. For Frank, who always had chosen men with strong work ethics to become part of his Woolworth organization, the thought of a wastrel (as he surely must have considered Jessie's betrothed) soon becoming a part of the family was anathema.

Regardless of her father's protests, Jessie was adamant in her determination to marry Donahue in February 1912. Totally frustrated by his daughter's stubborn refusal to heed his advice (why couldn't Jessie have inherited the soft, pliant characteristics of her mother, he must have wondered), Frank sulked and took to his bed in a manner reminiscent of his reactions to the severe depression he had suffered when, at age 25, he left his employment in Watertown to return to the farm for recuperation.

The executive and self-made multi-millionaire, accustomed to giving orders and having them promptly followed, had been unable to change Jessie's mind either by persuasion or coercion.[10] Just hours before the four p.m. wedding was to take place in his magnificent Fifth Avenue home, Frank lay on his office sofa in an orgy of sobbing and self-pity.

Frustration finally yielded to pride and "saving face," however, in time for Frank to return home, wash away his tears and gather up the vestiges of self-control that he could muster while his wife fussed over him and murmured little soothing nothings as she helped him get into one of the well-tailored suits that filled his closet. Reluctantly, he was ready at four o'clock to fill the traditional father-of-the-bride role in an at-home wedding as he gave his daughter, in white satin gown with a court train and lace veil, in marriage to James Paul Donahue.

The New York Times reported that the bride's two married sisters, Mrs. Charles McCann (Helena) and Mrs. Frank Hutton (Edna, who likely preferred — as did her husband — that Franklyn Hutton should be listed by his full name) were attendants. They wore huge leghorn hats and purple and white chiffon dresses over white silk as they carried pink roses. The two oldest of Helena's three children, six-year-old Constance and her younger brother, Frasier, served as flower girl and page.[11]

After a small reception at the Woolworth home, the newlyweds departed on their honeymoon. On return, the couple would reside where the bride's two sisters were living — in the Woolworth compound adjacent to their parents' mansion. Despite a few problems that had created rifts in family solidarity, togetherness remained the Woolworth theme and before long, young Donahue would become an employee of the E. F. Hutton brokerage.

Soon after the amalgamation of The F. W. Woolworth Company, the new company's founders had agreed to offer to the public $6 million, par value, of a total $15 million of preferred stock plus $7 million, par value, of a total $50 million of common stock which had been divided according to each founder's percentage of holdings. They also agreed to hold on to their additional stock for one year, except for a single reservation: the privilege of distributing $1,500,000, par value, of either preferred or common stock to their store managers and executives.

When the common stock was listed on the New York Stock Exchange in June 1912, only a few (already stockholders in the company through previous liquidation by original owners of the company) could purchase Woolworth shares. Within a day of the public listing, the common shares leaped upward to $84 a share. Nonetheless, the number of stockholders would expand gradually, and more quickly later as Woolworth managers, executives and founders' heirs would sell part of their increasing numbers of shares obtained through stock splits and dividends.[12]

It was not unlikely that Edward Hutton might have anticipated, as early as 1907 with the marriage of his brother Franklyn to Edna Woolworth, that his brokerage business could benefit from the Woolworth connection. And now, having Jessie Wool-

The founders of F.W. Woolworth Company in 1912, photographed at the time of the consolidation of Five and Tens. Seated, left to right: S.H. Knox, F.W. Woolworth and F.M. Kirby. Standing, C.S. Woolworth and E.P. Charlton. (John Compton Collection)

worth Donahue's husband employed by the firm, it could have seemed logical to Edward Hutton that the Woolworth connection would be strengthened. (When, in 1916, the older Hutton brother would marry Marjorie Merriweather Post, the cereal heiress, there definitely would be an improvement in the Hutton brokerage business.)

The problem, however, with taking Donahue into the business soon became evident because of Donahue's reluctance to take seriously any obligations to the workplace. He was no financier, nor did he wish to be. Instead, he was a big spender with a lust for entertainment and travel. In this, he was encouraged by his wife, Jessie, who was the most lighthearted and carefree of the three Woolworth sisters.

While the Donahues were enjoying their lengthy honeymoon, Frank Woolworth crossed the ocean again on the advice of his physician who, like most physicians in the early 1900s, prescribed an ocean voyage and treatments at the famed spas of Europe to restore good health. "Taking the cure" had become the byword for aristocrats in failing health as they trekked to Carlsbad, Hamburg and Marienbad for the baths purported to hold healing powers for the cure of nervous conditions, anemia, gout and many other ailments that less fortunate people tried to heal by drinking patent medicines touted as cure-alls.[13]

"Taking the cure" turned out to be not an entirely pleasant experience for an irascible Frank as the mentors at Carlsbad set out rules for his activities, exercising and diet. Unaccustomed to following rules, but rather to setting up rules for others to follow, he demanded that his wife should join him at once. Jennie complied. She came, accompanied by her cousin who had been one of the very first office employees hired by Frank — even before the arrival of Carson Peck.

Although a terrible disaster occurred at sea on April 14, 1912, when the "unsinkable" *Titanic* collided with an iceberg on the ship's maiden voyage and sank below the waves of the cold Atlantic,[14] it appeared that Frank refused to be intimidated by the tragedy because he would continue to travel across the Atlantic Ocean. But he had to have been chilled to some extent by reports of the loss of 1,500 lives in the *Titanic* disaster — among them the multi-millionaire from Fifth Avenue, John Jacob Astor, although his pregnant young bride, Madeleine, was placed in a lifeboat and saved.

Stories filled newspapers, citing the bravery of men who drowned in the disaster while women clambered into lifeboats. (And several pitiful stories found their way into print about the relatively few men — some even dressed like women — who tried to get into lifeboats ahead of females.) Deeply moved by the accounts of most men's heroism, many people questioned the advisability of suffragists staging a huge parade up Fifth Avenue (in the planning for quite some time but, as it turned out, occurring less than a month after the sinking of the *Titanic*). Did women really want equal rights? Should the women getting into the lifeboats have refused to take more than half the seats, giving up the rest to men?

But the suffragists marched as planned — proudly, up the avenue, ignoring a scattering of signs reminding them of the *Titanic* disaster.

Later that summer, Frank and Jennie (accompanied by their chauffeur) returned from Europe to New York and to the city's traffic congestion about which residents complained incessantly. Pedestrians put their lives at risk, it was said, when venturing out to cross certain streets overrun by motorcars, loaded streetcars, and horse-drawn wagons driven by impatient teamsters. The crossing at Broadway and 116th Street, intersected by an island providing entrance to and exit from a subway station, was known to be particularly perilous. One complainer stated in a letter to the *New York Times* that "It is a crossing compared to Hannibal crossing the Alps."[15]

Frank did not need to join the pedestrians menaced by wheeled traffic. The Woolworths' uniformed chauffeur provided reasonably swift and careful transportation for his employer as Frank was transported about the city in his Renault automobile. He kept another luxury automobile housed in a Paris garage for convenient transportation when he made one of his frequent trips to Europe. Frank was on the best of terms with his chauffeur; they were more like companions than employer and employee.

After his return from Europe, Frank checked on the progress of the Woolworth Building and, seemingly endlessly, discussed with perturbed architect Cass Gilbert several changes Woolworth wanted Gilbert to make.[16] Exactly how high had Gilbert made the building, Frank wanted to know. "I can't tell within a few inches," the architect demurred. "But it's about 787 feet."

"Well, I'll just put a corps of engineers to work, measuring," Frank retorted, intent on determining that the skyscraper would be the tallest building in the world. When asked about the Eiffel Tower, Frank discounted it as not really being a building, anyway.

He may have been satisfied with the height of his building, but he was unsatisfied with the state of his health as, once again, he and his chauffeur set off for Europe. Since his doctor had warned him that unless he curbed his prodigious appetite and stuck to other dietary and exercise rules he'd been given, he would not have long to live, Frank headed for a French mountain resort. He left Jennie behind because he was concerned about her vagueness and forgetfulness, both of which seemed to worsen when she was removed from familiar surroundings.

Frank was still overseas when his second daughter, Edna, gave birth to a baby girl on November 14, 1912, and named her Barbara.[17] Barbara Hutton—it was a name that would become well known to a worldwide readership of society and gossip columns as she would attain celebrity status in a love-hate (largely hate) relationship with a fickle public.

The Woolworth Building celebrated its opening on April 24, 1913, with a dinner for 900 people invited to honor architect Cass Gilbert that evening. Accustomed to travel in his own luxuriously appointed, private railway car, Frank saw to it that special Woolworth trains were prepared to bring guests to New York City for the opening event on the 27th floor, equipped for the occasion as a banquet hall, of his new tallest-in-the-world Woolworth Building. A couple of Woolworth Specials arrived from Washington, D.C., and from New England, delivering an assortment of dignitaries, friends, relatives and business associates who walked into the three-stories-tall foyer and gazed up at a vaulted ceiling of glass mosaic, then down again at niches in the wall which held grotesquely fashioned bronze statuettes, one of which depicted F. W. Woolworth counting his dimes. They admired the marble walls and terrazzo floors as they walked toward a bank of elevators that swiftly transported them up to the banquet hall.

It was a Friday evening of triumph for Frank Winfield Woolworth as 900 guests sat at the banquet tables and conversation hushed at the approach of 7:29 p.m.[18] At that moment, a Western Union telegrapher notified the White House that everything was in readiness for President Wilson to perform the magic touch that would flood the skyscraper (now touted as having 60-stories) with light. The President touched the button, closing the circuit and setting off a bell that rang in the banquet hall and in the depths of the engine room. At once, the skyscraper was bathed in light from 90,000 bulbs gleaming from every window and from the top of the tower out over the harbor like a gigantic illuminated sentry (792 feet, 241 meters high). A toast was drunk, an orchestra began to play the national anthem, and then the guests sat down to dinner.

Novelist F. Hopkinson Smith was the first to address the guests, paying tribute to American enterprise, genius and skill, exemplified by the erection of the towering Woolworth Building by a man who had been "a poor farmer's boy." He pointed out that Frank Woolworth had had no capital, no influential friends and had worked from 12 to 14 hours a day to achieve success. He was, the novelist concluded, "an everlasting example to the American youth."

WOOLWORTH BUILDING AT NIGHT. NEW YORK CITY.

Copyright 1913 by Irving Underhill. N. Y.

A nighttime view of "The Tallest Office Building in the World" is shown on a postcard. The Woolworth company itself manufactured many thousands of postcards sold at their stores. In an era when few people owned cameras, visitors bought Woolworth postcards and saved and displayed them in albums as mementos of their visits to New York and other cities. (Author's Collection)

A postcard view of the upper section of the Woolworth skyscraper in New York City, in which the visitors' "Observation Balcony" can be seen. (Author's Collection)

Frank Winfield was the next speaker, paying tribute to architect Cass Gilbert as "one of the greatest architects in the world." He also paid tribute to his early employers in Watertown — Moore & Smith, and had them rise to applause as he spoke of his former employers teaching him his "first and best principles."

"The business from which this building has grown began with a five-cent piece,"

The Woolworth office building towers behind the Brooklyn Bridge in a postcard picture. (Author's Collection)

Frank added, going on to say that when he came to New York in July 1886, he opened a very small account "with what is now the Irving National Bank." Later, he became a director of that same bank, he acknowledged as he credited the bank for helping to make possible the erection of the Woolworth Building. Despite the problems (largely regarding changes in plans for the building) that the architect had endured with Frank Woolworth, Cass Gilbert mentioned none of the last-minute changes when he spoke to the gathering. There could have been some irony in his statements, however, when Gilbert referred to the engineers' measurements of the building. (He did not mention that Frank Winfield had ordered what he called "a corps of engineers" to make the measurements when he was not satisfied with Gilbert's response that "it was about 787 feet high.") Instead, Gilbert said to the audience, "The reports of those engineers amuse me very much. If they are correct in their measurements, the building must be lopsided." He went on to indicate, humorously, that, in such a case, the building should be straightened up—an obviously impossible task.

If Frank winced at, or even noticed, the barb, he gave no indication. Perhaps he was too caught up in the excitement of the evening. And the rest of Gilbert's remarks were most complimentary as he went on to say that "Our object was to make the building beautiful without losing any feature of usefulness. I believe that there is vitality enough in our art to meet the modern commercial needs, combining the practical with beauty and art."

In conclusion, Gilbert remarked that "there was no financing of this building. Mr. Woolworth has paid for it all himself as he went along. His bankers told me that this building was unique here, and probably so throughout the country, for it stands today without a mortgage on it or a dollar of indebtedness."[19]

Mr. Gilbert's final remarks (that the $13.5 million building had no mortgage or as much as a dollar of indebtedness) refuted many earlier rumors that French financiers had supplied most of $8,000,000 as a first mortgage for the edifice. Robert M. Gillespie, it had been reported, had gone to Europe in the summer of 1911 for the purpose of financing the building after Frank Woolworth had supplied $5,000,000 of the necessary money. Gillespie had told a *New York Times* correspondent in Paris that he had raised the $8,000,000, largely in France, before he returned to the United States in August 1911.[20] But things changed betwixt and between August 1911 and the completion of the building in 1913. Not surprisingly, Frank Woolworth had clung to his tenets of remaining debt-free, although the illusory contributions of French financiers remained firmly fixed in the minds of many *Times* readers.

Despite the publicity and attention the magnificent Woolworth Building brought to its owner, Frank did not find fulfillment in the increased respect he gained. He was too worried about Jennie and her fading memory and increasing frailties. He took her to doctors and psychiatrists and hired a nurse to care for her. Often, she had difficulty in recognizing members of her own family. Frank also worried about his own health as he felt himself slipping back into the same kind of depression that he had experienced at different periods of his life.

Nonetheless, he bought an elegant summer home on 13 acres in Glen Cove, Long Island, in the hope that the beautiful surroundings would cheer both Jennie and him. But Jennie was fearful of leaving the Fifth Avenue house to which she had become accustomed. When their chauffeur drove them out to Glen Cove, Frank had to depend on his employee for companionship unless one of his daughters visited. Jennie seemed lost, afraid.

The senior Woolworths were grandparents to three more children now; Jessie's first son, Woolworth Donahue, born in January, 1913, and then baby Helena Woolworth McCann, a fourth child born to Lena that same year. Jennie Woolworth found it difficult to differentiate among the three youngest grandchildren, all so close in age — Barbara and her cousins Woolworth and Helena.

Despite his concern about his own health and that of Jennie, Frank had no pressing worries about Woolworth business affairs. Carson Peck stepped in more often now, when Frank was unwell, to carry out the duties of active president in his usual competent manner. By the end of that year, 1913, Woolworth sales would soar to more than $66 million.[21]

The Irving National Bank, of which Frank was a director, was one of the first tenants of the Woolworth skyscraper. The F. W. Woolworth Company occupied a section of one floor and the entire 24th floor, including Frank's 30-foot square private office — done lavishly in cream and gold complemented with bronze and marble — where Frank would reign over his kingdom from an oversized and elaborately carved mahogany desk.[22] Napoleon in his coronation robes, looking out from the oil portrait of the emperor that Frank favored, might have felt quite at home in the company of the valuable antique clock, reputedly presented to Bonaparte by the Czar of Russia, now set upon the mantelpiece of a massive marble fireplace that distinguished the office of Woolworth's head honcho. But the F. W. Woolworth Company was, as Frank pointed out, only one of many tenants who paid rent to the owner of the building, the Broadway-Park Place Corporation. Frank had organized the Broadway-Park Place Corporation while the skyscraper was being built, and the new corporation included sons-in-law Franklyn L. Hutton and Charles McCann among its directors.

On the evening of June 20, a deluge of rain and hail pelted the city as loud bursts of thunder and zigzag lightning forced people to run toward shelters. One bolt of lightning hit the steamship *France* and knocked down several stunned sailors. Another bolt struck and set fire to a trolley car, injuring the motorman and several passengers. Still another lightning bolt was seen to strike the Woolworth Building tower[23] and an observer phoned the fire department to tell them that the tower was on fire. When firemen arrived, they found no trace of fire, and determined that lightning had struck some of the electric wires on top of the tower and had set off sparks which had proven to be harmless. The building had been erected with every possible fire-deterrent device available, including its copper-clad dome. The Woolworth tower still stood, in all its magnificent height, like a beacon shining its lights out to sea. A visiting Englishman would describe the building as a "graceful immensity," comparing its beauty to that of the Cathedral of St. John the Divine.

Americans, at this point, had varying opinions on legal changes that had taken place in the year 1913. Largely, they approved the amendment that would now make it possible for citizens to directly elect their senators, but argued about the imposition of a new, graduated income tax. There were other dissident opinions (between capital and labor) about the gains of zealous reformers who had made some important advances in the past decade in regard to child labor restrictions and the providing of workmen's compensation by companies to protect workers injured in the performance of their jobs. But most Americans were unanimous in their opposition to anarchists, ever-present in the larger cities, who were committed, apparently, to the destruction of the government.

On the other hand, there were men of wealth such as Andrew Carnegie, the hard-nosed steel magnate turned philanthropist, who had provided the financial means for the building of a castle in The Hague, that year of 1913, where the peace of the world could be fostered, monitored and maintained. Americans did not yet know that their trust in The Hague would be misplaced … that, within a short time, the facade of peace among European nations would be ripped apart in a sudden explosion shattering to the entire world.

6

Heartbreaking Tragedy for the Woolworths

In January 1914 the Woolworth Building Safe Deposit Company of Manhattan, with $100,000 in capital, filed its certificate of incorporation with the State Banking Department.[1] Again, among the company's seven directors was the Woolworth triumvirate—Frank Winfield and sons-in-law Franklyn L. Hutton and Charles McCann.

On a Sunday morning near the end of June, it is likely that newsboys sold only a few more "Extra" newspapers than was usual on a hot summer day. Americans, it appeared, were not too disturbed about the report of the assassinations of Austrian Archduke Franz Ferdinand and his wife as the royal couple visited the Bosnian capital of Sarajevo.

For the F. W. Woolworth Company, too, business went on as usual. In July, the Merchants' Association of New York, of which Frank Woolworth was a long-time member, prepared to open an experimental school in the Woolworth building. The school would offer vocational education for girls and boys.

It was not until late July that hoarse-voiced newsboys were "in the money" as they ran to their suppliers for more "Extra" editions flaunting headlines predicting that war was on the verge of breaking out with powerful Germany backing Austria and with Russia and France backing Serbia. Still, American newspaper editors as well as politicians were expressing disbelief in the probability of war with words such as "inconceivable" and "incomprehensible" when, on July 28, Austria declared war on Serbia, followed very soon by Germany also declaring war. Russia and France, and then England, who had promised to protect Belgium from invasion by the Germans, were soon involved as well.

Within a short time, there were newspaper stories of ships being sunk by German U-boats, accounts of dreadful atrocities and lengthy casualty listings. Americans shuddered as they read the listings. Still, it was all happening "over there" and people who were not personally involved became more or less inured to the lurid headlines and stories of the European war while events occurring here in America took on only an echo of the destruction in Europe.

Average American citizens were disturbed, though, when a series of bomb explosions rocked apartment houses, tenements, courthouses and stores in various American cities, particularly in Manhattan.[2] Many bewildered and law-abiding citizens blamed the Black Hand for the destruction. Others blamed the increased terrorism on anarchists as St. Patrick's Cathedral on Fifth Avenue and the rectory at St. Alphonsus Church were bombed, among other religious institutions.

Sales figures for the F. W. Woolworth Company and its 737 stores rose to a total of $69 million by the end of 1914, regardless of the onset of the overseas war and the at-home disruptions.[3] The company paid an increased quarterly dividend in April 1915 as its shares advanced in value. These reports helped to cheer Frank Woolworth from another period of depression until he was shocked at the death of his close friend and associate Carson C. Peck of complications from diabetes on April 29, 1915.[4] Peck, in whose honesty and business acumen Frank had trusted totally for the past 25 years, was returned to his birthplace — Watertown, New York (where he and Frank had first met as poor but industrious young fellows), and was buried in the Peck family plot. Only two and one-half weeks later, Frank's cousin and successful Woolworth Company executive board member, Seymour Knox, also died.

Even before the deaths of these two men (both in their fifties) who had been so close to him, Frank had begun procedures to build a monument to the Woolworth name that would be far different from the giant Woolworth Building looming into the New York City skyline. This monument would be a colonial-type church, the Woolworth Memorial Methodist Episcopal Church, which would be built in Great

Organ devotee F.W. Woolworth ordered a fine pipe organ installed in the Woolworth Memorial Methodist Church, and had famous New York organist Frank Taft give a concert at the dedication ceremony in Great Bend, New York. (Jefferson County Historical Society)

Bend in memory of his parents, John H. Woolworth and Fanny McBrier Woolworth. The church was completed in 1915, after which Frank graced it with a $20,000 trust fund, the interest from which could be used for upkeep of the building. Some 80 years later, the church historian would say that Mr. Woolworth and his wife and daughters had come, in the Woolworth private railway car, to attend the September

The Woolworth Memorial Methodist Church at Great Bend, New York. F.W. Woolworth had this church built as a memorial to his parents, John and Fanny Woolworth. (Jefferson County Historical Society)

opening ceremonies for the church and for the organ recital that Frank, of course, deemed essential to any such important occasion.[5]

On July 6, 1915, a telegram arrived at the Woolworth executive offices informing the company that the Panama-Pacific Exposition had presented the Woolworth Building with the Exposition's highest honor, a gold medal, for present-day architecture.[6] A 30-foot-high model of the skyscraper previously had been sent out to the Coast and placed in the New York State Building at the Exposition. The skyscraper's architect, Cass Gilbert, also had been awarded a gold medal, the telegram reported.

By this time, Frank had taken up his full duties again in active management of his company in the void left by the death of Carson Peck. Because of complications caused by the war in Europe, the requirements of the presidency were especially demanding at this particular time after Woolworth imports (most importantly, its numerous imports from Germany for the Christmas season) were halted. Previous to his death, Peck had taken initial steps to confer with executives of American manufacturing companies about expanding their operations to produce hundreds of thousands of Christmas ornaments and decorations to supply Woolworth stores.[7] The ongoing challenge to Frank's inventive mind, at this point, likely spurred him to free himself, at least temporarily, from the self-defeating thoughts that had been occupying his mind and from his morbid concerns about the recent deaths of his peers and close associates.

Thanks to Peck's foresight, several American companies had rushed into production of colorful gewgaws and Christmas ornaments, thereby jump-starting a new industry in this country in response to Woolworth's needs. They made it possible for cash registers in Woolworth stores to jingle with sales to clamoring customers that Christmas season. While weary soldiers, overseas, continued to slog through the mud of deep trenches to the deafening roar of cannons, Woolworth enterprises tallied up even larger profits than in the previous year. Games were popular Woolworth items—from the perennial favorite "Old Maid" to the newer card game "Flinch." Sheet music at five cents a copy, reinstated into Woolworth stores in 1911 (after an earlier period of selling sheet music had failed), was boosted into major sales by Frank's idea of bringing pianos into the larger Woolworth stores so that hired pianists could beat out the tunes of "It's a Long Way to Tipperary," "Roses Are Blooming in Picardy," and "Mademoiselle from Armentieres." The demand for patriotic songs increased as the war progressed its exhausting way through four hellish years. And when American troops would begin to pour into France in 1917, "Over There" and, even the oldie from the Civil War, "When Johnny Comes Marching Home Again," were big hits for Americans.

On the home front in Europe, the ongoing war was making changes in the lives of women. In London, women had become licensed as omnibus and streetcar conductors because of the shortage of civilian men. But in Brooklyn, U.S.A., coroner E. C. Wagner was quoted in a newspaper as saying that American women should not be allowed to drive automobiles. Editorials and articles posed questions regarding the validity of women's signatures to legal documents. In early December 1915, Dr. M. M. Crawford made news by declaring she was retaining her maiden name for professional use when practicing as a physician after her marriage.[8]

The Woman's Peace Party, led by noted social worker and writer Jane Addams, was very vocal at this time, as were, of course, woman's suffrage spokespersons. Women were outspoken, too, in many unions, particularly the Human Hair Workers' Union, currently on strike for better benefits. Human Hair Workers were makers of hairpieces and popular hair amplifiers such as switches, braids, coils, chignons and the unattractively named "rats"—sold by Woolworths as well as other more "pricey" stores.

At Carson Peck's death, C. C. Griswold had been advanced to the position of general manager of the Woolworth Company (just one of the multi-positions Peck had held.) Now, there was another blow for Frank Woolworth to absorb as, near the end of January 1916, Griswold, too, died. For the first time, Frank chose to elevate a comparatively young man, 43-year-old Hubert T. Parson (who was not one of the company's old-guard nor was he from the Watertown environs) to the dual positions of general manager and vice-president.[9] A Brooklyn resident, Parson had gained Frank's trust and confidence since coming to work, at age 19, as the fledgling company's first bookkeeper in the small, congested Woolworth office only two years after Carson Peck had been summoned to New York. To Frank, the keeper of the flame, his selection of Parson for such an important position must have been in recognition of passing on the torch to a new and different generation.

In May, Frank traveled by train to Watertown for his company's annual meeting, staying in his usual suite at the elegant Hotel Woodruff. His old mentor, William Moore, paralyzed by a stroke, could not attend the meeting. Moore's condition worsened while Frank was in Watertown and when the old man died, Frank remained in Watertown for the funeral.[10] At that point, Frank decided that Moore's Corner Store, on the western corner of the town square, should be torn down. To replace it, Frank began making plans to erect a modern six-story building—another Woolworth Building.

In that same year, 1916, the huge Woolworth manor in Glen Cove, Long Island— where Frank enjoyed spending his summers since the war in Europe restrained Americans from traveling about on luxury liners—caught fire and burned beyond repair. But once Frank had begun to recover from the shock of the fire, he hired architect Cass Gilbert to build another Woolworth mansion at Glen Cove. This residence was to be a bigger, better, more impressive castle-like structure.[11] Never was Frank Winfield happier and more energetic, it seemed, than when involved in building plans.

On January 10, 1917, the Woolworth Board of Directors announced a quarterly dividend of two dollars per share on the common capital stock. Three weeks later, this was followed by another announcement that the F. W. Woolworth Company had leased "one of the finest and most valuable sites on Fifth Avenue" at 40th Street for the establishment of a "Five and Ten Cent Store deluxe."[12]

The new store, planned to be six stories high, would face the New York Public Library directly across Fifth Avenue, it was announced, and would be open for business in the fall. "There seems to be an impression that we are 'invading' Fifth Avenue," Woolworth Vice President H. T. Parson was quoted in *The New York Times*. Parson went on to explain that the very shops "that will now be neighbors to us, were our neighbors in the old days when Sixth Avenue was a fashionable shopping district ...."[13]

He pointed out that women of great wealth "who spend their mornings picking out new jewels" had the same need of hairpins and, even, clothespins, that poorer women had. Customer demand, he insisted, was the slogan for stocking individual stores. Woolworth stores did not intend to "compete with the so-called fashionable stores," he said, "any more than a butcher competes with a grocer."[14]

There was no denying, though, that "the rich are different." A caption in the same issue of the newspaper in which the announcement of Woolworth's plans for a Fifth Avenue store made news claimed that "Astor Baby Spends $86,034 in three years."[15] The expenditures of little John Jacob Astor, born four months after the sinking of the *Titanic* and the loss of his father, had exceeded the expenditures allowed by the guardians of the baby's $3 million trust fund. The child had been charged with such expenses as one-third of the combined taxes and maintenance of the 840 Fifth Avenue household he shared with his mother and her new husband. The baby also met the bills for an infant's ermine robe for $185 and a mink robe for $580 (likely from one or another of the elegant shops lining Fifth Avenue's exclusive shopping district) plus a variety of "roly-polys," mechanical chickens, balls and other toys that might have been — but probably were not — purchased at Woolworth's; rather, they probably came from one of the more pricey establishments.

On the worldwide scene, important events were occurring that made the question of who would buy what and where seem insignificant. In early February, Germany announced that it would resume its submarine warfare on any so-called neutral ships that might be bringing aid to the Allies. In response, President Wilson cut diplomatic ties with Germany.[16] The record of German U-Boat destruction increased with the March 22 announcement that 24 British steamers, each of a tonnage of more than 1,000 (plus 21 fishing vessels) had been sunk in the single week ending March 18.

Well before the end of March 1917, a state of war, for all practical purposes, existed between the United States and Germany. At the same time, a correspondent from Reuter's Amsterdam bureau reported that serious riots had broken out in Berlin because of scarcity of food. Employees were refusing to work in five munitions factories in Dusseldorf and would not return to work, they threatened, until their food rations were increased.

In Washington, the Senate Committee on Military Affairs was preparing to enact, at President Wilson's request, measures to bring the regular army to full strength. Vast numbers of college girls from Vassar, Wellesley and Smith signed up with The National League for Women's Service to become nurses, wireless telegraphers and clerks. Hospital classes organized by the American Red Cross were readied to instruct the girls in their duties. And former President Theodore Roosevelt was speaking out on the subject closest to his heart — American preparedness. On April 2, 1917, President Woodrow Wilson came before the Congress in a special session to ask for a declaration of war.[17] On April 6, the United States formally declared war on Germany.

Concerns about the mobilization of the nation and a universal draft, tremendous undertakings, now began to take precedence over the usual events in most citizens' lives even while there was an increase in outside-the-law activities of thieves who preyed on the wealthy. On the evening of April 17, the 810 Fifth Avenue home of Hamilton Fish (prominent politician who had served as Assistant Secretary of the Treasury) was burglarized by thieves who stole jewelry, estimated to be worth $75,000, from the gem collection of Mrs. Hamilton Fish. Reluctant, at first, to admit the value of jewels kept in their home, the Fifth Avenue couple finally admitted the loss of two platinum lorgnettes set in diamonds, platinum hairpins set in diamonds and sapphires and a Cartier wristwatch, and supplied a list of other jewels which police furnished to pawnbrokers in hopes of solving the theft.

American troops had begun training for future battles in France when, on May 2, 1917, a catastrophe occurred in the life of Frank W. Woolworth that minimized his concerns about his own failing health and that of his nearly helpless wife, Jennie. On that fateful May 2, his beautiful daughter Edna Woolworth Hutton, clad in a white lace dress, was found lying on the floor of her bedroom.[18] It was reported that her maid had found Edna's lifeless body there, next to a window, and that she had been dead for several hours.

For months, Frank Woolworth had worried about Edna — ever since, with her young daughter, Barbara, she had left her home in the Woolworth compound and moved into an apartment at the Hotel Plaza. He knew that his daughter and her stockbroker husband were not getting along. He knew, too, that Franklyn L. Hutton was drinking heavily and was seen frequently in the company of other women. How much time Hutton spent at the Hotel Plaza with Edna, Frank was not sure. But he had to have suspected that it was very little. It was obvious that Edna was unhappy, although she did not confide in her father.

This middle daughter, Edna, was not only the prettiest of Frank's three girls but the most artistic one who shared her father's passion for music. She also was very much like her mother, the quietest daughter and the one least likely to talk about her personal problems. The eldest daughter, Lena, was not only the most sensible of the three, but also the most dependable and thoughtful. Even though Lena had become a Catholic and had her children baptized into the Catholic Church, Frank would have had to admit that his eldest daughter was levelheaded. The youngest daughter, Jessie, (now the mother of a second son) had an unusually carefree disposition. "Never seems to worry; always in a hurry" could have summed up Jessie's joyous attack on life.

In the immediate wake of Edna's death, rumors spread quickly.[19] Rumors that little four-year-old Barbara Hutton had been the one who found her mother's body. Rumors that an unhappy Edna had been drinking to forget her troubles. Rumors that the death was a suicide, by poison.

If Frank Woolworth, using his prestige and money, could have put a quick end to the rumors, he likely would have done so. Whether he played any part at all in influencing the coroner's report has remained undetermined. The *Times* reported that Franklyn L. Hutton, "prominent member of the Stock Exchange, reached the hotel shortly after his wife's death from a visit to his summer home at Bay Shores, Long Island." Edna Hutton's death, the newspaper quoted the coroner as saying, was caused by "a chronic ear disease that resulted in hardening of the bones of the ear, causing suffocation."[20] Later, the coroner gave his opinion that an autopsy was unnecessary.

Since Edna left no will, her estate soon would be appraised at $617,220, almost entirely in Woolworth common and preferred stocks. Her husband received $205,740 of the estate. Daughter Barbara was awarded $411,450.

Edna's 1917 death was the first real tragedy in the lives of the very wealthy Woolworths, but before the end of the next year, the McCanns would suffer a terrible loss with the death of their eight-year-old daughter, Gladys.[21] And many other tragedies would strike the Woolworths, as happens so often in the lives of the super-rich.

The next tragedy was the plight of the motherless (and often fatherless) four-year-old Barbara Hutton, who would insist, in later life, that the rumors surrounding her mother's death were true — it was she who had found her mother's body in the bedroom. The child soon was passed into the care of her grandparents, Frank and the hazy-eyed, fuzzy-minded Jennie. To Frank, the little girl with the blonde curls and big blue eyes was a ray of light and sunshine in the great rooms and halls of the house on Fifth Avenue. To the child, her grandfather's attentions were welcome diversions from the overwhelming silence and gloom of the long hallways and rooms with high ceilings and massive furnishings. But all too often, the grandfather seemed distracted or lost in his own thoughts, sometimes as unaware of the little girl's presence, as was her grandmother.

Still, Frank Winfield continued to ride with his chauffeur each morning as he went to his office. He remained active, too, in the Liberty Loan Committee. In October 1917, he spoke to reporters regarding the work of the committee, saying that if the sale of war bonds did not prove to be an overwhelming success, it would be due to "inertia of the rank and file of the business men of the country."[22] Then he tempered this by saying that the large corporations and businesses seemed to be doing their part in purchasing the bonds.

"I am a great believer in thrift," he continued, attributing his success in business to his attempts to make every dollar work to best advantage. He pointed out that investment in the Second Liberty Loan was the finest example of thrift in which the people of the country could participate.

"War is the great business of the country this year and nothing else counts," he had concluded.

There was little evidence, if any at all, of thrift when the new Winfield Hall — Frank's 62-room Italian Renaissance mansion — had been completed at Glen Cove, Long Island, in 1917. Standing tall at three stories, the mansion boasted a huge fireplace at the entranceway and a magnificent staircase of highly polished marble. Lofty rooms, some with sculptured plaster and gold leaf ceilings, were styled for many different effects— rooms of different periods and in modes of different countries.[23]

By that time, the entry of America into the war had boosted the morale of the Allies, even though the United States had been unprepared for the fighting that lay ahead. By June, more than 17,000 American troops had landed in France and were training hard under the command of General John J. Pershing, while more soldiers were scheduled to arrive soon. In the meantime, life went on as usual for most Americans except for coal shortages that winter. At the end of 1917, the Woolworth stores had sold some four million pounds of candy at their popular candy counters while many of the nation's factories had begun spewing out all kinds of war supplies, from steel helmets and gas masks to tractors and airplane engines.[24] By that time, as the spring of 1918 wore on, American doughboys found themselves engaged in some of the biggest battles of World War I.

In early March, Americans were shocked to read of German raids, using mustard gas on Pershing's troops in the St. Mihiel sector of France and along the Chemin-des-Dames. Then, as longer American casualty lists began to appear in newspapers, the reality of the horrors of war sank deeper into the minds of appalled citizens.

As fall approached, a different kind of horror struck the United States after Spanish influenza — considered by American health authorities to be an old-fashioned pestilence that could not seriously affect a modern, healthy nation — was brought into the country on a Navy receiving ship. The flu epidemic quickly spread from the East Coast to the city of Washington, and on. Calls went out for nurses to come to army camps, to tent-hospitals set up on the Mall in Washington, D.C., and to school buildings and railroad stations being converted into hospitals for the hundreds of thousands of people stricken with the illness.

World War I ended on November 11, 1918, with the surrender of Germany. But the influenza epidemic wore on and spread. Churches, schools, saloons and theaters closed in many cities. A golden-haired Mary Pickford, looking out from large posters pasted over the closed doors of theaters, smiled at policemen and public-service employees, wearing gauze masks, as they passed by. And still, influenza victims were dying faster and in greater numbers from lung congestion than could be taken care of by undertakers. A pall of fear blanketed cities— even those as yet untouched by the plague.

When the epidemic died away almost as quickly as it had arrived, the death toll added up to some 22 million people in the entire world, including 548,000 Americans. But despite the plague, Woolworth stores (all 1,039 of them, with their 35,000 employees— mostly "girls") had tallied up more than $107 million in sales for 1918.[25]

7

Multi-millionaire Patriarch Dies

Because of the demands of World War I, Frank Woolworth's plans for the erection of a six-story Woolworth Building in Watertown had been delayed. Nor had he opened the Fifth Avenue, New York, Woolworth store as he'd previously announced. At the end of the war, though, the new store opened in the high-rent Fifth Avenue district across from the Public Library.[1] As yet, there was no progress on the Watertown building.

Once again, Frank had many things, other than buildings, on his mind. His granddaughter Barbara was no longer living with the senior Woolworths. Franklyn Hutton had decided to have his motherless child live with an aunt (Hutton's sister in California) after which Barbara would be enrolled, back East, in one or another of the private boarding schools geared to the education and training of daughters of wealthy parents.

Frank Winfield was concerned about the child, but even more concerned about his wife, who needed constant nursing care. The times when Jennie no longer recognized her own husband were occurring more frequently.

Since Woolworth stores would celebrate their fortieth anniversary in 1919, the company prepared an anniversary-sale brochure listing some of the stores' more popular bargains.[2] Harmonicas were longtime best sellers at Woolworth stores, but these were no longer advertised as "individually tuned to pitch at a small organ in faraway Germany" because the war, so recently ended, had not only made many German-manufactured goods unavailable but had pushed them into disfavor. Dust caps, with fluted edges, had been perennial favorites at Woolworth counters and had not yet completely gone out of style as they were bought by fastidious housewives who did not wish to have dust and cobwebs drift down into their long hair as they cleaned their homes. (Bobbed hair, of the early 1920s and the "flappers'" era, would, at this point, have scandalized the more conservative housewives who shopped at Woolworth's.)

Fels Naptha Soap was featured for heavy-duty cleaning and for washing clothes (usually via a washboard, also available at Woolworth's) as well as Ivory Soap (at five cents a bar) to protect both work-worn and delicate hands. Enamelware and crockery—both at ten cents a piece. For ladies' pastimes, embroidery goods at only ten cents per yard. Men's half-hose and women's hose at ten cents a pair. And spools of crochet

One time farm boy Frank Winfield Woolworth became a multi-millionaire before his death in 1919. (Courtesy of John Compton)

cotton (bought in volume from a leading supplier company named "Woolco") continued to be popular purchases by young brides who were no longer expected to work but to stay at home and crochet doilies and anti-macassars in their leisure time.

Before the end of the year, a report would be received from Paris claiming that a number of French medical men were certain that light silk and open-work stockings were responsible for much of the recent influenza epidemic among women.[3] But New York Health Commissioner Dr. Royal S. Copeland took exception to this opinion by studying records of the Health Department and unearthing statistics to show that women, especially young women, were not as susceptible to influenza as were men of the same age group. It was his opinion that the relationship between "light silk and open-work stockings" and influenza should be discarded just as had earlier predictions of the dangers of wearing high-heeled shoes (the fashion craze of 1913) which had women teetering along on four-inch French heels. It had been reported that the high heels would result in feet thrown out of alignment, possibly followed by nervous disorders and even mental derangement. Commissioner Copeland referred to those former reports as he noted that there had been no increase in the number of patients committed to mental institutions. He pointed out that even something as innocuous as face-veils had come in for criticism as the cause of impaired eyesight.

Dress, Copeland insisted, was not responsible for poor health, although he was of the opinion that "there could be dangerous ingredients in hair dyes that could have a harmful effect on the system."

Frank Woolworth's doctor had warned him that rotting teeth could generate many other health problems, including arthritic conditions. Still, Frank refused to visit a dentist. Perhaps he was motivated by fear and his distaste for surrendering control to a man who would loom above him (as he sat in a dental chair) with an array of instruments of torture set out on a tray. As a result, his rotting teeth had restricted his diet to soft and mashed foods and he was losing weight.

On Wednesday, April 2, 1919, Frank went to his office as usual in the morning, but left for home a few hours later when he did not feel well. By Friday, he decided a change of scenery (or possibly just getting away from the depressing sight of his

WOOLCO Quality Crochet and Embroidery COTTONS

WOOLCO Cordonnet
Article 1151

ALL sizes, viz.: 3-5-10-15-20-30-40-50-60-70-80-100-150 in white; Nos. 3 to 50 in ecru. A mercerized crochet cotton of highest possible quality and unsurpassed lustre. Used for lace collars, edgings for handkerchiefs, napkins, towels, pillow cases, underwear, hand bags, and copies of old laces. It is also used for heavy designs in tatting, for edgings for curtains, bureau scarfs, pillow cases, etc.

Colored Cordonnets may be used with good effect, as shown in Series No. 4, "Crocheted Yokes and Tatting," by Mary E. Fitch.

Nos. 30 and 50 only are sold in colors.

Price, 10 cents per ball. Postage, 3 cents a ball.

WOOLCO Tatting
Article 316

SIZE 70 only. One-eighth oz. balls, white and colors. This is particularly recommended for finer designs of tatting, and for edgings on handkerchiefs, towels, tea napkins, children's dresses, neckwear, and other articles.

Illustrations are shown in "Crochet and Tatting" book, Series No. 6, by Mary E. Fitch.

Price, 3 balls for 10 cents. Postage, 2 cents for 3 balls.

WOOLCO Broder Cotton
Article 199B

SIZES 20-25-30-40 in white. Size 25 in colors. This is used for the finer embroideries, for scalloping, and for embroidering monograms and initial letters on handkerchiefs, fine underwear, and household linens. It is also used for feather-stitching and for French knots. Illustrations are shown in Crochet Books Series, No. 7, by Mary E. Fitch.

Skeins, 2 for 5 cents. Postage, 2 cents for 3 skeins.

WOOLCO Cross-Stitch Embroidery
Article 1117

WHITE and colors. Size 25. This "Mouline" or 6-Stranded Cotton may be used for towels, doilies, runners, bureau scarfs, where handsome results are wished for in cross-stitch decoration. Fruits, flowers, figures of children, animals, birds, garlands, borders, and conventional designs are a few suggestions for decoration which makes this cotton popular. For illustrations, see Series No. 1 and No. 2 of "Cross-Stitch Designs," by Mary E. Fitch. Price, 3 skeins for 10 cents. Postage, 2 cents per 2 skeins.

A page from the 1917 Manual of Crocheting, published by the F.W. Woolworth Co. (Author's Collection) wife and her vacant stare) might help him to feel better. He ordered his chauffeur to drive him out to Winfield Hall at Glen Cove. There, he likely would have planned to relax by spending some time at his $100,000 Aeolian pipe organ in the beauty of his Baroque music room. True, he had an organ with sound and visual effects at his Fifth Avenue town house, but Winfield Hall was more majestic — a greater tribute to his success and, therefore, more uplifting to his spirit — than was the town house.

By the time he reached Winfield Hall, however, he had begun to shake with chills and fever.[4] Soon a doctor was summoned, but his ministrations had little effect in the absence of antibiotics, still unknown to the medical world.[5] Frank's condition worsened and his daughters, Lena and Jessie, and his brother, Sumner, came to be with him. On Monday afternoon, it was

The Woolco Girl graced the cover of the popular 1916 Woolco Knitting and Crocheting Manual. (Author's Collection)

clear that the patient was having breathing difficulties; he lost consciousness and died very early Tuesday morning, April 8, 1919, at age 66 — just short of his 67th birthday.

The next day's newspaper captions heralded the estimated value of Woolworth's estate as $65 million (which would be equal, roughly, to more than $1 1/4 billion in current markets) and the accompanying articles listed other achievements of the man who had built the Woolworth empire. He was, readers were told, president and the largest stockholder of the Broadway-Park Place Company, which owned the Woolworth Building and other New York properties. He also was a director of the Irving National Bank, the Irving Trust Company and the Pennsylvania Society. He was a member of the New York Chamber of Commerce, the Union League Club and the Lotos Club.[6]

Various sources attributed his death to stones in the gallbladder, nervous exhaustion, uremia, and septic poisoning. If it were influenza that had killed him — the terrible strain of illness that had killed more than a half-million Americans in 1918 (struck them down quickly and relentlessly and left people terrified of contracting the plague) — the doctors did not identify his illness as such.

Funeral services were held on the morning of April 10, only two days after death had occurred, and were conducted by Bishop Hamilton of the Methodist Episcopal Church of Washington, D.C., assisted by two other clergymen including the Reverend Dr. S. W. Brown of Watertown. Brother Sumner Woolworth, who had come from his home and business interests in Scranton, Pennsylvania, was among the few out-of-town, intimate family members who attended the funeral ceremony. But friends and business associates filled the music room of the Woolworth family home for the service while a Mrs. Herbert Witherspoon sang a few of Frank Woolworth's favorite Methodist hymns, including "Lead, Kindly Light" and "Nearer, My God, to Thee" accompanied by Frank Taft, famed New York organist.[7]

All Woolworth stores remained closed on the day of the funeral. What was surprising was the decision by Frank's chief competitor, S. S. Kresge, to pay tribute to Woolworth by closing Kresge stores during the time of the services.

At the close of the ceremony, the funeral procession formed and slowly wound its way to Woodlawn Cemetery. There, the remains of Frank W. Woolworth were placed temporarily in a vault. The elaborate mausoleum that Frank had ordered built for him and his family was not yet completed — an oversight by the Woolworth magnate who had wanted total control over every part of his dominion.

An even more important oversight dealt with an unfinished document — the will on which Frank Woolworth had been working shortly before his death, but which he never completed. "Woolworth Died with Will Unsigned" the *Times* trumpeted. Worse, "Demented Wife Gets All."[8]

The self-made multimillionaire who had reigned supreme over his Five and Ten empire had delayed too long in updating the brief handwritten will composed thirty years earlier. In that first, makeshift will, he had bestowed "all his worldly goods" upon his wife who now was totally incapable of comprehending the extent of her holdings.

It would be an understatement to say that the family was displeased with the kind of notoriety generated by public disclosure of the Five and Dime tycoon's will. Damage control rested in the capable hands of Lena's husband, Charles McCann, who met with reporters in his father-in-law's elaborate office on floor 24 of the Woolworth Building. Also attending, to hear McCann's statement, was a scattering of attorneys, Hubert Parson, and Jessie's husband, James P. Donahue, who already was becoming quite accustomed to being referred to in print only as "the other son-in-law."[9]

McCann began to read his statement to the assemblage: "Mr. Woolworth, prior to his death, had for some time been working upon a will which was just about completed, but due to his unexpected death he did not execute the same...." McCann went on to explain that the new will contained charitable and other bequests to relatives, friends and trusted employees of the Woolworth home. Woolworth's earlier handwritten will, which soon would be probated in lieu of the unexecuted will, had been made in 1889 (at the time of Frank's first trip overseas) and, if typewritten, would cover only a single page.

When asked by reporters about the provisions of the new will that Frank Woolworth did not complete, McCann was firm: "The family deem that to be a personal matter in which they alone are concerned."

At Frank Woolworth's death, his brother, Charles Sumner Woolworth, became Chairman of the Board, a newly created position to pay deference to the quiet but supportive younger sibling who had lived in his elder brother's shadow. With the passing of so many of the "Old Guard," a much younger man, Hubert T. Parson, advanced to the presidency of the company and became chairman of the executive committee.[10]

Before the last week of May, Frank Woolworth's infirm widow, Jennie, became ill with influenza at the home of her daughter Lena. At the same time, New York Supreme Court Justice Whitaker granted an application for Jennie's two daughters, Lena and Jessie, to become "the committee of Jennie Woolworth's person." It was their intention, they informed the court, to have their mother live with each of them for six months of the year.[11]

Less than seven months after the war in Europe had ended, the war at home by anarchists took on larger dimensions and began to terrorize American citizens. In June there was a series of bombings—the Pittsburgh home of Federal Judge Thompson was bombed and two other bombings in Philadelphia (one of a Catholic Church rectory) occurred on the same day. When a bomb badly damaged the New York home of Judge Nott, two people inside the house (thought to have been servants) were blown to pieces. Similar attacks followed in Boston where so-called "Reds" blew up the home of a Boston Justice who recently had sentenced anarchists to prison, shaking the complacency of Americans who had boasted of winning "the war to end all wars."

The government already was holding 90 Russian anarchists, slated for deportation, on Ellis Island. Emma Goldman, fiery leader of the anarchist movement who had been arrested and imprisoned for incitement to riot, had denounced World War I as an imperialistic venture and now, found guilty of conspiracy to violate the conscription laws, decided not to appeal her deportation order. It would take another decade, however, before the violence of the anarchists would begin to recede in this country.

Before the middle of December 1919, it became public knowledge that Woolworth heirs were required to pay the federal government $6,800,000 for inheritance taxes, plus $1,050,000 in New York state taxes. Woolworth Company President Hubert Parson, who also had been appointed committee of the property of the widowed Mrs. Jennie Woolworth, received permission to sell the Fifth Avenue town house to help pay inheritance taxes. The market value of the town house, Parson had stated, was $400,000; the value of Winfield Hall at Glen Cove, $852,666. There were other properties in Brooklyn, in Lancaster and Philadelphia, Pennsylvania, and in New Jersey. The widow's income from her husband's personal estate amounted to $10,000 monthly, Parson pointed out in explanation of the need for selling the Fifth Avenue house.

Before the end of the year, J. S. Bache of the J. S. Bache and Company banking firm agreed to buy the Fifth Avenue mansion.[12] In January 1920, the contents of the home (furnishings and paintings) were placed for sale at Silo Galleries. Three months later, all of the Washington Heights real estate holdings accumulated by Frank Woolworth were ordered sold at auction by estate administrators Parson and Woolworth daughters Lena and Jessie. The properties, grouped together at the intersection of St. Nicholas and Amsterdam Avenues, included the large Jumel Building, homes and apartment houses, and a number of vacant lots. Under Parson's direction, the Woolworth daughters agreed that it would be better to sell properties than to resort to selling their mother's Woolworth stock to meet tax bills.

There was a snag in the agreement with J. S. Bache, however, who, by March 1920, was suing to recover the $20,000 down payment he had made on the Fifth Avenue house.[13] In return, the committee of property for Jennie Woolworth sued Bache to compel him to keep his agreement to buy the house. To further complicate matters, the New York State Tax Department sued the Woolworth estate to recover 1919 income taxes. When it appeared that these suits would not be settled quickly, the Woolworth heirs mortgaged the Woolworth Building for $3 million to the Prudential Life Insurance Company.

By May 1920, both Lena and Jessie had become directors of the F. W. Woolworth Company — two of the very few women elected, at this point, to the directorate of any large corporations.[14] The combined interest of the two new directors in the company was estimated to be fifteen percent of the stock. At the same time, stockholders approved a plan to increase common stock capitalization from $50,000,000 to $100,000,000 along with payment of $15,000,000 of the additional stock as a 30 percent stock dividend on common shares. Lena McCann considered her elective office as a sobering responsibility. It is doubtful that fun-loving Jessie Donahue was sobered very much by the appointment. Her husband, Jimmy Donahue, already had eased himself out of the Hutton stockbroker offices and, likely, there was nothing but relief on the part of the Hutton brothers to see him go. Instead, Donahue had set up his own stockbroker office on Park Avenue; the only thing he needed was customers. They, apparently, were not numerous. Nor did Donahue actively seek them out; life without responsibilities was much more pleasant. And there was the Woolworth money, via his wife, Jessie, which enabled the Donahues to live the good life.

Well before the end of October 1920 there was some reason for the Woolworth sisters to feel a bit nervous about attending meetings of corporation directors. Secret Service and Department of Justice agents, plus detectives of the bomb squad at Police Headquarters, were guarding the Woolworth Building.[15] It soon became public knowledge that Postmaster Thomas C. Patten of New York had received a letter signed with the name "Knights of the Red Star, American Anarchist Fighters of New York." The letter stated that the government must release all industrial and political prisoners. Otherwise the Woolworth Building would be blown up.

The threat soon was erased when a Russian-born immigrant was discovered to have written the letter as a scare-technique. The man was arrested. On the same day of his arrest, three Finnish immigrants were fined for distributing anarchist posters in Harlem. The activities of anarchists were keeping authorities busily engaged.

There were other activities to keep police and federal agents busy, too, after the entire country had gone "dry" in January 1920. To satisfy the tastes of U.S. citizens who had no intention of obeying the new prohibition law, illegal speakeasies quickly began operating as bootleggers commenced to battle among themselves over control of various territories. More compliant citizens who obeyed the new "dry" law began to patronize, and socialize in, ice cream parlors, which rapidly proliferated around the country. They also bought much more candy, which increased Woolworth stores' already flourishing candy sales. A newsletter published by one large department store boasted that the nation's one-billion-dollars of annual confectionery sales at this point "ought to convert us all to sweets and make a return to booze forever impossible."

This rosy prediction was belied by a report from the New York Health Commission in December 1921, stating that there had been seven deaths in the New York area during the first eleven months of the year from wood alcohol poisoning but that during one single week in December, there had been five deaths from the same cause. Several other New Yorkers, including a 14-year-old boy, were hospitalized in serious condition from wood alcohol poisoning that same week of December.

At Woolworth's executive board meetings, Frank Woolworth's brother, Sumner, pushed the idea that the company should go ahead with the building of the Woolworth edifice that his deceased brother had wanted constructed in Watertown as a memorial to the Corner Store and its owner, William Moore. In 1921, the Watertown Woolworth Building would be completed as a memorial to both Moore and Woolworth at a cost of almost $1 million, continuing to serve as the site of the corporation's annual meeting. This new building boasted six floors as it reigned proudly over the westerly corner of the town square—a Woolworth store dominating the lower floor and eager tenants renting offices on upper-level floors.[16]

On October 17, 1921, Woolworth executives learned that agents of the Sinn Fein had summarily closed the corporation's Dublin, Ireland, stores that morning and had plastered signs on the Woolworth stores' walls. "Warning. These shops are selling boycotted goods," the posters proclaimed. When customers continued to enter the buildings, armed men came into the stores and ordered everyone into the street. Then they locked the doors while the Irish Republican Army saw to it that the crowd outside was kept moving.

It was the kind of hassle that Woolworth's had not anticipated when the company had opened stores in Dublin. But there was good financial news for the F. W. Woolworth Company that year as, after the Panic of 1920 had eased gradually, it was estimated that the company's sales for 1921 would total $147,500,000.[17] This was a gain of $6,600,000 over the previous year. And by 1922, the lagging stock market was climbing. As more working-class Americans found jobs, they began satisfying their aspirations to own player pianos, phonographs, and even static-ridden radios and slightly less-noisy automobiles—all of which could be purchased on credit terms. The fabulous 1920s were in full sway by this time as average Americans often were lured away from their player pianos, phonographs and radios at home by the attractions of newly erected and richly decorated motion-picture palaces. There, the full-throated music of three-tiered theater organs ringed with rainbow lights entertained theater patrons as they awaited the appearances of Mary Pickford, Colleen Moore, Harold Lloyd, or Richard Dix on the silver screens.

Young American women quickly adapted to the latest fashion—bobbed hair, a la movie actress Colleen Moore style, and, a few years later, to the flat-chested, boyish shingle-look and the short skirts of so-called flappers. Woolworth's sales of accessories also increased—compacts containing face powder and, even rouge (two cosmetics previously condemned by ministers of the gospel as used only by "ladies of the evening"), head scarves and "goggles" (the latter to protect the eyes of young

WOOLWORTH BUILDING, WATERTOWN, N. Y.

The six-story Woolworth Building in Watertown, New York, completed by the Woolworth Company in the early 1920s, shortly after the death of Frank Winfield Woolworth. (Jefferson County Historical Society)

people who rode about in the rumble seats of snazzy roadsters speeding along gravel roads on the outskirts of most towns).

In 1916, a federal child labor law finally had been passed, protecting children under 16 years of age from mine work, night work, and from working more than eight hours a day. Early in 1920, the suffrage movement saw success when women were, at last, given the vote. The 1920s were bringing serious considerations to the image-conscious and (or) reform-minded company executives at this point in America's slow but steady progress in providing employee benefits. For non-profit-sharing employees,[18] the Woolworth company set up a workers' benefit fund in 1920 for aiding needy employees. Two years later, the company established, for profit-sharing employees, a group life insurance policy with total disability provisions and with policyholders and Woolworth each paying a share of the premiums.

The status of the Fifth Avenue Woolworth mansion remained in limbo in early 1922 as a spokesman for the law firm of Wolf & Kohn gave an interview to reporters regarding the suit the committee representing Frank Woolworth's widow, Jennie, had brought against J. S. Bache in the Supreme Court of New York in an attempt to force him to complete the purchase of the Woolworths' Fifth Avenue home, according to their signed contract. The spokesman reported that it was estimated that one-fourth of the houses on New York's Fifth Avenue, extending from Sixtieth to Ninetieth

Street, "have had their titles rendered unmarketable."[19] This had occurred as a result of a recent decision by the Supreme Court of New York which then dismissed the Woolworth complaint and affirmed the previous judgment of the trial court.

At the time Frank Woolworth had built the house at the turn of the century, a permit had been issued by the Park Department authorizing the erection of a home that would encroach several feet beyond the proper building line. Frank Woolworth had paid a fee for this authorizing permit, but Bache's lawyers had contended that the encroachment belonged to the city and that "no department of the city could take the right to the Avenue away from the people."

Now, with the court's decision on the matter of encroachment, the Woolworths found themselves in a difficult position. Would they have to tear down the Fifth Avenue mansion, in which Frank Woolworth had taken such pride, in order to sell the valuable property?

8

"Everybody's Store"

By July 1922, the F. W. Woolworth Company was operating 1,174 stores in the United States and Canada and was anticipating doing a business that would total more than $160 million for the current year. (On the Saturday before Christmas, the company would report record-breaking sales of $3,119,645 for a single day, with anticipated gross sales for 1922 boosted to $167 million.)[1] Prosperous times encouraged the company to acquire another Fifth Avenue corner, this time at Thirty-fifth Street, with a 42-year, $12 million lease of an 11-story building, with basement and sub-basement, and the right to take possession in August 1929.

The successful financial picture did not prevent Charles McCann from filing a petition in the New York State Supreme Court on behalf of the Broadway Park Place Company, owner of the Woolworth Building, protesting the tax-rate assessment. The petition claimed that the $16,350,000 evaluation of the property and land was too high considering market value of the building and the decline of realty values in the area. It also pointed out that 12,000 persons inhabited the building, while 100,000 people moved in and out daily, causing steady "wear and tear."

Before the end of the year, the Supreme Court ruled on another Woolworth concern—that of allowing Jennie Woolworth (as requested by her two daughters and Hubert T. Parson) to exchange 50,500 shares of her 65,000 shares of Woolworth common stock for $5,050,000 of five-percent gold bonds of the Broadway Park Place Company. The bonds, part of an issue of $7,500,000 on the Woolworth Building property, were the only lien on the property except for a balance of $1,300,000 still owing on the Prudential Insurance Company mortgage.

The Court permitted the exchange, but Justice Gavegan temporized that the permission was not to be interpreted as approval by the Court of the specific action of the committee of Jennie Woolworth's property in the transaction.[2]

Woolworth's expansion movement peaked in May 1924, when Jennie Woolworth's nephew, Roy L. Creighton, headed a group that moved into Cuba to prepare to open the first of five Woolworth stores that soon would be built in that island country. Later in the year, the first store opened in Havana with sales of $7,000 (more than had been anticipated by Creighton) on opening day. And on the home front, the company continued its pursuit of expansion by undertaking a fifty-year lease of property in Astoria, Long Island, where it had plans to erect a new building.[3]

71

In the same month that her nephew had re-located in Cuba, 71-year-old Jennie Woolworth died, with daughters Lena and Jessie at her side, in the Long Island mansion where her husband had died five years previously.[4] Because she had been ill and out of touch with the rest of the world for so long, private funeral services were held at the mansion on the following day, after which Jennie was interred next to her husband and behind the great bronze doors of their marble mausoleum.

The only will ever executed by Jennie had been made in 1889, at the same time that Frank Woolworth had written his will previous to leaving on his first trip to Europe. But since Jennie already was incapacitated when Frank (designated as her sole heir) had died, her will was invalidated. One week after her death on May 21, 1924, the court appointed her two surviving daughters as administrators of their mother's estate, evaluated at $58 million at that point.[5] The estate would be divided among three heiresses: daughters Helena McCann and Jessie Donahue, and the 11-year-old Barbara Hutton — only child of deceased daughter Edna Woolworth Hutton.

Within a few weeks and after a more probing appraisal, the value of the Woolworth estate had grown to nearly $79 million. Each heiress (already in possession, in her own right, of sizable amounts of Woolworth money, with Barbara having inherited $2 million from her mother at the time of Edna's suicide) was now apportioned more than $26 million. At that point, the amount meant little to the very pretty, blue-eyed and blonde Barbara, who already was accustomed to all the trappings accorded a little girl of great wealth — nannies, chauffeurs, elaborate wardrobes, and training in etiquette and social graces by the staffs of exclusive boarding schools for young ladies. She had, in fact, everything except personal, loving attention from her father, without which the motherless only child would, in her lifetime, never be able to fill the void of an inner loneliness that continued to gnaw at her like an insatiable hunger in the midst of a whirl of parties for the elite, world travels and myriad love affairs. The hackneyed phrase "poor little rich girl" would be applied countless times in future newspaper items referring to Barbara, Doris Duke, Gloria Vanderbilt (a bit later) and a few others of their rarified domain — but, surely, to none more applicably than to the golden girl Barbara Hutton.

In late December 1924, the F. W. Woolworth Company made its estimation, as usual, of the amount of business that would be done for the year beginning January 1, 1925. The aggregate figure would be $90 million, the company predicted, adding that approximately $35 million of the total amount would be taken in during the month of December.

The increased volume of business fired company directors with even more enthusiasm for realizing the company founder's dream of expanding Woolworth stores into more cities and more countries. Frank Winfield Woolworth's dreamhouse on Long Island, however, presented a different kind of challenge to Woolworth heirs. The founder's 18-acre Long Island estate with its white marble castle (built at a cost of $2 million) was put up for sale at auction in June 1925. Four years earlier, Walter Chrysler of the Maxwell Motor Company had offered $800,000 for the properties, which included a nine-hole golf course, a bathing beach and extensive gardens. The heirs had refused that offer, asking for an additional $50,000. Now, only an estimated 50 people drove past luxurious estates of neighbors such as J. Pierpont Morgan to arrive at the auction of Winfield Hall. When bidding opened at $100,000, the responses from the small gathering were desultory. Attorney Charles S. Noyes finally submitted the winning bid, $395,000, acknowledging that he was bidding on the estate for a client he would not reveal. The client, it turned out, was Charles McCann, Lena's husband, who had attempted to avoid public disclosure.[6]

Since the McCanns had bought their own Long Island estate in Oyster Bay a year earlier, their reasons for buying Winfield Hall seemed unclear. The extensive gardens at Oyster Bay already gave Lena ample opportunity to raise the prize-winning flowers she loved to cultivate. Four years later, Winfield Hall was sold to Robert S. Reynolds, and later was turned into a museum.

The McCanns, whose activities rarely were publicized, chose to live quiet, family oriented lives at a time when many wealthy people, especially the newly rich and so-called "robber baron" type, lived extremely ostentatious lives. Lena's sister, Jessie, was, unlike the McCanns, of this latter, flamboyant type. She and her husband, James P. Donahue, were uninhibited social climbers who spent money recklessly to host lavish parties where illegal liquor flowed as if there never had been a prohibition amendment. Within these circles of party-type socialites, hostesses vied with one another to entertain people with European royal titles, even though, since the end of World War I, many of the titles had become almost worthless as far as money and valuable property were concerned.

The Harvard Advocate, joining the ranks of those who made fun of "drys" and of the prohibition amendment, held a contest in 1924 to stigmatize those who strictly upheld the amendment. A young woman by the name of Kath G. Welling won the prize for her suggestion — "spigot-bigot."

Young Barbara Hutton, when on "breaks" from the routines of boarding school, frequently spent time with her Aunt Jessie or Aunt Lena. Lena McCann was warm and loving to her niece, but it was fun-loving Aunt Jessie who captured Barbara's adoration because of her bubbly personality. Barbara's two Donahue cousins— Woolworth and Jimmy, both close to her own age — were fun-type youngsters, too.

But even happy-go-lucky Jessie must have been subdued when, only a few days after the lagging Winfield Hall auction in June 1925, the Woolworth townhouse on Fifth Avenue also was auctioned off to the highest bidder. With the sale of Frank Woolworth's elaborate home (assessed at $400,000) to a syndicate for $282,000, a representative for the syndicate stated that the property was still on the market and that he expected it would be purchased eventually as a private home, because "it would be a crime to demolish such a costly residence."

Since the demolishing of their parents' home was exactly what the daughters had feared might happen, they were relieved at the buyer's announcement. But they learned, on New Year's Day 1926, that the townhouse had been re-sold and that the mansion did, indeed, face the wrecking ball. On June 1, plans to "replace" the Fifth-Avenue home of the late F. W. Woolworth were made public. The replacement, slated for completion in the summer of 1927, was to be a cooperative apartment building, which would be sold on a 100 percent cooperative plan. Covering a ground area 27 feet by 110 feet, the building of luxurious, outsized apartments would loom 13 stories, plus a penthouse and roof garden, over Fifth Avenue.

The climbing profits of the F. W. Woolworth Company in the past few years of the prosperous 1920s inspired company directors to write off the last of what had been a total $50-million good-will asset in October 1925.[7] Soon afterwards, Barbara Hutton, now 13 years old, received approximately $10 million for the sale (engineered by her stockbroker father, the trustee of her estate) of 50,000 shares of her Woolworth stock in early 1926.[8] The shares were privately distributed by bankers at a little more than $200 a share. A March 2 *New York Times* headline announced that the "timely stock sale saved Woolworth heiress $850,000."[9] On that same day of the announcement, and largely due to the $10 million stock sale that had just taken place, Woolworth common stock dropped in value to $183 a share; within two months the stock took a deeper drop. In the meantime, Hutton had invested his daughter's money in various bonds and securities.

The estate of Frank Woolworth had been enriched by a 25 percent income tax rebate (in the fiscal year ending June 30,1925) when the Treasury Department distributed refunds to a number of prominent individuals. The Woolworth estate was paid $669,359 to head the long list of individuals collecting refunds, while John D. Rockefeller collected $457,870 and Secretary of the Treasury Andrew Mellon was paid $404,871.[10]

Barbara (plump, pretty, and definitely resembling her grandmother Jennie at the time she married Frank Woolworth) was too young at that point to appreciate, or even care about, the increased value of her inherited estate. And although she never would become personally involved in the management of her finances, she would, before too long and as she approached the end of her teen years, learn how to spend tremendous amounts of her assets without any concern for conservation.

In this same year of 1926, Franklyn Hutton married a woman who, regardless of her efforts to be friends with her husband's teenage daughter, filled a storybook stepmother-role in Barbara's jaundiced eyes. The young girl was not really "friends" with her father; yet she resented the intrusion of Franklyn's new wife into the desultory father-daughter relationship that had existed, largely, by occasional long-distance phone calls and by rare, brief visits from Franklyn to wherever his daughter happened to be staying at various times. His welcome at the home of either Lena or Jessie surely would have been only perfunctory; both sisters were well aware that the suicide of their sister Edna had been triggered by Franklyn's neglect of his wife and his pursuit of other women.

But after Franklyn's recent marriage, he seemed to take more interest in his daughter. He petitioned the Surrogate Court for money to buy, for Barbara, one of two adjoining duplex apartments in a Fifth Avenue building. The apartment would provide a 26-room home for Barbara. Franklyn and his wife would live in the adjoining, ample quarters.[11] In time, Barbara would lose her distaste for her stepmother (who was not of the society world where Franklyn Hutton might have been expected to find a wife) and would acquire some appreciation for the woman's sincerity.

Despite February's bitter cold weather, Woolworth stores reported a sales gain of $1,630,998 for the first two months of 1926 compared with the first two months of the previous year.[12] Woolworth's two major competitors, S. S. Kresge Company and McCrory Stores, reported sales gains, also, over the previous year. But the Woolworth Company had opened 67 new stores in 1925, bringing its total number of stores to 1,423. Kresge moved ahead, too, adding 48 stores to its roster, totaling 304 at the end of 1925. The McCrory and Kresge companies now had 183 stores and 166, respectively. Competition among the Five and Dimes was putting pressure on Woolworth but, determined to retain its lead, the Woolworth company was already looking ahead to expanding its operations into still another country — Germany.

Woolworth President Hubert Parson nourished ambitious plans for the expansion of the company in the United States, too. After all, the American economy was booming, the stock market was reaching unparalleled heights, and tempting credit plans continued to lure Americans into a frenzy of buying as production soared and people ordered washing machines, refrigerators, and new furniture for their homes. Although 59.5 percent of Americans had annual incomes of $2,000 or less in the latter years of the 1920s, some 8.2 percent of families had reached unprecedented yearly incomes of $5,000 or more. Spend, spend, spend appeared to be the byword for Americans who thought the good times would never end.

The first reports, in March 1926, of a $683,000 jewelry theft from Jessie Woolworth Donahue's suite at New York's Plaza Hotel (where, she claimed, her family had been living while repairs were being made to their Eightieth Street townhouse) [13] must have elicited at least of sigh of resignation from her sister, Lena McCann. The explanations of how and exactly when the theft had occurred were murky, at best, as they were printed in a series of articles. The explanations were complicated further by the sudden mysterious return of the stolen gems.

The resulting barrage of publicity picked up its pace when the "Gem Theft Case" finally was scheduled to be heard before a jury in November of 1926. So this last burst of publicity did not overshadow the October wedding that Helena Woolworth McCann was planning for her daughter Constance to Wyllys R. Betts Jr., son of a prominent, "old-money" New York family.

Constance, the first-born grandchild of Frank and Jenny Woolworth, had been carefully reared by her parents and then was graduated from the exclusive environs of Miss Porter's School in Farmington, Connecticut. After graduation, she spent a year at a finishing school in Paris, then made her formal debut to New York society and became a member of the Junior League. The groom was waiting at the altar in St. Patrick's Cathedral as the bride came down the aisle, following a lengthy procession by the St. Patrick's choir, eight bridesmaids, the maid of honor and a young sister of the bride (13-year-old Helena) and a sister of the groom, serving as flower girls.[14] Everything was properly and nicely executed with masses of flowers and even tall oak trees, with leaves in autumn colors, that had been miraculously transported into the sanctuary.

Some 1,000 guests attended the buffet reception at the McCanns' Eightieth Street home, after which the newlyweds sailed for Europe on the *Mauritania*. A Park Avenue apartment awaited their return to New York.

If the weddings of the three daughters of Frank and Jennie Woolworth had been given scant mention in newspapers, the wedding of their first granddaughter commanded respectful attention in the *New York Times*, which listed hundreds of guests' names in the lengthy account of the wedding.

Long before the newlyweds, Mr. and Mrs. Betts, returned to Park Avenue, Jessie Donahue appeared in court as the chief witness in the trial of private detective Noel C. Scaffa. Scaffa had been charged with compounding a felony when he had paid $65,000 in Donahue reward money for the return of Jessie's jewels and, it was charged, had withheld information from the police that might have helped solve the theft.

Jessie, who had built up a reservoir of self-confidence and assurance in her years of hobnobbing with social gadabouts, spoke in a firm, clear voice as she was asked about the jewelry theft. She recalled that she had returned to her Plaza suite late in the afternoon on the day of the theft and had gone directly into her bathroom, leaving the key in the outside lock of the entrance door to the apartment so that her masseuse could come in when she arrived. While in the bathroom she heard voices in the apartment, including the voice of her masseuse.[15] (She did not say anything about having heard the voice of her husband, although it soon would become known that James P. Donahue was in an adjoining room to the bedroom from which the jewelry had disappeared.)

Ten minutes later, Jessie said as she continued with her court testimony, she went into her bedroom for her massage and, soon after the masseuse left, she claimed she began to get dressed for the evening, but could not find her pearl necklace, valued at $683,000. Nor could she find her handbag, which contained a $30,000 ten-carat diamond ring.

It was quite possible that someone other than the masseuse could have opened the door to the apartment with the key she had left in the lock, Jessie admitted in response to a question from Scaffa's attorney. The attorney pointed out that Scaffa had received a phone call from a mysterious "Sam Layton" who told him to come to the Prince George Hotel. The caller, the attorney claimed, thereupon returned the missing jewelry to Scaffa without explanation, but on receipt of a generous reward from the Donahues, and paid by Scaffa to the mystery man, Layton. Scaffa brought the jewels to Police Headquarters and the office of Inspector Coughlin who then sent for the Donahues who, in turn, identified the jewels.

Jimmy Donahue was the next witness, claiming that Scaffa had suggested the offering of a reward. Accusations flew back and forth, from lawyers to witnesses and from lawyer to lawyer. Even as an attorney questioned Donahue about the reason why the theft was not reported to police for two days after it occurred, the actual thief remained unidentified. The story kept newspaper readers entertained and left the jury befuddled and unable to reach a decision as to whether Scaffa had compounded a felony. Defendant Scaffa was released on $10,000 bail with a date not yet set for a new trial.[16]

Before the close of 1926, the Woolworth Board of Directors declared a stock dividend of 50 percent at a time when the company could look back on an unusually productive year of business.[17] During 1926, 65 stores were added to the Woolworth chain and 45 more new stores already were under lease for 1927, including a corner site at Third Avenue and Fifty-ninth Street where a two-story-and-basement building already was under construction. The building would be occupied solely by the

F. W. Woolworth Company. Just one block away, Bloomingdale Brothers had purchased a corner lot on Third Avenue for their department store.

On Christmas Eve, 1926, Woolworth boasted of sales totaling $3,617,444 for the day. At the same time, the Woolworth business in England was doing so well that company director R. H. Strongman already was in Berlin selecting locations for new Woolworth stores in Germany.

The ban on allowing married women to teach school or to work in many stores and offices in the United States was echoed in Europe as well. In the spring of 1927, Lady Astor, defender of women's rights in England, was eloquent during a debate that raged in the House of Commons on Sir R. Newman's bill to prevent public authorities from dismissing married women because of their marital status or of refusing to employ them in the first place. As the debate ran on and on, Lady Astor boldly defended the bill by stating that, in matters of efficiency, mothers rated higher than some members of Parliament. Nonetheless, the bill was rejected.[18]

Hubert T. Parson, Woolworth President, spent considerable time in Germany in 1927, as preparations were made for opening several Woolworth operations in that country. There, Parson pointed out, the company could get quick access to some 98 percent of its stock because almost everything that would be sold by German Woolworth was manufactured in that same country. Woolworth's first 25-and-50-pfennig store in Germany was a two-floor leased building in Bremen, a busy port on the Weser River. President Parson reported back to New York from Germany that "The grand opening in Bremen attracted some 10,000 visitors to the store on July 29th."[19]

The Bremen store would be only the beginning of the German Woolworth chain; the company already had leases in various German cities for ten other stores that would open that same year of 1927, plus leasing the premises in Cologne that had been occupied by a major department store — Bergmann's. Since the English Woolworth stores tallied a 21 percent increase in the first quarter of 1928, it was expected that the company's German stores would do almost as well after the opening, in Cologne, of the eighth Woolworth store in early 1928.[20] In these prosperous latter years of the 1920s, Woolworth had no qualms about leasing 20 more locations in Germany, also designated to open in 1928.

Of the total 100 stores that Woolworth was scheduled to open in 1928, 75 were under construction by March of that year. And with Woolworth business assets growing at an unprecedented rate in these years and company President Parson predicting a 20 percent increase in earnings for 1928, the James Donahues bought a palatial Palm Beach home, Ceilito Lindo, located conveniently near the popular Bath and Tennis Club. If Jessie had any concerns about the variety of male friends visiting her husband and with whom her husband was seen in various clubs, there was no evidence of any such concerns in her passionate campaign to be a part of the upper echelon of Palm Beach social activities — many of them presided over by the Edward T. Stotesburys in their sumptuous, ocean-front, winter villa, El Mirasol, with aristocratic neighbors such as the Vanderbilts and Astors.

When Edward Stotesbury, President of the Society of Arts, arranged for operatic diva Geraldine Farrar to give a concert at the Paramount Theatre in Palm Beach on February 21, 1928, the Stotesburys entertained several notable guests in their plush

Woolworth store in Stuttgart. Germany had many Woolworth stores built before World War II that had to be rebuilt or replaced after the war. (John Compton Collection)

Paramount box.[21] Among others who entertained at various pre- or post-concert events were Jessie and Jimmy Donahue, who hosted a house-warming supper-dance at Ceilito Lindo following the concert. More than 200 people attended the house warming where Metropolitan Opera baritone Guiseppe Danise entertained them. Even Jessie's much more conservative sister, Lena, surely would have approved of the house-warming party that evening, but would not have approved of her sister's continuing, almost frenzied, pursuit of entertainment and parties, many of which she hosted at her Florida mansion. Jessie also gave frequent luncheons and teas on the Donahues' private beach, but these generally were more circumspect than some of the evening affairs.

Jimmy Donahue had no more time or inclination to pursue the stockbroker business that he had set up on New York's Park Avenue than he previously had when he worked for the E. F. Hutton Company in which his brother-in-law, Franklyn, was a partner with Franklyn's brother Edward. Nonetheless, Donahue's wealthy lifestyle came close to rivaling that of Edward F. Hutton, husband of Post cereal heiress Marjorie Merriweather Post Hutton, whose philanthropic works, particularly in her generous contributions and personal service to the Salvation Army, were frequently lauded in the media. Duly reported, also, were the swanky parties given by Post-Hutton in her 140-room Palm Beach, Italian stone mansion, Mar-a-Lago.[22] The magnificent home — a kind of masterpiece, even for Palm Beach — would be sold, years later, to Donald Trump, who would turn it into a prestigious club where wealthy members could rent a suite for $1,500 a night.

While Marjorie Merriweather Post Hutton busied herself with the Salvation Army, her husband, Edward, did a lot of golfing in California where he recently had set up an auxiliary stockbroker office. He was occupied also with making plans to sail the magnificent yacht, *Hussar*, that he was having built in Germany — 322 feet long and requiring a crew of 70.

DONAHUE RESIDENCE, PALM BEACH FLORIDA—128

Jessie Woolworth Donahue's estate, Ceilito Lindo, in Palm Beach, shown in a postcard photograph. The estate was one of the largest in the area. (Author's Collection)

· On May 1, 1928, Jessie Donahue and her sister Lena donated $100,000, in memory of their father, to the building fund for the Museum of the City of New York.[23] John D. Rockefeller Jr. was an even larger contributor, pledging $250,000 toward the new museum that would be erected on an entire block-front on Fifth Avenue. And on May 17, both Jessie and Jimmy Donahue, and surely Lena McCann as well, were relieved to see the end of the Scaffa case and its attendant publicity. At this fast-moving second trial, Scaffa was quickly acquitted of compounding a felony in bringing about the return of Jessie's jewels stolen from her Plaza Hotel suite.[24] On the same day that Scaffa was acquitted, the Woolworth Company held its annual meeting and announced that its net income for 1927 had been $35,350,473, with total sales for the year climbing to $272,754,045. President Parson soon predicted that the end of 1928 would show still another 20 percent increase in earnings. The financial outlook was rosy and an exuberant American public had great faith in its future.

In April 1929, and just previous to the early May date that the company would celebrate its fiftieth anniversary, Woolworth adopted a $50 million group-life-insurance program for its employees.[25] On May 5, a feature article in the *New York Times* (selling for two cents for a weekday copy) pointed out the humble beginnings of the Woolworth Company and contrasted those early times and struggles with the great success it currently enjoyed, symbolized by the towering Woolworth Building casting the brilliance of its thousands of lights against the New York skyline at night.

Still, there were other buildings in the planning for New York City that would loom even higher than the Woolworth edifice. A company founded to finance a tall Empire State Building planned to complete its project in April 1931. When the committee for this building learned that Walter Chrysler had secret plans to build a

Chrysler Building that would reach almost 1,146 feet, the plans for the Empire State Building were expanded to stretch to a still higher elevation.[26]

To emblazon its advertising of great sales in its anniversary year, the Woolworth Company used catchy phrases that had developed over the years to define itself. "Everybody's Store."[27] And later in 1929, "America's Christmas Store."

Even though the Kresge chain now had 364 five-and-ten cent stores and as many as 142 25-cent-to-one-dollar stores, which enabled Kresge to sell a much greater variety of goods, Woolworth stuck to the same five-and-ten-cent policy that had brought success and increased capital stock presently valued at $200,000,000. But the optimism of the business world of the late 1920s was shattered suddenly when the stock market tottered on Black Thursday, October 24, 1929. People panicked—not only businessmen and financiers with great amounts of money invested, but also "small" investors (storekeepers, waiters, office cleaners, and others with as little as a few thousand dollars in stock)—when the market crumbled into total collapse on Tuesday, October 29.

Before the market collapse, Woolworth already had contracted for the sale of ten-cent monthly magazines issued by Tower Magazines Inc. Tower claimed that many noted authors would be among the contributors to the bulky periodicals, each running from 128 to 132 pages. *The Homes Magazine, The New Movie Magazine, The Illustrated Love Magazine,* and *The Illustrated Detective Magazine* went on sale on Woolworth counters in November.[28]

Even while debates raged in Congress regarding tariffs and duties on certain imported goods, Woolworth President Parson issued a statement shaped to help restore confidence in the coming year. "Business cannot stop," he said, "because of the tariff uncertainty. We have got to buy goods, and our buyers have been advised to proceed accordingly, taking the chance that rates may be advanced."[29]

Labor spokesmen had been promoting more tariffs and duties on certain imported goods, pointing out that a trademark was a monopoly, and that labor needed protection against importation of trademarked products of American-controlled manufacturing plants in foreign countries. The owner of an American trademark, they insisted, should be compelled to produce his trademarked goods in the United States, or face heavy tariffs. In November 1928, Woolworth had won substantial reductions of duties on a number of imported items classed as toys and previously subject to duty at 70 percent. Since the sale of toys made up a significant part of its business, Woolworth was relieved with a new United States Customs Court ruling which lowered duties on imported magnifying lenses to 45 percent, on *papier-mâché* candy containers and figures of barnyard fowls to 25 percent, and on table croquet sets to 30 percent.

The public was made aware of the volume of business done in Woolworth stores by a partial listing, in the company's fiftieth anniversary brochure, of some of the quantities of merchandise sold in the company's 2,248 red-front stores. Millions of dozens of plain, blown tumblers in its glassware departments each year. More than 100 million razor blades and millions of mousetraps in annual sales. Some 600,000 yards of velour made into powder puffs for milady in cosmetics. The list continued, pointing out that approximately 11,000 bales of cotton used for Woolworth's towels kept 2,000 looms working 24 hours a day all year.[30]

This San Francisco postcard features the Woolworth store at the foot of Powell and Market streets, where cable cars were turned around by crews of muscular men so the cars could journey up the hill again. (Author's Collection)

A Pittsburgh Woolworth store at Liberty Avenue and Federal Street in the streetcar era.

Woolworth had weathered depressions and recessions in its 50-year history, and company officers looked ahead to the 1930s with little expectation of changing their pattern of doing business throughout the coming decade.

With 1929 sales of $303 million, they had no conception, as yet, of the years of turmoil and deprivations that the 1930s would bring to American citizens, and to the world.

Certainly, heiress Jessie Donahue continued her happy-go-lucky lifestyle in her usual *joie de vivre* manner without the slightest suspicion of the tragedy that would occur in her family soon after the arrival of the 1930s.

9

A Grim Decade Begins

A heavy, dark veil was drawing across the face of America, smothering the excesses and spending sprees of the 1920s and foreshadowing almost a decade of sobering, chilling years of a worldwide Great Depression. Within a year of the October 1929 stock market crash in the United States, 5,000 of the nation's banks collapsed and six million workers lost their jobs. By 1932, the toll of unemployed would reach 15 million.

Within just a few months of the collapse, some businessmen clung tenaciously to predictions of better times ahead. And regardless of what was referred to as the "dire prophecies of our economic preachers," O. H. Cheney, vice president of the Irving Trust Company with which Frank Woolworth had been so closely associated, addressed the American Bankers' Association in March 1930 to decry the "fatalistic spirit" of bankers and to call for a "philosophy of mastery and action."[1]

At the same March meeting, another banker said that the "Woolworth Company had nearly doubled its number of stockholders" in the few months since the market crash. Woolworth President Hubert Parson joined the spirit of "mastery and action" by continuing his expansion policies and announcing in June 1930 that the company had taken a $1 1/2 million sub-lease to expand its Newark, New Jersey, Broad Street store into an adjoining building.

Before the end of August, Parson proclaimed in print that, by the end of 1930, the Woolworth chain would have 65 new stores in the United States, Cuba and Canada. He pointed out that the company was increasing its business in Germany, with 55 stores operating there, and expanding in Great Britain with the opening of 53 new stores. Although he admitted that Woolworth inventories were lower by some $9 million than those of one year ago, he pointed out the advantage to Woolworth of being able to build up its inventories now in a lower-priced commodity market.[2]

However, shortly before the end of the drab year of 1930, the unemployment committee of the Trades Unions Unity League (an organization referred to as the "Reds" or "Communists" in newspapers) urged that masses of unemployed people should stage hunger demonstrations at Albany and Washington. Conference speakers announced that a petition with one million names would be delivered to President Hoover. The petition would demand $25 a week in unemployment insurance for out-of-work people, with the government also supplying $5.00 a week for each dependent of an unemployed person. Other extreme proposals were made, including free coal and rent for the poor, and a tax on all income of more than $5,000 a year and on all capital and property in excess of $25,000.

It was not an appropriate time for the rich to flaunt their wealth. Woolworth heiress Barbara Hutton, who became eighteen years old in November 1930, debuted to society at a lavish pre–Christmas party given by her father and stepmother for some 1,000 guests, as C. David Heymann (author of *Poor Little Rich Girl*) reports in his book. The party, Heymann wrote, took over the "entire first floor" at the plush Ritz Carlton in New York City. The constant popping of champagne corks proved that the rich were not only "different," but they were very "special," exemplified in this severe period of Prohibition laws. Nonetheless, Barbara, who at age 21 would inherit approximately $45 million, was now launched into society where she soon would learn of the complications that could be created in her life by notoriety resulting from her lifestyle of conspicuous consumption. Although tobacco heiress Doris Duke was even wealthier than Barbara, the prettier Barbara would attract greater publicity and resentment from the American public who shopped at Five and Tens and acquired a kind of proprietary interest in the young and vulnerable Woolworth heiress.

Because she often stayed at one or the other of her fun-loving Aunt Jessie's homes in New York, Palm Beach or Southampton, Long Island, Barbara had become very friendly with her cousin Woolworth Donahue and was especially close to her younger cousin Jimmy Donahue. Sixteen-year-old Jimmy had inherited all the sparkle exhibited by his mother, Jessie, plus a sharp mind that was given to clever banter and *repartee*. He loved to be center-stage and entertained youthful visions of becoming an actor or even a chorus dancer.

The usual openness of the Donahues became a united closed front, however, after they returned to New York from Palm Beach in early April 1931 in their luxurious railway car. Several days later, Jessie was admitted to a private hospital for more than a week during which no one outside the immediate family was informed of her ailment or condition. She was still in the hospital on Sunday, April 19, when her husband who, a newspaper report claimed, also had been in poor health for several days, had lunch at the Donahues' East Eightieth Street home with two friends and the older son, 18-year-old Woolworth. After lunch, the four men played cards (all the Donahues were avid poker and roulette fans) until James Donahue went downstairs.[3]

When the elder Donahue did not return to the poker game, his son went downstairs to look for him and discovered that his father had locked himself inside a bathroom. Ignoring Woolworth's pleading to come out, the father finally did unlock the door only to say, "Well, I've done it."

Donahue readily confessed to his friends that he had swallowed a number of pills. Inside the bathroom, they found a bottle marked "Poison" with the cork removed. While the son, Woolworth, ran to a telephone to call a doctor, Donahue's friends followed directions on the uncorked bottle and mixed an antidote of milk and eggs. By the time the doctor arrived, Donahue had swallowed the antidote and was begging his friends not to inform his wife of what he had done.

The physician, however, was concerned only with getting Donahue to the doctor's private hospital as quickly as possible. Two days later, with his condition worsening, the 44-year-old Donahue made his will, naming his wife as sole executrix of his estate "of undetermined value." Jessie was to receive the Long Island estate (Wooldon Manor) and "all tangible personal property and effects." The two sons would receive trust funds and, at age 35, each would inherit one-third of the residual estate, valued at the time of their father's death at $3,708,783. However, the value of the estate would be drastically reduced, very soon, by an accounting of several major debts amounting to $1,771,040 owed in large part to E.F. Hutton & Co. on marginal accounts.

Steadily weakening and with Jessie at his bedside, Donahue received the last rites of the Catholic Church administered by his cousin, Monsignor Stephen Donahue, secretary to Cardinal Hayes, on the morning of April 23. James Paul Donahue died shortly thereafter. Six hours later, the medical examiner completed an autopsy and reported that death had occurred from mercury poisoning by the ingesting of six tablets, each containing seven-and-a-half grains of the poison.[4]

That same night, Donahue's physician insisted that his patient had not committed suicide. "Mr. Donahue died of uremia," he claimed, "probably brought about by mercurial poisoning, but there is absolutely no evidence whatsoever that the poison was taken with suicidal intent."[5]

Reporters were told by Donahue's immediate family to get in touch with Franklyn L. Hutton for answers to their questions. But each inquiry was met with the response that Mr. Hutton was "out."

Funeral services were scheduled for the morning of April 25 at the Roman Catholic Church of St. Ignatius Loyola with the deceased's cousin, the Monsignor, officiating. A newspaper report stated that there were no priestly assistants at the requiem mass, no eulogy and no honorary pallbearers, but that some "3,000 people crowded into the church and several hundred stood outside."[6] There was a bit of the macabre about the size of the crowds, some of whom may have wanted to view the procedure of a mass celebrated by a Monsignor for a man who had committed suicide — an act officially condemned by the Church. This discrepancy was explained by clerics who pointed out that Donahue had not expired immediately but had lived long enough to repent his hasty act.

In addition to the widow and sons, the deceased's two brothers and five sisters attended the funeral as did the aging widower Charles Sumner Woolworth, still presiding as chairman of the Woolworth board of directors. Frasier McCann, son of Helena Woolworth McCann, was in church to represent the McCann family, and Barbara Hutton attended the service with her father and stepmother.

Soon afterwards, Barbara sailed with her stepmother for London where, in early May, she was officially presented to King George V and Queen Mary. The following day, she attended a garden party given by the Prince of Wales at Buckingham Palace. With these impressive formalities accomplished, the attractive five-and-dime heiress joined what Elsa Maxwell (famous party-giver and close friend of Barbara's Aunt Jessie, who was one of Maxwell's benefactors) called, in her autobiography, the "invasion of Europe" by American daughters of men of newly created wealth who were "looking for husbands with genuine or phony titles."[7]

Barbara had left for England only shortly before her Aunt Jessie responded to a $100,000 slander suit filed against her by a Jane O'Roark, claiming that Jessie Donahue had made slanderous statements about her.[8] The so-called statements included charges of Jessie having said that O'Roark had been an evil influence in James P. Donahue's life, had been responsible for having him "wreck himself" and was to blame for his suicide.

Denying that his client ever made such statements, Jessie's attorney was now asking the New York Supreme Court to require O'Roark to list just where and to whom the alleged statements were made. Only now that the slander suit became public knowledge did there seem to be a plausible explanation for Jessie's previously unexplained hospitalization shortly before her husband's suicide. It appeared that the merry-go-round of Jessie Donahue's life had finally jarred to a halt.

Nor was the Woolworth company itself immune to suits. Actress Louise Squire was seeking reparations from Woolworth at this same time because, she claimed, her scalp was scarred when a water-wave comb she had purchased in a Woolworth store exploded while she was drying her hair with electricity. Actor George Jessel testified on Squire's behalf, saying that her ability as an actress had been affected seriously because of her injuries.[9]

Although a company attorney claimed the actress was at fault for using the comb in connection with electricity and that the manufacturer, if anyone, was responsible, a New York Supreme Court decision awarded the plaintiff $25,000 two months later. Squire's attorney was quick to offer his opinion that the verdict "was the largest of its kind in this state." His opinion might have been correct — damage suits of this type were rare in any state during the 1930s, although breach-of-promise suits were filed frequently.

The O'Roarke suit against Jessie apparently faded into limbo (it may have been settled privately by Jessie to avoid further publicity.) Jessie and her two sons soon left their New York home, did not return to Southampton that summer, and, instead, departed for European travels—leaving behind the homes that held such unhappy memories of the husband and father's suicide.

Next door to the abandoned Donahue home in the Woolworth compound, Jessie's older sister, Lena, continued to live her quiet, unpretentious and family oriented life. She spent considerable time in spring and summer at the McCanns' Oyster Bay estate where she usually could be found in her flower gardens, nurturing her exotic blooms. In the spring of 1932, she won the Sweepstake Award from the Westbury Horticultural Society for her display of varieties of large trumpet narcissi, including three Lord Wellington specimens. With the arrival of autumn, Lena occupied herself with charity events and Daughters of the American Revolution affairs, and, in October 1933, with the birth of her first grandson to daughter Constance and her husband, Wyllys Rosseter Betts, Jr.[10]

Despite the continuing economic depression, Woolworth's five-and-dime business was not faltering, although, at a general meeting of the F. W. Woolworth Company of Ireland, Ltd., in London on June 2, 1931, it was determined that Irish Woolworth — its two stores in Dublin and one each in Cork, Belfast, Limerick and Kilkenny — would be liquidated voluntarily. There would be, instead, only one company issuing stock to the public for Great Britain and Ireland.[11]

Including the 53 new stores that the English company had opened in 1930, there were 428 British Woolworth stores in operation at the end of that year. Now, accord-ing to the plan for the recapitalizing and financing of F.W. Woolworth & Co., Ltd,. of England, English Woolworth would offer stock to the public, thereby changing the status of the private company it had been since its inception. The surplus for English Woolworth would increase by $78,000,000 while paying $27,000,000 to the parent company in New York, which owned the controlling interest in the English business. The American company also would receive 51.7 percent of the new ordinary stock issued, valued at $77,000,000.[12]

There was another, and more radical, change in Woolworth policies in early 1932, when the depression years were at their lowest ebb, as the company made its decision to experiment, in 100 of its 1,583 stores, with a new line of merchandise priced at twenty cents. President Parson was quick to announce that the new mer-chandise would be on display in all its stores by July 1, after manufacturers had sufficient time to catch up with production of the new goods for Woolworth.[13]

Parson pointed out that the purchasing offices in the Woolworth Building were jammed with salesmen — up to 400 a day, offering a variety of merchandise that could be sold in quantity for 20 cents each, at a profit. Reporters were told that the whole idea of stocking 20-cent merchandise had been an experiment that had begun in October 1931, in what was referred to as the company's Canadian "laboratory." By March 20, 1932, 20-cent merchandise accounted for 30 percent of sales in the selected stores, thereby guaranteeing the spread of the program throughout the Woolworth chain by July.

Hubert T. Parson soon was replaced as company president, however, by Byron D. Miller, who had begun his career as a learner in Woolworth's Brooklyn store in 1897.[14] Rumors circulated that Parson's retirement "for health reasons" was something other than had been stated. His extravagant personal lifestyle had become similar to that of royalty, his critics complained. They already were nervous about Barbara Hut-ton's lavish lifestyle and they felt that an unostentatious way of life should be more suitable for a Woolworth executive, particularly in those early 1930s years of the depression.

Woolworth lunch counters, however, were very suitable for the needs of hungry customers, who hunched over their stools to eat hot, savory sandwiches accompanied by cups of coffee provided for a total of twenty cents. And despite 1932 being the most depressed year of the Great Depression, Woolworth sales figures for the year, in the United States, Canada and Cuba, amounted to $249,892,861.[15] Net profits were $21,560,734 — down from $25,200,252 in 1931. Even though 1932 had been a declin-ing one, economically, Woolworth still paid its stockholders a dividend (amounting to $2.40 per share that year) as it had paid annually ever since the founding of the com-pany. And by the end of 1933, net profits would rise again to $28,690,884. So, too, would problems rise to confront the Woolworth organization, particularly in Germany.

Lunch counters and savory hot sandwiches were far removed from the exclu-sive hotel dining rooms and pricey restaurants where Barbara Hutton customarily dined as she traveled about Europe, often accompanied by the cousin she found so amusing — Jimmy Donahue. Under the aegis of her Aunt Jessie and social arbiter Elsa Maxwell, Barbara had become a part of the whirl of parties and sporting events that enlivened the world of moneyed pleasure-seekers "on the continent" before returning to her New York apartment in late November 1932 with her stepmother, Irene. Irene had been commissioned by her husband to go to Italy and bring Barbara home because there were rumors that the girl was involved in a love affair with Count Emanuele Borromeo-d'Adda of Rome.

Still not 21 years old and not yet in command of her own finances, Barbara's return to New York was for only a brief time. Near the end of January 1933, she arrived in Los Angeles with the wife of New York publisher Morley Kennerly. Barbara, who wrote poetry, (much of it in sentimental fashion) could well have relished associations with people who had connections with publishers.

As the two women, bound for Australia, stepped onto the San Pedro pier, Barbara parried questions from reporters. Was it true, they wanted to know, that she was engaged to an Italian count? The count, who had followed Barbara from Italy to America, had told them that the two were informally betrothed, the reporters said.

"I'm not going to marry anyone," Barbara replied, and, just as the count appeared on the pier, she added that her denial was final. Still, the count walked with her as she went on board and the couple continued to talk together for a while.[16] But reporters lost interest in the titled Italian as he remained uncommunicative when he came back down to the pier and watched as Barbara sailed off, bound for summertime in Australia. From there she would continue her international lifestyle, moving from country to country as, again, she followed the seasonal travels of restless, and easily bored, wealthy Americans.

While Barbara traveled, the Woolworth Company experienced an unusual year in 1933. Its stores in Germany, where the company had been conducting successful businesses for years, were being menaced in various cities. With the March 24, 1933, opening of a new Woolworth branch store in Halle, Germany, a crowd gathered and threw stench bombs into the store as employees opened the doors to the public. The crowd became so threatening that police, failing to restore order, temporarily closed the entrance doors. Even larger crowds prevented police from re-opening the doors that afternoon.[17]

Woolworth stores were not the only businesses under siege in Germany at this time. Hitler's campaign of terror had begun. American newspapers were reporting, in front-page stories, that German city-owned hospitals were instructed to dismiss Jewish physicians and other Jewish employees on their payrolls. Windows of Jewish-owned stores were smashed and properties destroyed. And only a few days after the attack on the new Woolworth store in Halle, a Nazi group picketed a Woolworth store in Berlin as storm troopers, wearing boots and uniforms marked with swastikas, stood in front of the doors.[18]

By this time, Woolworth officials had learned that rumors about Woolworth being Jewish-owned were circulating throughout Germany. Under pressure from the Nazis, six Woolworth stores were forced to close their doors. Only when the company went to great lengths—embarrassing itself enough to place a poster in the window of a closed Berlin store, stating that Woolworth was not a Jewish enterprise and was not operated with Jewish capital—could that store be reopened.

The secretary to the Woolworth Company's president went further in a statement issued in New York. "Mr. Woolworth was born in Jefferson County, New York, of English stock and his ancestors had been in America since 1600. He was not a Jew."[19]

The highly respected, Nobel prize-winning Albert Einstein spoke out from Antwerp to say that the economic and social existence of Jews in Germany was "extremely difficult," but that he did not believe the present rulers of Germany were anxious for war. Nonetheless, Einstein stated that Germany was no place for him as long as the persecution of Jews continued.[20]

In Brooklyn, 3,000 Jews adopted a resolution to boycott German-made goods "until the reported atrocities against Jews in Germany shall cease." In Lawrence, Long Island, leading clergymen of Catholic, Protestant and Jewish faiths signed a resolution calling upon the United States Department of State to demand an investigation into reports of mistreatment of Jews in Germany.

At this same time, American cities had their own problems with unrest as strikes proliferated with workers and unions demanding better pay. A cleaners and dyers' union of 10,000 members was threatening to strike. Tobacco workers were demanding a minimum wage of $13 a week. And by this time, President Roosevelt and the Department of Commerce were working hard to bring more employers under the provisions of the NRA Blue Eagle, specifying employees' right to organize into unions and to bargain collectively with employers.[21] On September 1, 1933, every unit of the International Telephone and Telegraph Company and 1,800 Woolworth stores went under the Blue Eagle. But as early as July 16, Woolworth executives had announced that its minimum wage of $7.50 a week would be boosted to $10 a week in Pennsylvania, West Virginia and Ohio, accompanied by a general increase in wage scale.[22]

On the same September 1933 date that the German government announced that police and militiamen would begin clearing beggars from Berlin streets, the Woolworth Company in Berlin pledged 25,000 marks (almost $9,000) to the German Community Chest to combat cold and hunger in the coming winter. Woolworth also pledged to furnish 21,000 hot meals beginning in November and extending to January 1934. The better relations that Woolworth expected would result from its gesture of good will were not immediately evident. Following a German newspaper's article claiming that American Woolworth stores were displaying window-signs asserting "Not one piece of German goods in our stores," the German government undertook an investigation, which asserted that Woolworth stores had, indeed, continued to purchase German goods. At the same time, an Austrian film, booked to open in Berlin, was banned abruptly when it was learned that an actress and a music composer were Jewish.

While the year 1933 had seen an increase of employment in the United States, particularly in the latter months of the year, Woolworth's problems had expanded as, in October, a bomb exploded in one of its stores in Havana, Cuba. No one was injured because the store had been closed temporarily after its employees went out on strike. But plate-glass show windows shattered and the main entrance to the store was damaged.[23] Following the explosion, there were threats that more American-owned properties would be bombed by Cuban terrorists in a campaign that was only beginning.

Just before the end of December, and very shortly after Woolworth reopened the same Havana store (with many new employees) that had been bombed in October, enraged former employees, who had not gone back to work at the store, staged a riot that resulted in injuries to one young woman.[24] The following morning, native Cuban laborers, armed with clubs and stones, attacked the headquarters of the National Federation of Labor (made up largely of foreign members). The attackers broke down the door of the building and began beating occupants of the headquarters. When some of the members escaped to the roof and then leaped to adjoining roofs, the raiders turned their fury to the destruction of furniture and fixtures while Cuban police failed to interfere with the work of the attackers. Terrorist bombings were now becoming nightly occurrences in Havana as a part of the struggle between union organizations and businesses, many of which were owned by Americans and other foreigners.

In the United States, where Franklin Delano Roosevelt had been inaugurated as president in March 1933, many changes had taken place during that first year of his presidency including the repeal of the Eighteenth Amendment and the establishment of the national slogan — "Follow the Blue Eagle." Nonetheless, hard-fought labor-business struggles would continue to overshadow the country throughout the dismal decade of the 1930s.

10

Protests, Demonstrations and Strikes

While the dark years of the depression wore on, punctuated with union-management strife and upheavals, Woolworth heiress Barbara Hutton returned again to New York City in March 1935. At this point, she had been flaunting a royal appendage to her name for nearly two years, that of Princess Barbara Mdivani. The acquisition of the title had become possible by way of her income from many lucrative investments made from her original Five-and-Dime inheritance, which had attracted the attention of Prince Alexis Mdivani. Mdivani, formerly of the Georgian Soviet Socialist Republic, had then pursued Barbara on her restless quest for excitement and pleasure around the globe.

In the spring of 1933, when Franklyn Hutton had received news from Siam (now Thailand) that his 20-year-old daughter was planning to marry Prince Alexis Mdivani, Hutton was concerned and not without cause.[1] Anyone who had the slightest connection with the international society set knew of the three Mdivani brothers' propensity for latching on to susceptible American heiresses or high-salaried Hollywood motion-picture stars to help support the brothers' fondness for extravagant lifestyles. The brothers had been dubbed the "marrying Mdivanis" for obvious reasons. Prince Alexis had been divorced recently from Louise Astor Van Alen, an American heiress who had presented him with a million-dollar settlement. Both his brothers had married American motion-picture actresses.

Franklyn Hutton was very much aware that on his daughter's twenty-first birthday in November 1933 he would no longer be Barbara's guardian, as she would assume full control of her entire inheritance. He quickly convinced Barbara to delay the wedding until he could meet with her and Mdivani in Paris.

Despite the father's arguments to stall the wedding until his daughter was 21 years old, Barbara and her prince were married in Paris in a June 1933 civil ceremony witnessed by Franklyn Hutton and his wife. This was followed shortly afterwards by a formal wedding in the best traditions of a royal couple at the Cathedral of St. Alexander Nevsky with a half-dozen priests officiating at the Orthodox Russian rites. Invited guests and the curious filled the huge church to overflowing. Outside the church, crowds of people collected to try to catch a glimpse of the princess-bride while 200 pairs of eyes (as the number of gendarmes was reported) kept watch over the mob.[2]

Stories of the elaborate wedding, the following reception at the Ritz Hotel, and the departure of the newlyweds to India (as a part of their trip around the world with cousin Jimmy Donahue in tow) occupied columns in American newspapers read by ordinary citizens who shopped at Woolworth stores. They learned of the bride's gift to the groom — a collection of polo ponies, and the Prince's gift to his Princess— a jade necklace to augment her precious collection of gems.[3] Letters expressing hate and disgust for Princess Barbara began to compile at the offices of Woolworth's board of directors. The directors, in turn, were embarrassed by the notoriety of the heiress who, despite the liberal spending she'd already done, would receive approximately $45 million on her twenty-first birthday (thanks to her father's fortuitous investments of her money over the years.)

It was not too surprising, then, that when the Mdivanis had returned to New York shortly before Barbara's twenty-first birthday to celebrate with a birthday-bash at her Fifth Avenue apartment, a rash of protests— some by way of newspaper editorials— broke out in fever-like proportions. The protests raged against Princess Barbara's exorbitant expenditures at a time when "starvation wages," it was claimed, were paid to shop-girls in Woolworth stores. It seemed that average Americans who bought safety pins, dishpans and shaving brushes at Woolworth's felt a proprietary interest in the well-publicized extravagances of the "poor little rich girl" (now dubbed "America's wealthiest heiress") who, through no initiative of her own, represented her grandfather's company in the public eye.[4] The hate and threatening letters would continue to shadow the pleasure-seeking life of the Woolworth heiress whose every move was followed by reporters and photographers.

Barbara's cousin, Woolworth Donahue, was traveling in a different part of the world in these years, spending many months on an African safari, but without much of the publicity that surrounded Barbara. Even when he went on to India where he picked up a cheetah and then moved on to Cannes, where he walked about with his cheetah on a chain,[5] his exploits did not garner the notoriety that attached itself to Barbara.

Woolworth stores had their own problems with general unrest that prevailed in the early and middle 1930s. Near the end of May 1934, some 1,500 men and women staged a demonstration outside New York's Welfare Department Building. The demonstration rapidly exploded into a riot as police, several of whom were injured in the fracas, tried to control the demonstrators. On June 2, the same group of people held another demonstration outside the Welfare Department Building. This time, a large police detail of mounted men, patrolmen and detectives maintained order, keeping close watch until the leaders of the demonstration moved on to City Hall to talk to Mayor Fiorello La Guardia. The Mayor was not conciliatory. "You want people to starve to serve your own ends," he accused.[6]

Whatever the demonstration leaders might, or might not, have wanted, it was a fact that starvation deaths had occurred throughout the country. New York City hospitals had reported 95 deaths from starvation in one year — 1931.[7] There was no recording for those, including children, who had died quietly of starvation in sparsely populated areas of New York State and various other states.

When the Woolworth organization was challenged by the Non-Sectarian Anti-Nazi League to Champion Human Rights, who demanded disclosure of the company's policy regarding the importation of merchandise from Nazi Germany, Woolworth President Byron D. Miller responded by telegram on March 20, 1934. The telegram stated that Woolworth had discontinued importation of such goods "owing to extreme sales resistance."[8] In 1933, the company had purchased from Germany only 1.25 percent of its merchandise, company officials pointed out, mainly Christmas tree ornaments and Easter novelties, which now would be supplied by companies in the United States. Depreciation of the dollar in foreign exchange had contributed to the change in Woolworth's buying policies.

Again, there were repercussions. The West German Observer, while insisting it would not call for a retaliatory boycott of Woolworth stores in Germany, let it be known, in print, that it was the duty of "every decent German" not to buy anything from a firm that had "so abused our hospitality."

More repercussions followed. Woolworth stores in Kassel and Chemnitz, Germany, closed as demonstrations spread. Crowds picketed other stores, smeared paint across store-fronts, and smashed windows in what was termed by Nazi leadership as opening a counter-offensive against "the malicious Jewish boycott drive in America."[9] The cycle of closing and reopening stores in Germany would continue to be a matter of pressing concern to Woolworth officials.

Despite the notoriety generated by Princess Barbara's royal lifestyle, her Aunt Lena McCann and her family went on quietly with their unspectacular way of life. When the McCanns' younger daughter Helena married Winston Frederic Churchill Guest on June 2, 1934, in the beautiful garden setting of the McCanns' Oyster Bay, Long Island, estate, the next day's *New York Times* gave significant space to the event. The newspaper described the marriage as uniting members of two families "prominent in society of New York, Palm Beach and England."[10] The groom, who had graduated from Yale and gone on to acquire a law degree from Columbia University, had other significant credentials as well, including that of lineage since he was a second cousin to Winston Churchill.

Like Princess Barbara's husband, Helena's new husband was an international polo player and had invited fellow-polo players, including the bride's brother, Frasier McCann, to serve as ushers at his wedding. But the bride's polo playing relative-by-marriage, Prince Mdivani, was not among the ushers, nor even among the guests. It was rumored that he and Princess Barbara already were having marital problems that would have prevented the couple from attending the wedding to hear the Paulist Choir sing at the ceremony while the McCanns' friend, Professor Alexander Russell of Princeton University, performed at the pipe organ. Lena McCann previously had donated an organ, in memory of F. W. Woolworth, to the Princeton University chapel as just one of her many philanthropic gifts, most of which were done without fanfare.

In a lifestyle similar to that of the previously married McCann daughter, Constance, this younger daughter, Helena, had the customary schooling given to children of aristocratic families — at private boarding schools in the East and Miss Porter's School in Connecticut before going on to Italy for another year of studies. Now, the

McCanns could expect that their daughter's marriage to a young man of impeccable background would be a stable union that would carry on the traditions of their family. There was no indication of public resentment toward the wealthy, but circumspect, McCanns as newspapers carried accounts of the McCann-Guest wedding.

At this point, Franklyn and Irene Hutton were concerned about Barbara for two reasons—her faltering marriage to Mdivani and her health.[11] She had gone on a rigid diet when Prince Alexis told her she was "fat"—a fact that she freely discussed with those close to her, including her Aunt Jessie and society's pace-setter, Elsa Maxwell. Barbara's diet was so extreme that some sources have stated she ate no solid foods, that she subsisted on coffee and cigarettes.

Princess Barbara's round face thinned; pounds melted from her body until she achieved an emaciated look that still did not end her exaggerated quest for slimness. The diet would have a lasting effect on her health. Even before she entered a London medical clinic in early June 1934, her father was on his way to England. The ever-present contingent of reporters was on hand with questions when Franklyn and Irene arrived in Southampton. Prince Mdivani was there, too, awaiting the Huttons' arrival. Reporters detected no signs that anything was amiss between the Huttons and the prince as Hutton confided to the press that "Prince Mdivani ... is a great fellow."[12] Then the three entered a motorcar and departed for London.

But Mdivani was no longer with his in-laws when the Huttons entered the clinic to see Barbara. And although Franklyn and Irene spent considerable time inside the clinic, Hutton refused to make any comments about his daughter's health when the couple emerged from the building.

In the sheltered atmosphere of the clinic, the young princess surely was far removed from labor problems at home in the United States (if, by this time, Barbara ever thought of the country in which she was born as "home"). In 1934 the turbulence of nationwide textile strikes and a series of strikes by the American Federation of Labor (AFL) against automobile companies in Detroit and Flint, Michigan, would lead in a few more years to a new kind of strike—sit-down and, later, sit-in strikes which would greatly affect the Woolworth company.

Soon after his inauguration as president in 1932, Franklin D. Roosevelt had become busily occupied in setting up his Works Progress Administration with money from the five-billion-dollar Emergency Relief Appropriation Act that he had steered through Congress. By 1934, out-of-work Americans looked forward to part-time employment under various combinations of letters—WPA, PWA, NYA, CCC and others, but quickly learned that $44.00 monthly (the amount paid to most WPA laborers) would not cover bills for rent, electricity, heat, food and other necessities. Glue-on soles (sold in quantity at Woolworth's) for shoes became popular items as they were affixed to children's shoes that, often, were already too small for the wearers. For gifts, if the Woolworth shopper could afford to buy a gift, economically priced beach pajamas (their use not confined to the beach) were a much desired and stylish item. Or the pajamas could be made from patterns and yard goods, both available at Woolworth stores.

Although, under the WPA program, there were some good results (schools and roads were built) much of the work in the northern sections of the country, during the bitter cold of winter, was only make-do type work. Laborers, supposedly doing road work, had to spend most of their time gathering wood to keep fires blazing to protect themselves from freezing in an era when thermal-underwear and insulated clothing were unheard of, or could not have been afforded if they had existed.

Apart from organized strikes, however, unemployed and poor Americans rarely resorted to resistance or violence in those tough years of the depression. Although there was a sharp increase in bank robberies, most unemployed men did not smash store windows to get groceries or boots for their children. They did not storm relief offices, set up by Roosevelt, to demand rent money or food orders. After duly registering at the offices and having relief "investigators" sent to their homes, they generally were outwardly passive (though rage smoldered in their bellies) when an investigator saw a radio in a home and insisted that the applicant must sell the radio (a luxury) first and use the money for food before re-applying for aid. And despite the "gangster" image of America that had largely arisen in the Prohibition era and continued to exist, that undesirable image was not seen in the faces of average Americans caught in the pain and long-lasting squeeze of the Great Depression.

Out-of-work men and those who worked only a couple of days a week for the WPA hung around barber shops, tire and vulcanizing shops and even gas stations (where the flow of customers had stagnated) to meet with other guys to play checkers, parchesi or, possibly, cribbage. A new board game called Monopoly had debuted at the 1935 Toy Fair but many of the jobless continued to play checkers and cribbage because they could not afford extra expenditures for Monopoly, enticed as they might have been by its play money and rental properties. They could not have imagined at that early date that Monopoly, translated into many different languages, would become one of the best-selling games in the world.

However, a new board game called Chinese Checkers that could be played by two, or as many as six, players, also became a craze in the 1930s. Woolworth's shelves and counters were filled quickly with the new economically priced game, which sold out so fast that the manufacturing company shipped some 15,000 games, each equipped with a good supply of colorful glassy marbles, to Woolworth stores every month.

Mostly, though, Woolworth's Five-and-Dimes continued to be the mainstays for purchases of necessities by hard-up Americans. They bought razor blades. Can-openers. Flannel by the yard for making diapers and kimonos for infants. Pinking scissors, spools of thread and skeins of wool to make "soakers" and sacques. Baby bottles and pacifiers. (By this time, it was considered unsanitary to pacify an infant with homemade "sugar tits.") Although the annual number of births had declined in the depression years and many people had to get by with "make-do" baby supplies, Woolworth's nursery sales were good, and the company finished the year 1934 with total sales of $270,684,797 (up approximately $20.5 million from its worst year of the depression, 1932) and with 1,957 stores in the United States, Canada and Cuba.[13]

Beginning in 1932 with the kidnapping of the Charles Lindbergh baby from the child's nursery and the subsequent finding of the little boy's dead body not far from the Lindbergh home, extortion threats and, sometimes, actual kidnappings terrorized wealthy American families. Some of the families, seeking safety, moved to England, as did the Charles Lindberghs.

There was little fanfare at first when, on May 28, 1934, the *Toronto Daily Star* carried a report on Page 21 of the birth, two months early, of five scrawny babies— identical quintuplets (from one egg)—to an Ontario backwoods woman, Mrs. Oliva Dionne.[14] It is likely that the same-page report of the marital difficulties of Princess Barbara Hutton Mdivani received as much or more attention than did the birth of the premature quintuplets. Within days, though, the tiny babies' struggles for survival began to attract the awed interest of Canadians, Americans and western Europeans.

The premature baby girls could not live, the pundits said. Most prematurely born babies, even in single births, died in the 1930s. And now, five of them? How could they beat such great odds—fed by eye droppers in a drafty house with no electricity nor plumbing as the wizened infants lay curled together in a blanket-lined basket, supported on kitchen chairs, in front of the opened oven door of a cook stove for heat?[15] This contrivance was their incubator? There were cynics who cursed fate for having brought into existence five "skinned-rabbit-like" creatures (as the country doctor who delivered and tended them was said to have described the tiny, underdeveloped girls) to join a poor and already populous family. But even cynics joined the ranks of millions who avidly read newspapers' daily accounts of the quints' barely discernible progress. The birth of the fragile infants and their fight for life seemed to symbolize the battles for survival of the great masses of the jobless trapped in the grinding poverty of the Great Depression. "Miracle babies," the infants were called. Even the most jaded of newspaper readers were heartened to learn of a half-ounce gain by Yvonne or saddened by a half-ounce loss by Marie. No one could imagine at this early date that the Dionne quintuplets would, within another year, become enchantingly plump toddlers; that they would give rise to a new and flourishing Northern Ontario tourist industry and would be visited by royalty; that they would become more popular than movie stars—that, indeed, they would become child movie stars. And Dr. Dafoe, the man who had delivered them as babies, had become their father figure while the Ontario Government provided a home and nursery along with proper nursing care and protective guards.

The Dionnes' likenesses in picture books could be purchased at Woolworth stores where they were piled high on sales counters. Even the new "Betty Boop" dolls, with their bowed lips and long-lashed eyes, could not outsell the Dionnes at Woolworths as 1935 moved into 1936. Boys, of course, preferred their perennial favorites, tin soldiers and, now, the new tin "G" men.

Although the government-built compound which housed the Dionne quints was very near the farmhouse where their parents lived, their father felt forced to resort to various desperate means (including crawling through a drainpipe to try to sneak inside the seven-foot-high fence enclosing the nursery compound) to see, or try to snap a picture of, his famous offspring.[16] There were rights involved with photographing the so-called "quints," and rights concerning other controls that would bring the Woolworth Company into court in September 1938 in regard to the Dionne picture books that the company had purchased in good faith.[17] (For the last two years, the quintuplets' books had surpassed those featuring the curly-headed darling of Hollywood, Shirley Temple.) By a ruling of the Ontario legislature, the quints now were under the direct control of the government in all respects. Any rights that Papa Dionne or his representatives attempted to sell were of questionable value.[18] But the suit against Woolworth and Kresge stores, as well as Pathe News, would be quickly dismissed, possibly because of rising public sentiment that the Ontario government was unfairly barring the Dionne parents from any control over their famous children.

Charles W. Deyo became the new president of the Woolworth Company in December 1935 as President Byron D. Miller retired at his sixtieth birthday.[19] Deyo had begun working in 1902 as an assistant stockman in the London, Ontario, store of Seymour Knox, whose sizeable dime-store company had merged with that of his cousin Frank Woolworth and four other associates to form the F.W. Woolworth Company in 1911. Deyo brimmed with ideas for expansion and growth of the company as economists were predicting that the worst of the depression years were behind the country. Moreover, President Roosevelt's National Industrial Recovery Act (which pressured employers to raise wages, shorten hours, and ban child labor) was declared unconstitutional by the Supreme Court in the 1935-36 era, so Deyo was partially relieved of some of the restrictions that businesses had viewed negatively.

Shortly before Deyo had become president of the company, but while he was chairman of the board (retaining that prestigious office when he became president), he had promoted the idea of removing all price limitations from Woolworth merchandise — a change that company officials claimed was accomplished in November 1935.[20]

In New York City, new Woolworth stores soon were in the planning stage to accommodate expanded lines resulting from removal of price limitations. Among the new stores was one at Broadway and 190th Street and another in Times Square. A far-reaching program of modernization and enlargement of existing stores also was begun as, in 1937, an issue of ten million dollars in Woolworth debentures was sold and would be retired three years later.

In the interim, the financial future for Woolworth appeared to be rosy as the country began its slow climb out of the depression years. Rosy, that is, except for the troublesome and headline-making entanglements of the heiress who could not be disassociated from Woolworth enterprises in the public eye, even though her investments in the company that bore her grandfather's name had been non-existent for a number of years.

When Princess Barbara Mdivani had arrived in New York City in March 1935, accompanied by her cousin Jimmy Donahue, she had been surrounded by bodyguards and was quickly driven to her Aunt Jessie's commodious Fifth Avenue apartment. Barbara had not forgotten her earlier arrival in New York, two years previously, when her Rolls-Royce had been attacked by a crowd of women who beat at the automobile with their fists as they screamed taunts at its occupants—the Prince and Princess Mdivani. But in early 1935, Prince Mdivani was not at Barbara's side. Only her cousin and her personal servants accompanied her. She spent only one night at the Donahue apartment before boarding a flight for Reno, Nevada.

Princess Barbara created headlines in the American press by losing her royal title in ten minutes in May 1935 by way of a Reno divorce from Mdivani on grounds of extreme cruelty.[21] Ten-minute divorces were nothing new to Judge Thomas F. Moran of Reno. He had banged down his gavel many times recently to dispense equally quick divorces to such personages as Jack Dempsey and to Mrs. Marshall Field.

But the day after the Mdivani divorce, the former Princess Barbara became, instead, Countess Barbara with marriage in Reno to Count "Kurt" (as newspapers reported the count's first name) von Haugwitz-Reventlow of Denmark.[22] Only a couple of days before the wedding, the count, surrounded by New York reporters, had firmly denied any intention of marrying Barbara, declaring that he was a "misogamist." This unusual statement by the tall, stern-looking Count Kurt (some 17 years older than Barbara and a winner of the German medal, the Iron Cross, for bravery in World War I) apparently attracted even greater numbers of reporters and photographers to follow the newlyweds on their wedding day and enticed others to pursue the couple after the newlyweds arrived in San Francisco. The count, who did not suffer public displays gladly, determined to do everything he could to thwart reporters and photographers. This would be a turnabout for Countess Barbara who, while married to publicity-seeking Alexis Mdivani, had freely posed for photographers and turned a smiling face toward cameras like a Hollywood starlet responding to strobe lights.

While still in San Francisco, the count handed out typewritten slips of paper with what he said was the correct spelling of his name. The first name was Court, he informed reporters. Not Kurt or Curt, as had been reported previously. With that, Count Court and his countess left on a motor trip, headed east. But Count Court might have accomplished more if he had informed the Danish press, also, of the correct spelling of his name because as late as August 2, the Danish press was still referring to him as Count Kurt von Haugwitz-Reventlow.

By early June, the restless couple arrived in Paris where Barbara told reporters she was "awfully happy" with the count who was "the most charming man I ever met."[23] At the same time Count Court or Kurt announced that they would live in Europe because of the prevalence of gangster activity in America. Even though a number of wealthy American families had moved to England or to the continent for similar reasons, many people were inflamed by the Countess Barbara turning her back on America and, in the haters' opinions, traveling about in luxury on Woolworth money — the hard-earned nickels and dimes of working men and their families.

Early August found the traveling threesome (now joined by Barbara's cousin, the gregarious Jimmy Donahue) in the count's ancestral castle in Denmark where Count Court expected to get away from reporters. He was dismayed to become more aware in those first few months of marriage that Barbara did not share his disdain for the press. Nor, certainly, did her cousin Jimmy who seemed to the count to be an ever-present and ostentatious third person intruding into the privacy of the newlyweds.

But Barbara leaned on her cousin for companionship and now that she was expecting a baby, Count Court did not want to upset her by haggling about Jimmy Donahue. Normally a controlling man, the count tried to restrain his dominating tendencies. Despite his public remarks that he had not married Barbara because of her money, the proud Count Court had to have been sensitive on the subject of finances since he had been the recipient of a $1 1/2 million gift from his bride plus a trust fund for one-third that amount. The money-gift meant very little to Barbara who was fretting, now, about gaining weight during her pregnancy—the weight she had dieted so rigorously to lose.[24]

Barbara had not yet become accustomed to the old-world castle and the Haug-witz-Reventlow estate in Denmark when she was stunned, in early August, by the news of an automobile accident that had taken the life of her former husband, Prince Alexis Mdivani. Details of the grisly accident filled newspaper pages. Driving his car at his usual reckless speed along the Corsa-Figueros Road leading out of Spain, with a woman companion seated beside him, Mdivani accelerated his roadster as the car flashed past a truck and struck a culvert. The roadster leaped into the air and hit a tree before the chassis, ripped away from the front wheels and axle, bounced over several times, then crashed into a ditch. Mdivani's head had gone through the wind-shield. The woman passenger, Baroness Maud von Thyssen, survived with injuries to her face for which she would sue the Mdivani estate.[25]

Countess Barbara received news of the decapitation of her former husband at the Warnemuende, Germany, railroad station whereupon the count and countess, accompanied by Donahue, withdrew into Barbara's private railway car. The railway car promptly was sidetracked onto a ferryboat headed for Gjedser, Denmark, where the Haugwitz-Reventlows would take refuge in the secluded baronial estate that now was supposed to be home to Barbara.

A week later, reporters questioned the count after his arrival with Barbara at a Copenhagen hotel. The count informed reporters that his wife was "most depressed" and that "her nerves have completely broken down over recent events."[26]

A visit to Rome in late September was intended to cheer Barbara. Donahue was with the Haugwitz-Reventlows, of course, because Barbara found solace and enter-tainment from his presence. The Roman political climate of late September 1935 was the subject of controversy in the League of Nations as Great Britain sent a war fleet into the Mediterranean in an attempt to deter Mussolini in his intended invasion of Ethiopia. Count Kurt von Haugwitz-Reventlow (who seemed, by this time, to have abandoned his insistence on being recognized as Count "Court") observed several Black Shirt Fascisti outside his hotel on the evening of September 26, and responded to their presence in an unusual manner. "Viva Ethiopia!" he shouted several times.[27]

The Black Shirts rushed to the hotel entrance where hotel employees tried to hold them back until police arrived. Threatened with deportation for his behavior, the count protested that he had not been serious; that he was only joking. Although known for his austere, stern demeanor, he escaped deportation for his "joke," mak-ing it seem quite possible that his earlier distribution of typed notepapers, asking California reporters to spell his name correctly as "Court," might also have been as much a joke as his pre-marital admission to the press could have been when he claimed that he was a misogynist.

However, when perennial jokester Jimmy Donahue shouted the same fiery words, "Viva Ethiopia," a few days later at a demonstration by a group of Fascisti,

Italian police nabbed him, escorted him to the French border and deposited him on a Paris-bound express train. Donahue retained his aplomb, though, jauntily remarking that he had a home in Paris and would promptly go there. (Actually, he went to a hotel.) When questioned by police about the incident, Donahue's cousin Barbara and her husband said only that they liked Italy and admired Premier Mussolini. On October 2, The *New York Times* published a report that James Donahue regretted his recent actions in Rome and would ask Italy's pardon.[28]

Only a day later, newspapers around the world carried front-page headlines reporting that Mussolini had rallied 20 million Fascisti and had invaded Ethiopia. American newspapers headlined President Franklin Roosevelt's promise to keep the United States "unentangled."

Early November found the Reventlows back in London where they rented a townhouse and settled down to await the birth of their child. They also would make plans for a London home suitable for a Woolworth-Reventlow heir — a home impressive enough to rival the palaces of English royalty.

In that same November, cereal heiress and Salvation Army philanthropist Marjorie Post (Hutton) divorced her stockbroker husband, Edward F. Hutton, after 15 years of marriage, the birth of one daughter, and, it was rumored, the discovery of her husband in a compromising situation with a maid at Mar-a-Lago (Marjorie's Palm Beach home.)[29] She quickly took possession of her former husband's famed yacht, *Hussar*. The prized yacht (so-called largest pleasure-sailing yacht in the world) was re-named *Sea Cloud* by Marjorie. E. F. Hutton promptly resigned his cushy position as chairman of the board for General Foods Corporation and married Dorothy Dear Metzger. But his former wife had married Joseph E. Davies a month earlier. The only mention of Franklyn L. Hutton in the newspaper account of his brother's divorce and remarriages was the reminder to the reader that Franklyn was a brother to Edward, and that Franklyn also was the father of Countess Kurt Haugwitz-Reventlow.

By this time, Franklyn was accustomed to seeing his name in print where he was frequently heralded (however remotely) as the father of the young countess. Whatever his paternal oversights were in the earlier years of his daughter's life, though, he appeared to be a concerned parent in recent years to a willful daughter with a penchant for hasty marriages, quarrels with husbands and, soon, equally hasty divorces.

Woolworth sales for 1935 had amounted to $268,750,483, a decrease of 0.7 percent from 1934. The company also had added 23 more stores to its roster in the United States, Canada and Cuba and extended its group life insurance program to include all employees who had completed one year of service, thereby adding some 30,000 people to the program.

Although company papers would insist that Woolworth officials had adopted its no-price-limitation policy on merchandise in 1935, as late as February 1936 the company announced that it would "keep its 40-cent price policy"[30] and would extend the 40-cent policy to 1,900 of its stores.

For the first time, the establishment of price policy at Woolworth stores appeared, to the American buying public, to be murky. The company's wordy explanation that management had received authority to go beyond the former established price ranges without the necessity of additional action being taken by the board hardly clarified what the public might expect to pay for items at Woolworth's Five-and-Tens in the near future. People could remember clearly that it was only in 1932 that the company had advanced its top-selling price to twenty cents; it advanced its selling price to forty cents in its numerous stores in February 1936. They could remember, too, that Christmas 1935 had found some Woolworth stores already selling "component" items at one dollar and slightly more. They began to wonder if the "Five and Dime" aspect of Woolworth stores would fade away and disappear.

In a clarifying attempt, the company announced on June 14, 1936, that all units would handle articles up to $1.00 in an experiment "to keep the 5-10 cent trade."[31] There would be no limit set by the Woolworth organization, it was said. Former limitations were removed to enable the company to adjust itself to any "merchandising changes the future may require, including the possibility of inflation," company officials stated.

In early February 1936 Countess Barbara had been more than mildly interested to learn that her former brother-in-law, Prince Serge Mdivani (brother to the recently decapitated Prince Alexis Mdivani), had married Princess Louise Astor Van Alen, the American heiress who had been the first wife of his unfortunate brother, Alexis. Only one month after the February marriage in Florida, Prince Serge was equally unfortunate. He was killed while playing polo when his horse collided violently with another mount.[32] So quickly had the hand of fate destroyed the two hard- and fast-living Mdivani brothers. The restless, party-going, pleasure-seeking set that followed the sun around the globe was obsessed, for a while, with gossip about the macabre deaths of the brothers. But by the time Princess Barbara Haugwitz-Reventlow was confined to her London bedroom (outfitted with special hospital equipment) for the cesarean birth of her first child in February 1936, the two Mdivani brothers were nearly forgotten by the high-society set. Now the awed conversations were of Barbara and her child, a healthy boy born on February 25,[33] and of Barbara and the ominous reports about her health.

Franklyn and Irene Hutton were in London with Count Kurt when the child was born. Relieved that the infant was in good health, their concerns for Barbara increased as, four days later, the public learned that the countess, hospitalized by now, was dangerously ill with internal bleeding.[34] For weeks, Barbara languished with a questionable prognosis until, one month after the baby's birth, her condition began to improve. The child was almost four months old when the count and countess took him to the chapel of Marlborough to have him baptized as Lance (at his mother's insistence) Haugwitz-Reventlow.[35]

Since Barbara had been very ill in early March when her Aunt Jessie Donahue and Aunt Lena McCann were honored guests at the opening of two new galleries at the City of New York Museum, Barbara was unable to attend the ceremony. One of the galleries was named for F.W. Woolworth in recognition of gifts made to the endowment fund of the museum by his daughters. The exhibit depicted the gradual evolution of trade from Indian barter to the big stores of the present.[36]

Another very small family gathering of the McCanns took place on August 23, when their son, Frasier, was married in a quiet evening wedding ceremony to Carol Ware of Pond Ridge, New York, at the bride's mother's home.[37] The bride was a graduate of low-Haywood School of Stamford, Connecticut. Frasier had prepared at St. Paul's School for Princeton University and the couple now planned to reside in Bridgewater, Connecticut.

Cousin Jimmy Donahue also remained in London at this time, indulging his passion for stage productions by investing money in a musical revue, Transatlantic Rhythm, scheduled to open at London's Adelphi Theatre on October 2, with scores of celebrities attending. The celebrities packed the house, but the curtains remained closed.[38] Backstage, the cast of American stage and motion picture actresses and actors milled about in turmoil. Torch-singer Ruth Etting had stalled the proceedings, announcing that she would not go on stage until she was paid the $1,500 owed to her by Jimmy Donahue.[39] Donahue, for his part, declared that he was not willing to "sink any more money into the show," pointing out that expenses had mounted well past the budget.

The waiting audience grew restless as a director pleaded with Etting and other reluctant participants to go on stage. They would be paid tomorrow, they were promised. The curtain rose, a half hour late, and the actors, including the fiery actress Lupe Velez and comedian Lou Holtz, performed. "A brilliantly hollow entertainment," the London reviewer wrote for *The Times*. Miss Etting was paid the next day and promptly left on the Normandie to return to New York. Jimmy Donahue boarded the same ship and there was little doubt that Count Kurt Haugwitz-Reventlow was pleased with his wife's cousin's departure from England.[40] When a so-called "anonymous" American backer supplied enough money for the revue to continue, Dorothy Dare (under contract to Warner Brothers) replaced Ruth Etting, and Jimmy Donahue, on his way to New York, could not have cared less whether the revue continued or expired. He had sold his interest in the revue to a syndicate, he told reporters, and received a part of his $50,000 investment back. But he remained committed to going into theatrical production in New York on a bigger and better scale, he added.

It was quite evident that the objections of his mother, Jessie Woolworth, to her son's continued interest in the theater had little effect in discouraging Jimmy in his attempts to be a successful entrepreneur in the show-business world. It is likely that she thought his stage ambitions of his late teens in performing as a chorus dancer might have ended after he danced, at age 20, in a Broadway musical (Hot and Bothered) which closed within ten days of its opening. Now, she was not pleased with his talk of going into another theatrical production in New York, nor was she willing to underwrite additional expenses that he might incur. It was even more likely that, despite her own fun-loving disposition, Jessie Woolworth was disappointed with the lifestyle choices that both her son and her niece Barbara were making.

11

Woolworth Hit by Sit-downs

The Dionne quintuplets were almost three years old in January 1937 and an enamored public read every detail (the adorable little Emilie Dionne had cut still another tooth) published about their carefully managed lives. The five identical miracle-toddlers now owned $543,046 in bonds, their earnings were reported by the Ontario government to be nearing the $1 million mark and a bill was to be introduced into Parliament by which the quints would be copyrighted.[1] They were displayed to long lines of visitors twice a day, each slowly moving line of people able to observe the little girls in their play-yard while the quints had no way of knowing that they were being watched. A disturbing element had come into the famous children's lives, though, as a plot to kidnap the quintuplets was disclosed. Although a kidnapping did not occur, their picture-perfect lives would take many downturns as the five sisters grew out of their charmed toddler years into adulthood.

The average reader of *The New York Times* may have taken more interest in Emilie Dionne's new tooth than in the 1936 Woolworth financial report published in February 1937. The Woolworth hierarchy was pleased to get past the depressing financial report for 1935 and to announce that sales for 1936 had advanced three percent as the company's stock values moved up from $3.20 a share to $3.35.[2]

At this same time, unsettling events were occurring in the heart of the country's automotive industry (the Detroit, Michigan, area) as a wave of contagious sit-down strikes began and soon would spread into other businesses, including stores.[3] In late 1936, 65 General Motors plants were immobilized as huge walk-out strikes shut production down in various states. The GM plant in Flint, Michigan, was unique, however. There, 6,000 workers called for a sit-down strike four days after Christmas, then defied a company order to evacuate the buildings. Thousands of pickets cheered the sit-downers with noisy demonstrations outside the occupied plant. Supporters from other unions set up a field kitchen just outside the gates and hauled ten-gallon milk cans to the site, half of the cans filled with chili and half with hot coffee, while guards tried to keep control of the plant gates. Dragged into the controversy, Governor Murphy made it clear that he remained an advocate of the rights of labor to collective bargaining, but said that he was responsible also for preventing unnecessary injury to industry, commerce and transportation.

Sympathy strikes spread into other automobile and automobile-supply plants after the General Motors strike ended February 11, with eight days, including nights, of constant bargaining talks.[4] General Motors agreed to recognize the union, not to discriminate against strikers and to set up a grievance procedure. The workers strode from the plant in triumph behind a blaring brass band.

On February 27, shoppers in Detroit's crowded Woolworth store at the heart of the city's hub were stunned by blasts from a shrill whistle and by rough and tough union organizer Floyd Loew's strident shouts. "Striiike!" Years later, Loew would recall to this writer how quickly cash registers banged shut. He recalled lines of customers, purchases in their hands and not yet checked at registers, looking about in confusion while union agents herded them toward the doors. News of sit-down strikes in the plants was becoming quite ordinary to Detroiters by this time, but now they were confronted with the first sit-down clash that directly involved citizens going about their everyday shopping errands.[5] Department heads and managers were equally confused as they, too, were escorted, or propelled if necessary, out the doors while employees took over the building. Clerks quickly followed instructions to unwind long sections of wrapping paper, taping the paper across the front and side windows of the building so that curious observers could not see what was going on inside the store. Countertops, too, were covered with paper.

The February 1937 sit-down strike at the main Woolworth store in Detroit was the first such strike in the nation at a department store. The waitresses at the lunch counter appear to be enjoying their break as they sit on the counter and smile for a picture. (Walter P. Reuther Library, Wayne State University)

Waitresses and clerks settle down on mattresses placed on the floor to read for a while before they go to sleep for the night. (Walter P. Reuther Library, Wayne State University)

Local executives of the company quickly descended upon the Woodward Avenue store where union leaders confronted them and insisted their demands had to be met. The executives left, saying there would be no talks until the store was evacuated.

Evacuation was the farthest thing from the occupying forces' minds. By this time, shop-girls had turned on radios and were singing and dancing in the aisles. Later, unionists brought in mattresses and placed them in the aisles so that more than 100 female strikers could curl up for the night, observing a union-enforced 11 o'clock curfew.

Morning dawned with the sit-down looking much less romantic to the shop-girls, who complained of getting little sleep as they tried to make themselves presentable with the help of bobby pins, compact mirrors, and lipsticks. The store manager returned on Sunday morning to talk with a union leader who threatened to expand the sit-downs into all 40 Woolworth stores in the Detroit area if the union's demands were not met.

The union's goals sounded great to Woolworth employees—a 10 cents-an-hour raise, a 48-hour week, company-supplied aprons for soda fountain and bakery girls, and a 54-hour week for stock boys and men employed in the basement. But the close quarters, three-to-a-mattress sleeping arrangements, and, most of all, worries about the possible loss of weekend dates were taking their toll among the strikers who seemed to renew their energies only when photographers were admitted to the store to take photos which, it was rumored, would appear in *Life* magazine.

Photos of the first Woolworth sit-down strike in the nation did, indeed, appear in *Life* but, before that time, a second Detroit Woolworth store was struck and strike leaders were threatening again to take the strike nationwide unless it was settled by the following Saturday. At that point, New York City unionists were demonstrating in front of some of that huge city's Woolworth stores, urging a boycott of all Woolworth stores in New York pending the results of the Detroit strike. But in Detroit, other sit-downs were occurring by now in restaurants, department stores, and hotels—a rash of them immobilizing sections of the city.

Michigan's Governor Murphy warned strikers that force would be used to remove them from the buildings they occupied. Businessmen and newspapers warned that anarchists were taking over the city, which, they claimed, was swarming with outside organizers, agitators and labor racketeers. The bad publicity cast a shadow over unions and a deep split between the AFL and CIO occurred after AFL President William Green proclaimed its policy of disavowing sit-down strikes. Reluctantly, the Detroit unions began to search for other protest techniques that could substitute for the sit-downs.

However, Detroit's Woolworth strike was settled before the Saturday deadline set by the union. The company agreed to pay striking employees for work time lost during the sit-down. The union agreed to accept a five-cents-an-hour raise and won its other objectives, including a 48-hour week and a one-week vacation with pay after a year of employment, as all Detroit-area Woolworths were brought under union hiring policies.

A plague of strikes continued to spread throughout the Midwest, infecting cigar-making plants, the meat-packing industry, and Chicago's taxicab drivers with strikers forcefully stopping cabs, seizing patrons and yanking them out of the taxis.

Despite the many unions that had been organized in New York, both New York City and Boston remained relatively untouched by major strike fever until, on March 18, some 50 employees of the West Fourteenth Street, Manhattan, Woolworth store and 20 employees at the Sutter Avenue, Brooklyn, Woolworth building began a sit-down. They refused to wait on customers in response to the arrival and orders of union organizers.[6]

Unlike the Detroit strikers, some of the young New York salesgirls did not join the strike, but paraded about the Manhattan store shouting "No strike," while others simply left the store to avoid confrontations. But the strikers were prepared with signs that read: "Miss Hutton counts millions while Five-and-Ten girls count 10 and 12 dollar salaries."

When the store manager ordered the "No strike" employees to go back to the counters, only 20 clerks returned. Customers had disappeared and the doors were locked behind them at 11 a.m. When the store reopened 25 minutes later, groups of strikers were stationed at each door to ask customers not to enter. Outside, pickets moved along the sidewalk, asking people not to patronize the store. In mid-afternoon, unionists delivered food to the strikers, but at six p.m., when the doors were locked for the night, ten private patrolmen, hired by the store, stood at the doors to turn away sympathizers who tried to bring in food and cots. Then the strikers began calling their protest a "hunger strike," sending a telegram to Countess Barbara stating that: "Hunger strikers in New York store ask your intervention for a living wage." No response came from the countess. Nor was there any indication that she was turning her attention from her parties and travels to any philanthropic interest in the well-being of the self-proclaimed "hunger strikers." Detroiters who had participated in the Woolworth sit-downs in that city appreciated the effects of the propaganda that had been distributed by newspaper accounts of the "hunger strike" and the telegrams sent to Countess Barbara. But they also regretted the lack of unity among the workers in the New York Woolworth stores since they believed there were too many New York workers who were not supporting the union.

To add to the disenchantment, the so-called hunger strike had been discounted when a large gathering of pickets on the Thirteenth Street side of the huge store found a way to get food and bedding into the building by having pickets climb up to a ledge and open six windows some 15 feet from the ground. Then the growing numbers of picketers threw packages of food and blankets and folded cots up to the strikers while private guards were unsuccessful in blocking the picketers' efforts. The next morning, the police entered the store in force, evicted the striking occupants and arrested three union officials and more than 50 "girls," who put on their best displays of screaming and weeping while onlookers repeatedly booed the police.[7]

New York Mayor La Guardia sent telegrams to Woolworth officials and to the Department Store Employees Union of the AFL requesting them to meet with him to effect settlement of the strikes. "The responsibility is now placed squarely on both sides to indicate a willingness for immediate adjustment," La Guardia stated.

After a week of negotiations during which Woolworth stores in Providence, Rhode Island, held sit-downs, the union and representatives for Woolworth reached a tentative agreement, which was announced on March 30, 1937.[8] The agreement would cover more than 4,000 employees in New York City's 123 Woolworth stores. The pact provided for the reinstatement of 80 sit-down strikers "without prejudice" and for the dropping of court action against them. (A similar strike in five New York variety stores of the H. L. Green Company had ended recently with the same kind of provision.) The contract established a 32 1/2 cents an hour minimum wage for regular workers and 30 cents for apprentices, compared to 30 cents and 28 cents previously. It also provided for a 48-hour work week.

Nonetheless, there remained many serious problems to threaten the slowly improving economy of the country. A coal strike was pending. Even the WPA was having a strike problem as 52 technical workers (not workers who had been hired from the relief rolls) were arrested when the Architects' Federation held a sit-down at the end of that tumultuous month of March.

By July, Woolworth officials had more than sit-downs to worry about, as an Independent Retailers and Wholesalers Association was formed in Westchester, New York, to campaign for anti-chain store legislation.[9] This was not the first organization of its kind to be formed. Over the years, antipathy had increased among independent storeowners against the chains—Woolworth, Kresge, A&P stores and many others dealing in varieties of goods. Independent merchants were convinced that taxation was the most effective tool in restraining the chains.

One proposal for tax-technique was to tax the chains by the numbers of stores each chain had in each state—with increasingly bigger taxes for each additional store. The Empire State was not alone in having anti-chain associations organized: Florida,

California and other states were home to such organizations. James Brough, in his book on the Woolworths, tells readers that beginning in 1934 and continuing for the next seven years, "500 anti-chain bills would be introduced in state legislatures" throughout the country.[10] Such bills kept the directors of Woolworth and other such enterprises busily occupied in planning counter measures. Nor had the pressure of Woolworth strikes disappeared from the scene as late as December of that year of turmoil —1937. Two Woolworth stores in Brooklyn were closed on December 16 by the Department Store Employees Union while pickets walked the protest line in front of 35 other Woolworths that remained open. The State Industrial Commissioner ventured to say that an improved minimum-wage offer by the company, presently paying a $15.60 minimum per week to its New York workers, might solve the dispute.

The union, proposing a minimum wage of $16.50, and a ten percent raise for those making more than the minimum, was miffed when the company refused to discuss the proposal with the mediation board. The strike order was issued then, plus a demand for a minimum wage of $21, a 20 percent raise and a 40-hour week. The union also pointed out that its demands were reasonable since the State Labor Department recently had determined that a working woman, living with her family, required a weekly wage of $20.73 for "adequate maintenance and protection of health." A working woman living alone would require $23.36.[11]

Pickets carried signs decorated in green and red to celebrate the season while strikers sent a radiogram to Countess Haugwitz-Reventlow, asking for her intercession with the Woolworth Company for a "living wage" for its employees still enduring "starvation wages." The Countess, though, was much more concerned at this time with her personal finances than with the finances of Woolworth employees. Just two days earlier, she had made a one-day visit, by ship, to New York where she renounced her American citizenship before a federal judge.[12] This act created an even worse image for the countess in the eyes of the American public despite her attorneys' claims that taxes and "various legal complications" related to her dual citizenship (the United States and Denmark) had prompted her to take this seemingly drastic step out of concern for the conservation of her assets. At the same time, Count Kurt discovered that he would be required to sign a waiver to any rights to his wife's inheritance. Nonetheless, an agreement was reached that he would receive $2 million in the event of his wife's death or $1 million in case of a divorce.

Actually, the loss of American citizenship would make only a small difference in Barbara's present tax status, but would make a considerable difference in taxes that would have to be paid by heirs in the event of her death.[13] She had a young son and his future to consider now. Moreover, she had come dangerously close to death after giving birth to her child. All this was pointed out by wiser heads to Barbara, who rarely, if ever, had given any thought throughout her life to her finances, which always had seemed to grow rather than to diminish. It is quite likely that she gave an equal lack of thought to the radiogram from striking Woolworth employees which reached her after she had left New York aboard the liner *Europa* on its way to Cherbourg, France. There, she confided to reporters that she and the count would spend the holidays in Paris and then go to St. Moritz, Switzerland. Later they would visit India where she would begin studying the Arabic language.

The Count and Countess Haugwitz-Reventlow arrived in Bombay, India, at the end of January 1938.[14] They had been in India only a short time when Barbara met a prince who flattered her after he read some of her poetry and complimented her on the sensitivity of her writing. Her husband quickly ran out of patience with his wife's susceptibility to her admirer's fawning attention and likely thought that she was spending much more time with the prince than at her studies of Arabic. Barbara soon admitted publicly that she had given up her Arabic studies as newspapers began to pick up on a series of arguments and problems between the count and countess—problems that would continue even after the Haugwitz-Reventlows' early–April return to London, where the countess's splendid new home awaited them.

The Georgian-styled Winfield House (named for Barbara's grandfather, Frank Winfield Woolworth) reigned over 12 1/2 acres of gorgeous gardens that rivaled the remarkable gardens of Buckingham Palace. The home's luxurious interior, featuring Eastern treasures and embroideries displayed behind glass panels, Chinese jade pieces in glass-paneled recesses in the heiress's enormous many-windowed bedroom, and a reception room with carved timber paneling, included a six-room "apartment" for two-year-old Lance and his nurse with its own kitchen and a nursery padded with pink kidskin.[15]

On their return from their lengthy trip, the count and countess settled into their impressive home in which they could have been very comfortable with their staff of servants to wait on them. However, their time together at Winfield House was destined to be not even as lengthy as their most recent trip, which was not surprising to those who read the published statement the count gave to his attorney in early July, 1938. "If I blow my brains out," he said, "everybody will have known that Barbara drove me to it."[16]

By the end of 1937, the F.W. Woolworth Company had netted $33,176,509, an increase over the previous year.[17] Sales, not including those of its European subsidiaries, were the largest in Woolworth history, with 2,010 stores now operating in the United States, Canada and Cuba.

However, storm clouds on the international scene had grown more threatening to the world in 1937. The Japanese shelled British vessels on the Yangtze River in late December, and Japan's assurances that the shelling would not be repeated were looked at with suspicion. Before the end of December, newspaper headlines announced that the British premier was issuing a stern warning to Japan and that President Roosevelt was not willing to preserve "peace at any price."[18]

The S. S. Kresge chain of five-and-ten-cent stores recently had publicly announced that they would no longer order Japanese-made goods. Woolworth officials quickly said that no orders for their chains had been placed recently for Japanese goods, and if there was consumer resistance to the goods, which was expected, there would be no orders placed in the future. The Sino-Japanese conflict already had resulted in various American labor organizations boycotting Japanese-made products. Civic clubs such as the Boston Kiwanis Club were announcing that they would exclude Japanese-made toys from their Christmas gift bags.

However threatening the world situation appeared to be, the Woolworth Company went ahead with its plans for expansion and improvement. Some of this expansion and improvement was made possible by the private purchase by a life insurance company, in August 1937, of the $10 million debentures issued by the F. W. Woolworth Company a few years earlier.[19] The company opened its new and largest six-story store, with a floor area of 3,400 square feet, at Fifth Avenue and Thirty-ninth Street in February 1938 with a blitz of advertising.[20] Eight New York newspapers, using quarter- and half-page Woolworth ads, boasted of the new store's mezzanine lounges, powder rooms and rest rooms. The ads pointed out that the store had installed the first escalator to be used in a variety store and that the latest in electrical air-cleaning provided 99 percent pure air for the benefit of customers and employees. The granite and terra cotta building would take the place of the previous Woolworth's store at Fifth Avenue, which was closing.

The company emphasized again that, with the exception of some novelties still stocked in the store, there would be no Japanese goods sold at the new store. By February 1939, a U.S. government report from the commerce department would state that the importation of toys from Japan had dropped by 60 percent. Before the end of the year, German toy manufacturers were voicing fears that there could be a permanent market loss in their sales. Other problems had arisen earlier when an American exhibit of new toys drew flack from various quarters because the display of ever-popular tin soldiers contained, "for realism," mutilated soldier figures.[21]

For the F. W. Woolworth Company, sales had boomed in 1938. The company announced that goods selling at prices up to one dollar would be available to customers and, in a number of instances, component-prices of an item would be quoted separately, bringing the total price "well above" (in the company's carefully phrased language) the one-dollar figure, with delivery service available as far as Westchester County.

More stores were in the planning for the East Coast. In a million-dollar deal, another modern building to be leased, long-term, by Woolworth was to be erected in Jersey City with a guaranteed minimum rental fee, plus a percentage of sales, paid to the building proprietor by Woolworth. Woolworth would also occupy a smaller newly erected building on Main Street in White Plains, Westchester.

Despite these and numerous other expansion plans in 1938, an entirely different matter was creating concern for Woolworth officials that year. In late September, a $1 million lawsuit against Woolworth and Kresge chain stores, Pathe News and Dr. Allan R. Dafoe (the doctor in charge of the Dionne quintuplets' medical care since their birth) was scheduled to be heard before a jury.[22] The damage suit had been brought by Ivan I. Spear, a Chicago promoter, who, his attorney claimed, had signed a contract with Oliva Dionne, father of the children, only two days after the quintuplets' birth. Spear's attorney also explained that the contract had given Spear exclusive rights to "exhibit" the children, with Mr. Dionne receiving 23 percent of the income and the Dionnes' parish priest collecting 7 percent. In addition, Oliva Dionne would receive a weekly payment of $100, but only two such payments had been made, the lawyer claimed, because Mr. Dionne had been forced to break the contract when Dr. Dafoe and the three other defendants (including Woolworth) had "conspired" to force the quintuplets' father to back out of the agreement.

Although two witnesses for Ivan I. Spear testified that soon after the quintuplets were born, Oliva Dionne had contracted with Spear to bring the babies to Chicago for exhibition at the Century of Progress Exposition, Federal Judge John P. Barnes ruled, on the second day of the trial, that there was no evidence presented to prove a conspiracy on the part of Dr. Dafoe with the other three defendants. The judge pointed out that although it was true that Dr. Dafoe had interfered with arrangements made by others regarding the quintuplets, the doctor was responsible for the lives of the babies and he had been fulfilling those responsibilities by his actions. Judge Barnes directed the jury to arrive at a not-guilty verdict for all the accused, and when this was done, the case was dismissed.

The Woolworth Company was looking forward to profits of more than $30 million in 1938. Toy sales remained as they always had been — a major source of Woolworth profits. In October, a pre–Christmas display by toy manufacturers indicated that a flood of new and innovative toys (many of which Woolworth stores would be selling) would bring about a Christmas bonanza. "Untearable" picture books for tots, and a miniature cradle telephone with a dial and a bell that rang when a button was pushed. A doll that blew bubbles when a pipe was placed in its mouth and the stomach was squeezed. Higher-priced streamlined scooters. A remote-control airplane with a revolving propeller and a long arm attached to a control tower. And the perennial favorites — chemical sets, medical sets and musical instruments, from drums to four-octave organs.

However, Woolworth officials had been experiencing serious concerns for its 82 flourishing stores in Germany. Because Hitler had forbidden having Reichsmarks drained away from Germany, two million dollars of 1937 profits had to be removed, now, from American Woolworth's income accounts, leaving 1938 net income at less than had been expected — $28,584,000.[23]

On the international scene, even more important events were increasing the general sense of uneasiness in Europe. Czechoslovakian army troops had been forced to mobilize in the spring of 1938 in response to German troop movements interpreted as menacing to the Sudetenland, which had been part of Czechoslovakia for some 20 years but had belonged to Germany previous to World War I. Already, France was committed to aid the Czechs if Germany invaded. It was likely that Britain would follow.

In June 1938, Countess Barbara remained at Winfield House while her husband went to Geneva, Switzerland, for what he called a "rest cure." There, he admitted to reporters that he and his wife were having difficulties regarding the future education of their two-year-old son.[24] From Switzerland, he traveled to France and registered at a Parisian hotel. Countess Barbara, it was reported, had hired a police guard to patrol the grounds of the well fortified Winfield House because, she claimed, her husband had threatened to kidnap his son.[25]

Although the count vehemently denied that he ever had made such a threat, Franklyn Hutton arrived in London to try to settle what he called "just a marital tiff" between his daughter and the count.[26] While Barbara consulted with her banker and her lawyer, the senior Hutton arranged to confer with Count Kurt in Paris. "There is too much nonsense going around about the whole affair," Franklyn told inquiring reporters. Still, rumors abounded that the countess (a Danish citizen by marriage to the count, who was German by birth but became a Danish citizen in 1924) was reported to be seeking a divorce in the Danish courts.[27] The Danish newspaper *Politiken* claimed that, under the marriage contract, the countess had reserved the sole right to administer her fortune.

Certainly she appeared to have been profligate in the past in regard to her fortune. When a tax appraisal had been made of the estate of her deceased husband (Prince Alexis Mdivani) in her first marriage, the appraisal had found the estate to be worth nearly $3 million, more than $2 million of which had come from Barbara's fortune in the form of two trust funds. In addition, she had given him many expensive gifts.[28]

Surely concerned, too, by increasing fears of war breaking out, Barbara and her attorneys had attempted to regain American citizenship for the countess on June 29, 1938. Hit with another barrage of bad publicity regarding this move, the heiress explained to reporters that her recent renouncement of American citizenship had been arranged by her attorneys and was purely a money deal. In Washington, the chairman of the House Immigration Committee declared that he would oppose any attempt by Countess Haugwitz-Reventlow to regain U.S. citizenship by what he called "short-cut" methods. Only days later, the Danish lawyer who had been summoned to London by Barbara told a reporter that "Nobody in the world, not even the count and countess, can say yet whether there will be a divorce. If neither the count nor countess petitions for a divorce in addition to their judicial separation, they will remain separated but not divorced...."

From that point, the dispute between the embattled couple created flamboyant newspaper articles read avidly by people on the continent and in the United States. Charges and counter-charges during the count-countess court case filled columns in newspapers. The case wore on with more dramatics even as Barbara was sobered by a ruling in Denmark that the Danish courts had jurisdiction over the couple's matrimonial difficulties. The English courts, on the other hand, claimed jurisdiction over the child, born in England, since his mother had made him a ward "in Chancery."[29]

By the end of July 1938 and after Barbara had withdrawn some of her more flamboyant charges against her husband, it was announced in London that a separation agreement was signed between husband and wife with the final divorce decree remaining in the hands of the Danish courts.[30] The London agreement assigned to the count the final decision as to his two-year-old son's future education, religious training and the overseeing of the boy until he became of age, while Barbara handed over a substantial, but publicly undisclosed, amount of money for the child's education and other expenses. Temporarily, custody was granted, in part, to Barbara with the provision that young Lance, when of school age, would divide holidays between his parents.

While Europe teetered on the brink of war, September 29, 1938, headlines in American newspapers announced "German Liners Called Home. Thousands of Tourists Stranded." Americans wondered, could this action by Germany be a preliminary to another European war that might involve the United States?

Jessie Donahue had returned to her Fifth Avenue apartment early in 1938 when she learned of the serious illness of her older sister, Lena. After a brief illness, 60-year-old Lena McCann had died on March 15[31] as quietly as she had lived at her East Eightieth Street home in what was left of the compound that her grandfather, Frank W. Woolworth, had built to foster family togetherness. Three priests conducted a solemn high mass of requiem on the day of the funeral, while Bishop Stephen J. Donahue and Lena's pastor at Oyster Bay, Long Island, participated in the mass from inside the altar rail. The burial site was the McCann mausoleum in Woodlawn Cemetery.

Less than two months later, Jessie Donahue, who had left her home in the family compound following her husband's suicide years earlier, sold the period furniture, Flemish tapestries and *objets d'art* from her former home at auction at the Parke-Barnet Galleries for $55,398. For the past few years, she had been living in her Fifth Avenue apartment when she was in New York, but much of the time she was at her Palm Beach home or, like her niece Barbara, traveling throughout the world.

Before the end of September as war with Germany seemed inevitable, many Londoners began leaving the city which, they were convinced, would be attacked by German airplanes as soon as war broke out. Others, who had no intention of leaving London, took the precaution of getting fitted for gas masks while laboring men busily dug trenches and hauled sandbags.[32]

On November 9, although the "Munich Agreement" had temporarily eased fears of the immediacy of war breaking out, the so-called "Night of Broken Glass" (*Kristallnacht*) occurred.[33] Nazi thugs unleashed their fury in both Germany and Austria on that date as they burned synagogues (many of them in Vienna), arrested Jews and murdered hundreds of them, and plundered Jewish homes. The terrible night signified the start of the Holocaust and the herding of thousands of Jews into railroad boxcars to be shipped to concentration camps.

Less than two weeks later, a communication from Rome quoted *The Tribune*'s statement as saying that "as is known, President Roosevelt is of Jewish origin," among other claims charging that no country in the world, including the United States, would admit Jews. In that same month of November, however, Great Britain offered to lease 10,000 square miles of land in Guiana for settlement by Jews from Germany even while newspaper headlines lamented that "Liquidation of the Jews Goes On."

The passion aroused in Britain by *Kristallnacht* gradually languished as the British people, desperately eager to believe that peace still was possible, did not have the last of their illusions destroyed until Hitler invaded non–Germanic lands in Czechoslovakia in March 1939. Within two days, Czechoslovakia was conquered. Despite such gloomy news, more pleasant plans for a celebration of the quintuplets' fifth birthday were published in both Canadian and United States newspapers. Excitement rose as it was reported that the quints were learning to curtsy in preparation for their presentation, together with their parents and Dr. Dafoe, to the King and Queen of Great Britain when the royal pair arrived in Toronto.

Behind the scenes, though, the children's father was preparing to launch charges against Doctor Dafoe regarding funds obtained from contracts.[34] Only a month later,

Dionne did file suit and at the end of December Dr. Dafoe resigned as guardian of the quintuplets, but he would continue to serve as their personal director.

By this time, Adolf Hitler had taken a decisive move toward war with England when he moved his troops into Poland on September 1, 1939. Honor-bound to declare war on Germany if the Nazis moved against Poland, Britain fulfilled its pledge and declared war two days later. Immediately, an evacuation plan was activated which took thousands of British children on trains to rural parts of the country for safe-keeping. Unaccustomed to rural life, some children yearned for London. "Where's Woolworth's?" they whined.[35]

Barbara had remained at her London residence with her son, Lance, although she had traveled in other countries frequently even while the world seemed poised on the brink of war. But after the American embassy notified American citizens in London (including Barbara, who no longer was a citizen of the United States) of the strong possibility of war, she was given permission by Count Kurt to remove her son to the safety of his mother's native land, although he insisted on making the trip with them, and then would return to Denmark.

Reluctantly, she left England after storing her furniture and arranging for bank-storage of her jewelry. With her son and the husband from whom she was separated, an entourage of servants and the assurance that her Danish passport would admit her to the country of her birth, Barbara boarded an Italian liner in Genoa because of the possible danger of a German U-boat attack on English or American ships.[36] (One month earlier, on September 3), the British passenger liner *Athenia* had been sunk in an attack by a German U-boat and 28 Americans had drowned.)

Barbara was still aboard ship when President Roosevelt ordered United States ports and territorial waters closed to belligerent submarines "to keep the war from American shores."

At this same time, Barbara learned of the notices that her father, Franklyn Hutton, had placed in newspapers. The notices stated that he would no longer be responsible for debts incurred by his wife, Irene.[37]

The mixed-up affairs of the Huttons (why was the daughter aboard the same ship as Count Kurt from whom she had separated under a barrage of publicity? people wondered in confusion) became even more bewildering when, a month later, Franklyn Hutton placed another public notice disclaiming his previous newspaper statement. He had been mistaken, he confessed, in evaluating debts accumulated by his wife.[38]

However much the hierarchy for the Woolworth Company may have been disconcerted by the notoriety generated that year by the founder's granddaughter, Barbara, and by the insistence of the public on linking her name ("the Woolworth heiress," as she was invariably identified in newspapers) to her grandfather's company. Woolworth's 1939 celebration of its sixtieth anniversary was a proud affair. During the year, Woolworth enterprises had expanded to include a total of 144 stores in Canada, more than 750 in Great Britain, eight in Cuba and 82 in Germany under the corporation's control. At the conclusion of the year, a new high in sales had been reached—$319 million.[39]

It would not be long before the United States, too, would be actively involved in World War II and the company's expansion and store-improvement programs would be cut back drastically because of building material and labor shortages during the war years. Annual stock dividends, too, would be cut back to $1.60 during wartime.

12

Marriages, Divorces and a Real War

Countess Barbara was one of the few guests present at the Florida residence of her Aunt Jessie to witness the wedding ceremony of her cousin Woolworth Donahue to Gretchen Wilson Hearst in late January 1940.[1] The bride was the mother of a young son, John, and had been divorced less than two years previously from John Randolph Hearst, third son of publishing magnate William Randolph Hearst, after charging Hearst with having an ungovernable temper that "shattered her nerves and impaired her health."

Barbara's favorite cousin, Jimmy Donahue, was on hand to serve as his older brother's best man. The 86-year-old great-uncle, Sumner Woolworth, supportive as always of his deceased brother Frank's family, had come to perform the duty of giving the bride away. The ceremony itself was both brief and unspectacular — vastly different from the marriage ceremony uniting Gretchen Wilson and John Randolph Hearst that had taken place seven years previously at the Hearsts' palatial San Simeon ranch in California.

The newlywed Donahues had met while Gretchen Hearst visited Jessie Donahue in Cannes and Biarritz, and after Woolworth had returned from nearly two years of big-game hunting in India and Africa, a hobby frequently indulged in, also, by Barbara's father, Franklyn. There had been no betrothal announcements prior to the wedding, although Donahue had been the subject of two previous betrothal announcements to other young women — the first ended by agreement of both parties, the second quickly denied by Woolworth. Now, with marriage to Gretchen, Woolworth was taking on the responsibilities of becoming a stepfather to a six-year-old boy who would be expected to share in the vast Hearst fortune.

The former Gretchen Hearst's second wedding had been planned hastily, with only family members invited, including the bride's former mother-in-law, who had come to offer her good wishes to the newlyweds. As was usual in reports of socialites' weddings, a newspaper account included background information pointing up any so-called family relationships of note, including, in this case, the fact that the bride was a descendant of Thomas Jonathan (Stonewall) Jackson, and the groom was a nephew to the late Mrs. Charles E.F. McCann and a cousin to the three McCann offspring — Frasier McCann, Mrs. Winston F.C. Guest and Mrs. Willys Rosseter Betts, all duly listed though not in attendance.

Two weeks later, while Barbara remained in Palm Beach following her cousin's wedding, she was pestered by newsmen who wanted to know if she had plans to marry well-known golfer Robert Sweeney, with whom she'd been seen frequently. She denied having any such plans, saying only that she was looking forward to receiving a final divorce decree from Count Haugwitz-Reventlow from the Denmark courts — perhaps as early as the following day, she added in a hopeful voice.[2]

The Haugwitz-Reventlow divorce had not yet been decreed by Danish courts when the final accounting for the estate of Prince Alexis Mdivani was presented, almost five years after the prince's death. Family squabbles had delayed the accounting until, on March 7, 1940, the estate's value was reported in *The New York Times* as only $150,613, of which his former wife, now Countess Haugwitz-Reventlow, would receive the amount designated in the deceased prince's will — one-half ($75,000) of his estate. The remainder of the comparatively small amount would be distributed among his several sisters, one remaining brother (Prince David, now being sued by his former wife, actress Mae Murray, for custody and support of their son) and to the widow of the deceased brother, Serge Mdivani.[3]

In April, Barbara left Florida for Hawaii. Her latest male companion, actor Cary Grant, also vacationed in Hawaii at this same time. The two had met, it was said, through introductions by international socialite Countess di Frasso who, during an extended romantic liaison with the young and gauche Hollywood actor Gary Cooper, had transformed the man into an urbane gentleman approaching the Cary Grant type.[4]

Following the Hawaiian vacation, Barbara and Cary were seen together frequently in California where the pair denied any romantic attachment. Both were credited with contributing to the British and European war relief — Barbara donated ten ambulances to the British Red Cross and donated generously to the American Red Cross War Relief and the French Underground cause. Grant turned over his entire earnings for a Metro-Golden-Mayer motion picture he had recently made ($62,500) to the Red Cross for relief in England — the country of his birth.[5]

Despite her own gifts to the Red Cross, Barbara surely felt much less like "Lady Bountiful" when she was forced to file with the federal government under the new alien registration law.[6] Claiming she was too ill with influenza to comply with the law, she was humiliated when a deputy arrived at her Beverly Hills home to question and fingerprint her as an alien and to register both Barbara and four-year-old Lance.

She had other concerns as well. A month earlier, Count Kurt had arrived in New York and, when interviewed, would say only that he was seeking data on his divorce status.[7] Immediately, Barbara was suspicious of the motives of her second husband, whom she had found to be unrelentingly dictatorial during their marriage. Despite repeated declarations by both that they now had a friendly relationship, she knew this was not so. She knew, also, that Denmark had been invaded and occupied by German troops in early April, at which time Copenhagen had been occupied. Certainly the count had reason to leave for the United States, just as she and Lance had re-located. She knew, too, from news reports, that in early June, two more American ships bearing 2,684 American refugees from Europe sailed for the United States. Almost 2,000 of the anxious passengers were picked up in Italy, but others, still remaining in Italy, were nervously hoping to get out of that Axis country by way of another American ship.

In July 1940, Woolworth directors became wary when the widow of Samuel Gompers, founder of the AFL, was appointed as an organizer for the United Retail and Wholesale Employees of America, an affiliate of the CIO.[8] Gompers' job, specifically, was to organize employees of the F.W. Woolworth Company. Nonetheless, despite the stepped-up union activity against Woolworth and the threat of the country being involved in the European war, Woolworth directors were looking forward to a big year for their company. They knew that wholesalers were anticipating the best Christmas sales volume in the past ten years, particularly in toy sales, as American companies continued to produce a normal output of toys, many of them with a patriotic theme.

Back in 1875, there had been only two American factories that manufactured toys, neither of them producing dolls. The Woolworth Company had played an important part in encouraging the growth of toy factories even before the turn of the century. In the modern world of the 1940s, the homemade toys of an earlier era — corn-husk rag dolls, and whistles and slingshots whittled from trees — were far removed from the plethora of American-manufactured toys now available to children.

In October 1940, 100,000 toys were displayed by the Toy Manufacturers of the United States at their show in New York City. A patriotic theme prevailed as even simple toys — balls, kites, balloons and drums — flaunted red, white and blue colors. Miniature battleships, tanks, anti-aircraft guns and cannons — modeled after United States Army and Navy equipment — were big hits at the show, although complaints were compiling that war toys stimulated violence and an eagerness for war in children.[9]

That same year, Woolworth stores found that play-sets featuring railroad stations, stores and farm life in America sold very well, as did hobby kits and games such as backgammon that could now be played by more than two participants. Woolworth buyers also had ordered, much earlier in the year and before an expected price increase, such popular items as wheel goods, sleds and metal toys which could be expected to be in short supply later because of defense requirement demands for steel, aluminum and brass.

The entire country became more alert to the possibility of war when the first peacetime conscription act was passed in September 1940. Young men were required to register for a draft that was intended to raise an army of 1,200,000 for the United States.

When the year 1940 drew to its close, though, the Woolworth predictions of a record year would not be met. In fact, Woolworth's net profits of $24,104,815 would mark a distinct downward trend.[10]

Well before the end of the year, Barbara Hutton was spending a great deal of time with Cary Grant in her rented, but luxurious, Beverly Hills home when she learned of her father's serious illness. Immediately, she flew to Franklyn Hutton's

5,500-acre plantation near Charleston, South Carolina. At age 63, Franklyn died on December 5, 1940, of cirrhosis of the liver.

Like her father, Barbara drank quite heavily. And because of her fragile nervous condition, she relied on sedatives to get to sleep. Her stepmother, Irene Hutton, now, as always, could be depended upon to offer support at a time of crisis. Jessie Donahue arrived promptly, too, offering comfort to her niece, along with Franklyn's sister and his brother, Edward F. Hutton, who lived on a nearby plantation with his wife.

Retired from business for many years, the avid sportsman Franklyn had always had many interests and responsibilities (in addition to managing his daughter's Woolworth fortune until she became of age) to keep him busily occupied. He had traveled extensively, many of his travels taken up with big-game hunting as he rented shooting preserves in various foreign countries. Still, his obituary notice pointed out that he was "best known to the public because of the prominence of his daughter, Countess Barbara Hutton Haugwitz-Reventlow, a Woolworth heiress."[11]

The Episcopalian funeral service took place in the capacious living room of the plantation manor, with mounted trophies of the hunt looking down fiercely on the assembled mourners and guests. Shortly after the day of the funeral, Franklyn Hutton's will, naming his wife as executor, was filed in probate court.[12] Despite the conciliatory and soothing terms in which the will referred to Franklyn's only child, the daughter was not pleased with the manner in which her father had chosen to dispose of his properties. When a second will was filed for probate several days later, there was no change in the father's only provision for his daughter: wishing her a "loving father's blessing," he had explained that any amount of money he might give her would be "quite inconsequential" in the light of her own assets. His entire estate would go to his wife.

Barbara was incensed by this exclusion, likely seeing it as another rejection by the man who had given her scant attention as a motherless child. She did not accept the perceived rejection well, particularly since she had loaned her father considerable money over the years. Despite the money with which she had gifted two husbands, with no hope of return, she determined to recover the loans she had made to her father by way of a court suit. However, when Irene Hutton expressed her willingness to repay whatever money her husband had borrowed from his daughter, and did so, the two women were, in part, reconciled.[13]

Despite Barbara's assessment to reporters in early 1940 that she was expecting her final divorce decree very shortly ("perhaps, tomorrow") the decree was not handed down until March 1941.[14] Then Count Kurt applied for United States citizenship, again making Barbara nervous because, he said, he wished to spend the summer with his son, Lance, which the count had every right to do according to the custody agreement. Moving into the St. Regis Hotel in New York, Count Kurt took the boy to his summer camp in the Adirondacks. In the fall, he had plans to go into his own business in New York City, he stated.

By July 1941, the management people of the Woolworth Company were being much more cautious in their outlook for anticipated financial returns. At that time, company directors decided to cut its quarterly dividend by one-third, payable to stockholders in September.[15] Higher Canadian taxes, higher British taxes which would reduce the dividend paid to the parent company, and an increase in United States Federal tax rates, plus the war situation, had occasioned the cut in dividends "in order to maintain a strong financial position," the directors explained.

Despite the ever-increasing threat of the United States becoming involved in the European war, the suddenness of an attack at Pearl Harbor by Japanese war planes on December 7, 1941, stunned Americans and seriously crippled the U.S. fleet. Simultaneously the Japanese launched surprise naval and air attacks on U.S. bases at Guam and at Midway and Wake islands while the Japanese army attacked Hong Kong, Malaya, Thailand and the Philippine Islands. When President Roosevelt called for a formal declaration of war against Japan, war against the United States was declared by Germany and Italy as the conflict quickly encompassed the world. Even the Woolworth Building was affected by the declaration of war. The skyscraper's observation tower, which had attracted an average of 300,000 people annually from all parts of the world, was closed to visitors as a precaution against spies who might signal foreign ships.[16]

In the first few weeks of the war with Japan, the bulky *New York Times*, now selling for ten cents a copy, carried expanded coverage of major gains by the enemy. The Philippines fell to the Japanese, followed by Malaya and the Netherlands Indies, while the British were forced to give up Hong Kong on Christmas Day. Then Thailand surrendered to the Japanese. Reality set in for Americans as they realized that the Japanese soon dominated a chain of Pacific Islands and that American young men would have to fight their way across these same islands to reclaim them from the enemy. It was not until late April 1942 that U.S. naval and air forces would win their first major victory in the Battle of the Coral Sea.

But U.S. forces faced a series of major battles that only began in August 1942, when a successful land action was taken by U.S. forces against Japanese forces that had previously seized the Solomon Islands. In the meantime, casualty lists in newspapers shocked Americans into a realization that the war would be a lengthy and difficult one.

Despite the cautious approach to 1941 by Woolworth directors, the company completed the year with a large increase in sales before deductions for increased federal income and capital stock taxes, plus excess profits taxes, all of which totaled $13,730,000 — more than twice the amount of federal tax deductions for 1940. Still, net profit for 1941 leaped to $26,114,372 while stock dividends increased to $2.69 a share.[17]

British Woolworth's sales for 1941 had risen to $7,958,259 before taxation. But Woolworth's investment in its German subsidiary had now been written down to $1.00, as was the depreciated value of the Woolworth warehouse in Germany.[18]

Shortly before the end of 1941, a New York toy designer secured a patent on a "blackout" doll that would make it possible for children to play in the dark while the doll glowed with a phosphorescent light when normal lights might be extinguished during air raids.[19] Even while the designer pointed out how effectively children's fears of darkness could be eliminated by use of the toy, a rash of protests followed news of the "blackout" doll offering and there was little demand for the toy.

"The year 1942 will present perplexing problems for the management to solve," Woolworth Chairman Charles Sumner Woolworth declared in his understated manner. Metal, leather and rubber toys and other goods would be in short supply, he pointed out.

By late June, 38-year-old Cary Grant, in a class of 300, received American citizenship, expressing his wish to get his affairs in order so that he could volunteer his services to the United States military.[20] Less than two weeks later, he was married to Barbara Hutton in a small, quiet ceremony presided over by a Lutheran minister at the Lake Arrowhead home of Grant's agent.[21] Just days earlier, Grant had signed a pre-marital agreement; he signed it willingly because he wanted none of the baggage that accompanied marriage to a super-wealthy woman who could then assert control. A traumatic childhood in England during which his mother had been confined to a mental institution appeared to have damaged his trust in women. Now that he was a successful and wealthy actor in his own right, he required no money from a wife. What had appealed to him about Barbara was her fragility and need for a man upon whom she could lean for strength. The newlyweds returned quickly to Barbara's luxury home so that Grant could start work at his studio the next day in the film *Once Upon a Honeymoon.*

The following month, the 47-year-old Count Haugwitz-Reventlow married Margaret Drayton, a great-granddaughter of the late Mrs. William Astor.[22] As was the case with the Hutton wedding in June, newspaper reports of the Haugwitz-Reventlow wedding in July were accompanied by a summarizing of the previous Reventlow-Hutton marriage and its matrimonial problems.

Cary Grant, who, apart from making necessary public appearances, liked privacy in his life, was already beginning to discover that the fragile Barbara had a will of iron when it came to planning and executing parties in the large home which was admirably suited to entertaining. Grant could be a charming host to his close friends, but when he came home after a day's work at the studio, he was not pleased to find the house filled with people, many of whom he did not know and did not care to know. It annoyed him, too, that Barbara employed so many servants in the house. To her, it seemed an essential part of running a large household; to him it was another privacy intrusion. He realized that Barbara was in control of her own money and how she chose to spend it, but he was a frugal man who hated waste and ostentation. He began to retreat to his own room to find the privacy and control he felt he needed.

Perhaps it was taking this British-born man longer than he had expected to "settle his affairs," as he had said when he became a citizen; or perhaps it was his age, nearing 40 years, that kept him from being accepted as a volunteer to the U.S. Army Air Corps, but Grant remained as he was—a motion picture star, with a large following of movie fans, who made many appearances at military bases. He was more than that, though, to Barbara's son Lance when Lance was at home with them. Grant became a companion to the boy—even a role model, taking an interest in his schoolwork and his hobbies and gaining the boy's devotion. Barbara was appreciative of that but Count Haugwitz-Reventlow was not.

After Charles E. F. McCann, son-in-law to Frank W. Woolworth, had joined his wife, Helena, in death, the auction sale of the McCanns' collection of English, French

Wedding picture of Barbara Hutton and Cary Grant. (Authors Collection)

and Italian works of art created a stir among art lovers in November 1942. A gold tea and coffee set, a wedding gift from Emperor Paul I of Russia to his daughter, was sold for $11,000. Tapestries, Oriental rugs, English furniture and other items brought the total sales to $266,382.[23]

The war wore on and more ordinary U.S. citizens, who did not need to deal with disposing of works of art, learned, instead, to live with gasoline, meat and sugar rationing. A treat for the average New Yorker in 1942 was sitting at one of the long lunch counters at Woolworth's and ordering a turkey dinner with a generous serving of turkey and dressing, mashed potatoes and giblet gravy, cranberry sauce, a vegetable and hot roll. All for thirty cents.[24]

There were no new cars on the market at this time; tires for older cars were difficult to acquire. Silk and the newer nylon stockings could not be bought. Shortages of materials such as rubber made it difficult for mothers of young children because they could no longer could find rubber pants or rubber sheets on Woolworth counters. As replacements, a kind of papery-textured plastic-type pants and sheets were sold at Woolworth's which were most unsatisfactory for keeping a baby or a baby's bed dry. And if a mother wanted to buy a stroller for her child, she had to settle for a wooden-wheeled conveyance that clattered and jounced along the sidewalk.

During the war, nearly half of Woolworth's male employees would enter the armed forces and some female employees joined the WAACS or WAVES. In the absence of so many male employees, more women were hired to fill their positions. By the end of the war, women would be managing more than 500 Woolworth stores.[25]

Woolworth sales for 1942 were higher than they ever had been, but higher federal income and excess profits taxes, interest, foreign exchange loss (the exchange rate for the British pound had dropped to $4.02 1/2 to the pound) and other charges had reduced total Woolworth earnings to $23,538,739. This was the lowest level of earnings since the depression year of 1932. Woolworth shares were now equal to only $2.43 each.

In the war with the Japanese, there was some good news in late November 1942, as U.S. troops made gains to recapture Guadalcanal in the Solomon Islands. But it would take a full year before the Japanese were pushed out of all bases in the Solomon Islands.

Newspapers carried glowing, patriotic reports of the Dionne quintuplets making their stage debut in Toronto in a Victory Loan drive, and, in early 1943, enrolling in the Junior Red Cross. But the management of the F.W. Woolworth store in Elizabeth, New Jersey, made less patriotic news when it was fined in police court for having kept lights burning through the blackout test in April 1943.[26]

When, on September 8, 1943, news of the armistice between Italy and the Allies was announced, American manufacturers of neckties, and even of men's robes and hats, were excited about the possibilities of obtaining fabrics (largely silks) from Italy, which had on hand large quantities of fabrics made especially for shipment to America before the war had broken out. Their enthusiasm was hardly dimmed at the thought that the warehoused goods likely could not be sent overseas to America for several months. After all, it could take several more months for the Allies to push German forces out of Italian territories above Rome. But pedal pushers, the latest American style craze, were one of the few items that did not seem to be in short supply. The low-priced, below-the-knees, women's and girl's pants were piled high on Woolworth counters.

In early September, the Office of Price Administration charged the F.W. Woolworth Company, along with J.C. Penney Company, J.J. Newberry Company and McCrory Stores Corporation, with selling women's clothes in excess of maximum prices set by the Office of Price Administration. A federal judge issued temporary restraining orders.[27] The OPA had forbidden sales of women's clothing during the spring season at higher prices than were charged in March 1942 for garments in the same category. It was not a simple matter for merchants to keep track of such restrictions.

In 1943, volume of toy production in the United States had reached some $200,000. A year later, estimates of volume production were reduced by 25%, according to trade experts. The War Production Board had hinted that it would consider resumption of the use of steel and iron for toys, to save lumber and manpower. However, conditions did not indicate any such resumption in 1944. Still, some 400 exhibitors brought toys of wood, paper and composition to the March 1944 American Toy Fair, although scarcities in wood, paper, cartons and some fabrics, especially cotton goods, had made their job a difficult one.[28]

In that same year, 1944, 88-year-old Charles Sumner Woolworth resigned as Woolworth's chairman of the board. C. W. Deyo, who had been president of the company since 1936, now became chairman of the board as well.

Two months later, Barbara Hutton Grant was fighting her own not-so-private battle with former husband Count Haugwitz-Reventlow with whom the son, Lance, was living in Pasadena. The count had filed a suit for enforcement of an earlier order by England's High Court of Justice granting him control of his nine-year-old son's education and religious schooling.[29] Barbara was upset by an order from the Superior Court that made it obligatory for her to appear in court to answer charges that she had used "coarse or vulgar language" in the presence of her son.

Grant, too, was disturbed at the notoriety that might reflect on his own image as an urbane gentleman, and likely was even more upset by his wife's bitter raging at what she interpreted as Reventlow's never-ending and relentless campaign to take her child away from her. She had to have wondered if Reventlow's vindictiveness was driven by his discovery that Lance had found, in Cary Grant, an attentive father figure.

Despite Barbara's denial in court that she had used profanity in Lance's presence, or that she had spoken of Reventlow to the boy in a derogatory manner, the court issued a temporary restraining order by which she had to abide when her son was present.[30] Still, at the end of June and just one day before Lance was to be handed over to his mother for her six months of custody time, Reventlow suddenly withdrew his suit to control the rearing and education of the boy. It did not seem that the rapid-fire barrage of charges and counter-charges would slow, however, because an angered Barbara stated that she remained determined to move ahead with a new suit for complete custody of her son.

Perhaps it was this expression of determination by Barbara that motivated Reventlow to leap back on the battleground and, instead of returning Lance to his mother, to rush off to Canada with the boy. Now his former wife would find it necessary to fight for custody through the Canadian courts, he stated boldly.

Barbara's attorneys postponed action against this challenge because, they announced, Mrs. Grant was ill. Cary Grant was tiring rapidly of the constant notoriety and of his exposure to the raw edges of his wife's ragged nerves. He found it impossible to soothe her. Instead, she had her attorney file a plea against Reventlow for child stealing.[31] But the plea was refused by the district attorney in Hollywood who said that Reventlow had not violated any California law when he took his son to Vancouver, British Columbia.

To Grant, it must have seemed that the newspaper presses of the entire country — if not the world — were grinding out grating phrases that constantly leaped out from newspaper pages. "Cary Grant's wife" or "now married to movie star Cary Grant." Regardless of any tempering advice that Grant might have offered to his wife, Barbara pressed her attorneys to file for full custody of her son on the basis that Reventlow was unfit to have charge of the boy.

Her accusations against her former husband were inflammatory, as she charged him with having an ungovernable temper and of assaulting his son on various occasions, even in the presence of other people. He had possessed, she claimed, a "hypnotic influence" over her and a great desire to get control over a "substantial part" of her fortune. She pointed out the amount of settlement money that she said she had transferred to Reventlow's bank account at various times, amounting to almost $3 million.[32] This was not enough for him, she stated; he continued to expect more.

The constant turmoil was too much for Cary Grant to accept. He packed his bags and vacated his wife's home. It was, Barbara said in a familiar routine, a friendly separation; just a case of incompatibility.

Before the end of the month, Reventlow had left Canada and moved to a Boston hotel with his wife and his son who, he said, knew nothing of the ongoing custody battle. The boy, he insisted, would be enrolled in a Boston school.

Maddened by her former husband's behavior, Barbara tried to get a temporary injunction restraining Reventlow from benefiting from the trust fund she had given him at the time of their separation six years previously. Two weeks later, Barbara and Cary reconciled and quietly left town, presumably for a "second honeymoon," Grant's RKO studio reported.[33]

Christmas approached and, although metal remained in short supply, Woolworth's toy counters were filled with model airplanes, now painted in colors other than olive drab in keeping with the trend away from war toys.[34] Toy planes and tractors, made mostly of wood and plastic, appealed to boys while dolls and stuffed animals, with cotton instead of kapok filling, were expected to be big sellers for girls. Electric trains, sleds and roller skates were reported to be first on the "wish lists" of youngsters, but the metal shortage would not allow their manufacture.

Retailers' main problems were making sure they complied with latest rulings by the OPA, which had set maximum prices for toys as those of March 1942. Any recent changes in models of toys requiring price rises had to be checked out first with the government agency.[35] Because in 1943 the OPA had concentrated on food, clothing and furniture prices, toy prices had not been closely regulated; some toy prices of 1944 would be even lower than those of the previous year.

Barbara's favorite cousin, Jimmy Donahue, who had been residing largely in Florida since his European travels had ended for the duration of the war, was ordered to report to his New York draft board for induction into the armed forces early in November 1944.[36] Immediately Jimmy requested a transfer of his selective service record to Florida where, he said, he was developing plans to set up a civilian airfield, which he referred to as a major war effort. He had learned to fly airplanes in 1939, he stated, and had been flying for two years with the Civil Air Patrol in Florida.

After being carried on the Army Air Force reserve inactive list while he had flown with the patrol, Jimmy had been released from that list the previous May. When the New York draft board refused the transfer request, Jimmy had no recourse except to report to the New York board at eight in the morning (an unearthly hour for Donahue). Newspaper photographers were on hand to shoot photos of his march along Park Avenue to the induction center where he was sworn into the army.[37]

Private Donahue got through the rigors of basic training and discipline, and had been in the army less than five months, stationed at Camp Dix, New Jersey, when he got into trouble. Jimmy and a corporal friend and three civilian men, one of whom was a salesman, went to an apartment where, apparently, drinks were plentiful. At 1:30 a.m., the salesman was thrown from an automobile onto a street corner where he was found, semi-conscious and only partly dressed, wearing his trousers backwards. He had suffered a head cut and was taken to a hospital.[38] What could have been a serious charge against the two Camp Dix soldiers, however, was dismissed by a grand jury after the salesman failed to press charges because Jessie Donahue had bought his silence for almost $250,000.[39]

Even before the latest misadventures of Donahue appeared in print, his cousin Barbara and Cary Grant separated again. This time, Barbara had moved out of her home on February 26. The couple issued a unified statement that seemed to express Grant's restrained attitude: "We can be happier living apart."[40] Only days later, Barbara suddenly dropped her suits against Reventlow and yielded custody, control and supervision of the religious and academic education and upbringing of young Lance to her divorced husband.

According to the new agreement, Lance would live with his mother in California during the 1945-46 school year. Then he would return to his father and attend an Eastern boarding school after which he would divide vacations and free time equally between his parents.

Even while Americans looked forward to the end of the war with a weakened Germany fighting on two fronts, they had to continue dealing with the problems of rationing and food stamps. Blue stamps for processed foods, red stamps for meats and fats, stamps of other colors for sugar, shoes and gasoline. Still, they knew their rationing complaints were minuscule compared to the hardships borne by other countries.

Youngsters learned to accept shortages, too. At Easter time, a chocolate bunny was impossible to find. Instead, inedible bunnies molded from wax or soap and bought from candle manufacturers adorned store shelves. Woolworth stores had a good supply of decorative wooden rabbits, also. Youngsters in the Stamford, Connecticut, area who played the old-fashioned game of marbles were surprised to find not a single "glassy" was available in dime stores in the area. Engineers at the nearby Sorenson & Co. Inc., makers of transformers for navy radar equipment, had scouted the stores for plain glass marbles after Sorenson's engineers had discovered that the marbles could be used as an essential part of a container housing a high-voltage transformer. Other materials had been tried, but they trapped air when the container was filled with oil. Only marbles worked.[41]

Soon after the Russian Army began its final push against Berlin on April 19, 1945, the last German defenders surrendered to the Russians on May 2; five days later the German High Command unconditionally surrendered to the Allies. The European war had ended but the fierce campaign against the Japanese continued.

In Berlin, where the Allied armies had not yet arrived, the Russians seized the machinery, products and retail goods of eleven American businesses. The businesses included three F. W. Woolworth stores.[42] Russians had suffered greatly during their long war with Germany, and their stripping of German businesses was viewed as a part of reparations due them.

The Woolworth Company already was looking forward to post-war expansion and had announced its plans to raze the Lancaster, Pennsylvania, six-story building that had been constructed in 1899 near the site of Woolworth's first Five-and-Ten. A replacement would be built, company officials said, after the first of the year, 1946, as soon as restrictions allowed new construction.[43]

In the meantime, the United States accused Japan of committing atrocities, including torture, starvation and massacre of prisoners of war held in their camps. In the camp at Palawan, it was disclosed that 150 prisoners had been burned and murdered.

In August, Marine Captain Winston F. C. Guest, former top polo player and husband of Helena Woolworth McCann's daughter (also named Helena), brought honor to his family when he managed to land his plane, carrying an Allied humanitarian-aid team, on a heavily mined airfield at Canton, China. In December, he would be decorated with the Soldier's Medal for his heroism.[44]

By the end of August, Barbara Hutton Grant, still a Danish citizen and surrounded by news cameramen, appeared at the courthouse in Los Angeles with famous divorce lawyer Jerry Giesler. There, she testified before Superior Court Judge Clarke in a divorce suit charging Cary Grant, the actor many American women viewed as the "ideal man," with mental cruelty.[45] She pointed out that he had snubbed her dinner guests, preferring to eat his dinner in his upstairs bedroom because her friends were annoying to him. His behavior made her very nervous, she complained. And yes, she had required the services of a doctor because of it.

An interlocutory decree was granted and Barbara would be a single woman once again — though likely not for long, according to her history.

The war with Japan ended that same year, soon after President Truman decided not to risk many more lives of American servicemen in an invasion of Japan, but, rather, to have an atomic bomb dropped on Hiroshima on August 6, 1945. When the Japanese did not quickly surrender, a second bomb was dropped on Nagasaki three days later. President Truman did not declare V-J Day officially, though, until September 2 when the surrender was signed and the Emperor ordered his subjects to obey all commands issued by General MacArthur.

Because of the quick expansion of business after the war, women employees were not demoted when men (except for the 119 male employees who had lost their lives) returned to their jobs at Woolworth. There were enough managerial and supervisory positions available, as the company planned post-war expansion, to keep everyone working.[46]

13

Post-war Labor Problems

In 1945, stretching through the final months of World War II and beyond, Woolworth's net profit for the year increased to $23,587,267 with total sales reaching the $477 million mark. There was a boost, too, in dividends received by American Woolworth for 1945 from its British subsidiary—amounting to $3,579,494, an increase of $397,720 over the previous year.[1]

In the aftermath of the war, the OPA relaxed its price restrictions, one of which had rolled back restaurant prices to whatever charges restaurants had listed in the week of April 4 through 10, 1943. This meant that the average restaurant could charge only five cents for a cup of coffee with cream and sugar. This particular restriction really had no effect on Woolworth restaurants, which would continue to charge only a nickel for coffee for more than another decade.[2]

Woolworth Company officials were elated in anticipation of improved business prospects for 1946 now that manufacturers would be able to supply war-scarce items along with new products that were being developed with the use of plastics and nylons. Plastic pin-wheels on sticks soon would replace the celluloid little pin-wheels that kids bought at Woolworth years earlier and attached to their tricycles. But businessmen did not yet realize that, after the patriotic hiatus of workers' demands during World War II, the optimistic views of big-business soon would be overshadowed by renewed clamoring from unions for better wages and benefits and, even, by internal and bitter warfare among unions themselves.

To Barbara Hutton, the relatively peaceful months immediately following V-J Day must have appeared to her as an opportunity to reshape her self-centered, spendthrift image into the form of a philanthropist. On December 9, 1945, Barbara had made an offer to President Truman to donate Winfield House—the Regents Park mansion she had built in London and named for her grandfather—for use as a United States embassy. Since the lease on the present embassy in London would expire in 1947, her offer seemed to be a fortuitous one. President Truman called it "patriotic and generous" as he officially accepted the gift on August 1, 1946.[3]

In the meantime, Barbara donated four valuable, early eighteenth-century paintings, by Antonio Canaletto, to the National Gallery of Art in Washington, D.C.[4] By this time, the "patriotic" heiress was no longer living in the United States or staying in the elaborate home she had bought just outside of Mexico City while she was married to Grant. As soon as possible, she returned to Paris and to the lavish suite in which she had lived, earlier, at the Ritz. She wanted to pick up the threads of her former life among those she chose to think of as the "literati," which likely included as many phonies as did the Monte Carlo "hangers-on" or those who trekked from one country to another, following the polo circuit.

Again, Barbara often was in the company of her cousin Jimmy, who owed his allegiance to her for the many times she, along with his mother, had come to his financial aid when he was in trouble. Soon, though, the amiable and amusing Jimmy would be occupied much of the time with working his way into the intimate circle of friends surrounding the Duke and Duchess of Windsor.

During the war years, the home of the Duke and Duchess had been in the Bahamas—the islands to which the duke had been banished (and named governor of) after he, newly crowned King Edward VIII of Great Britain, had abdicated the throne in December 1936. He chose, instead, to marry "the woman I love," the formerly twice-wed American divorcee Wallis Simpson.

At the end of the war, the Windsors speedily left the Bahamas to return to Paris —the city they loved even though, like Barbara Hutton, they traveled incessantly, frequently coming to Palm Beach or other cities in the United States.[5] Americans who thought of the English as "snobs" would have had to admit that American Palm Beach residents vied with each other to host the most exclusive and expensive parties to which the Windsors might deign to accept an invitation.

Moneyed Americans fawned over the favored couple and curtsied to the Duke and Duchess, addressing them as their "Royal Highnesses," even though, at this same time, the British royal family was firmly denying permission for the Duchess of Windsor to be addressed by the title of "Her Royal Highness."[6] In fact, those few of the society set who maneuvered to reach the pinnacle of friendship with the Windsors were elated when permitted to address the couple as "David and Wally." More ordinary Americans gathered in great numbers to catch a glimpse of the splendor of the Windsors as they arrived in New York by ship or in Washington, D.C., or Palm Beach by train or luxury automobile.

Barbara Hutton had met the Windsors and had entertained them on a few occasions. After her cousin Jimmy was released from the Army into his more natural habitat, he soon succeeded nicely in his campaign of attracting the admiring attention of the Windsor royal pair, particularly of the strong-willed Duchess, who appreciated Donahue's flair for comedy and clever repartee.[7] Jimmy and the royal pair soon became a nearly inseparable threesome. As a result, the amount of time that Jimmy could spend with his cousin Barbara would become limited in the early 1950s by the whims and summons of the Duchess of Windsor. And because of Jimmy's reputation for developing strong attractions, however temporary, to males (a reputation similar to that of his father), his increasingly close friendship, particularly with the Duchess, created much less gossip than it might have as the trio traveled about, even if Donahue was not as careful as most homosexuals of that era to remain "in the closet." Despite Donahue's reputation, the closeness of his friendship with the Windsors (particularly with the Duchess) became the source of scandal and knowing whispers among the society set.

During and in the wake of the terrible war with its casualty lists of many thousands of young men, change had encroached further and inexorably into the ultra-lavish lifestyles of wealthy patrons of the arts and of owners of palace-like structures (no longer worth the millions that had been poured into them in an earlier era) that lined the shores in Palm Beach. In the early spring of 1946, Jessie Donahue, almost sixty years old, placed her $1,000,000–plus Palm Beach home on the market.[8] A syndicate purchased it for $101,000. The house, it seemed, was as much a "white elephant" as had been her suburban New York mansion (left vacant after the death of her husband in 1931) that also was sold at a loss.

While, in her late years, Jessie Donahue was occupied with unloading properties that had become cumbersome and relatively unimportant to her, average working-class Americans were occupied with more mundane matters. Young married veterans, newly discharged from the armed forces, were scrambling to find low-priced housing and mortgages that they could afford at a time when suitable homes were scarce. Soon, under provisions of the G.I. bill making mortgages more available to veterans, builders turned their attention to constructing economically priced, small houses to satisfy the demand from young married couples. At the same time other problems, largely wage-and-hour issues, were persisting and expanding.

During the previous November of 1945, New York State had issued a minimum-wage order of 52.5 cents. The order also contained several other provisions, including overtime pay — which applied to women and minors working in retail trade. Leading Five and Dime chains, including Woolworth, joined together in the spring of 1946 to pose objections to the order at a hearing before the State Board of Standards and Appeals.[9] Among objections cited by the chains was the argument that Five and Ten stores should be allowed to pay 50 cents an hour because there was an "obvious difference" in quality and skills between a saleswoman in a smart Fifth Avenue shop and a chain-store counter girl. Another argument cited for not paying the minimum wage specified for part-time workers was that Dime Store workers likely had less experience and skills than full-time "girls." The arguments were not effective; the order was defended by the state board as "constitutional and fair," and it was pointed out to the chains' representatives that 75 percent of all retail shops affected were obeying the order and that 90 percent of the workers in retail shops already were collecting at least the legal minimum pay.

Frank W. Woolworth's brother, Charles Sumner Woolworth, would not live to observe the rapidly escalating problems of post-war labor-management relations. He died in January 1947 at age 90.[10] Nor did he live to see the gradual decline in front-page exposure of the Dionne Quintuplets, who had been moved into a new seven-bedroom, brick home with their parents and siblings and, in 1947, into what was termed a "normal life" with less publicity as the girls attended a special convent-school with ten students.

Even Sumner Woolworth's grandniece, Barbara, had been able to avoid undue publicity for a time following the granting of the final Hutton-Grant divorce decree on September 1, 1946. Only two days later, it became apparent that Barbara had interests other than Paris when a newspaper item disclosed that the Woolworth heiress had bought a once-grand Moorish castle in Tangier overlooking the Strait of Gibral-

tar, at what the restless heiress would call a "bargain" price (reported to be somewhere between $75,000 and $100,000.) [11] Shortly afterwards, Barbara moved to that
internationalized zone not far from Casablanca.

If the heiress had not become a central figure in the "literati" circles of Paris,
perhaps she thought she could find fulfillment in the exotic atmosphere of Tangier.
Because Tangier was a relatively inexpensive place to live, the city was continuing to
attract artists and writers, many of whom were of the existentialist variety such as
Paul Bowles, who affected the hairstyle and various mannerisms (including the use
of long cigarette holders) of Noël Coward. Tangier also became the home of the drug-
addicted grandson-writer of American inventor William S. Burroughs of adding
machine fame. [12]

Barbara's cousin Frasier, of the publicity-shy McCann clan, rarely occasioned a
news story but did so in 1946 when he and Jeremiah C. Ingersoll bought a veterans'
monthly magazine named *Salute*. [13] Almost immediately, ten major staff members
resigned from their positions. New staffers were hired to replace those who had
resigned, and claims that the dispute had been triggered by editorial, not political,
differences soon became questionable. Leaks disclosed that many staffers, regarded
as liberals, resented what they considered were Communist party influences that
would, they believed, direct the journal to adhere to Communist party lines.

As journalists and commentators continued to urge a long occupation of defeated
Germany to avoid another Nazi takeover, once again the manufacture of toys, porce-
lains, leather goods and jewelry, bearing "made in Germany" labels, was taking place
in that country. These goods were intended to reach the United States in time for
the Christmas season of 1946. [14] In this way, the destitute German nation could obtain
dollars to pay for food imports being shipped out by the United States.

In June 1946, 62-year-old Alfred L. Cornwell, who had worked for Woolworth
ever since he began as a 21-year-old "learner," was named president of the Woolworth Company. [15] Although post-war America soon would be plagued by strikes, the
reign of President Cornwell was destined to be one of unprecedented growth to
annual sales of $700 million in 1954 when the company would celebrate its diamond
anniversary.

Even before the end of June 1946, the new president had to deal with an unexpected and short-lived strike by Woolworth employees in Havana, Cuba, wherein
the strikers demanded, but did not receive, a huge wage hike of 40 percent to 60 percent. In August, Woolworth and many other companies were affected by a major
crackdown on cleanliness in food establishments as part of a campaign by New York
Mayor O'Dwyer and Health Commissioner Weinstein, who expressed their goals of
making New York City "one of the cleanest and healthiest cities in the world." The
campaign was "a witch hunt," one restaurant owner complained as he became one
of 700 owners fined in the first round-up. The F. W. Woolworth Company was publicly embarrassed when the lunch counter in its Fifth Avenue store was fined $350
because of harboring roaches and unclean dishes. [16] The company issued specific clean-
up orders but two months later, two more Woolworth stores at Third Avenue and
at Lenox Avenue would be among many other restaurants fined for sanitary code violations.

On the national scene, workers' strikes were looming and, according to business owners, threatening the economy of the country and the well being of its citizens. An ongoing seven-months-long strike against a Phelps Dodge Copper Products Company in New Jersey (where workers were demanding an 18 1/2 cent hourly wage increase) showed no signs of ending even after a worker was shot in the neck. In early August, Long Island Railroad trainmen threatened to strike and a general maritime strike was called by the Seafarers International Union and the Sailors Union of the Pacific for early September. A truck drivers' strike in New York City on September 3, 1946, cut the delivery of food for a short time to display the union's "muscle," while truckers refused to accept a wage increase of 18 1/2 cents an hour recommended by Mayor O'Dwyer. With the truckers stalled, the Railway Express Agency established an embargo on express shipments within New York City in order to prevent overloading its facilities.[17]

A report from British Woolworth that its profits for 1946 amounted to $36 million was followed by another report in February 1947 that its top price-limit of six pence would no longer be in effect.[18] The parent company was encouraged by these reports to expand British Woolworth operations. Before the end of 1947, there would be 811 stores in England, Scotland and Wales—a remarkable recovery from wartime destruction of British Woolworth stores caused by German bombs.

From St. Moritz, Switzerland, Barbara Hutton created a stir by making a public announcement of her forthcoming royal marriage on February 20, 1947.[19] She would marry 34-year-old Prince Igor Troubetzkoy next month, she said, right here in St. Moritz where the prince was occupied with his writings on psychology. The prince's father, she confided, had been living in the United States ever since he left Russia previous to the Russian revolution.

Within a week of the announcement of her imminent wedding, she sold to a Greek shipping magnate her 1,250-ton yacht, recently returned to her by the British Admiralty that had requisitioned it during the war. But Barbara's earlier plans to be married in a month, by way of a ceremony befitting royalty, were suddenly and drastically changed when she and the prince, who never had been married previously, became husband and wife on March third in a Zurich registry office during a ceremony so brief that the bride never removed her mink coat.[20]

In an after-ceremony gesture, the prince donated 500 Swiss francs "for the poor" to a registry employee, adding that he would like to offer more but his money was running out. A newspaper report noted that the prince and princess left the office with their two witnesses and went into a pastry shop to celebrate, in a most non-royal way, with coffee and cake before the newlyweds checked into a hotel in the Alps above Zurich.

That summer of 1947, the month of July was marked by more labor-management problems and strikes. Negotiations between Woolworth and Local 65, Wholesale and Warehouse Workers Union of the CIO, had broken off on June 21.[21] The 334 warehouse employees at two Woolworth warehouses were not satisfied with the company's proposal offering a 35-hour workweek and a $55 minimum weekly wage, along with better holiday and vacation clauses.

Well before Woolworth and the union reached terms for ratification by union members, the country was gripped by many other strikes pending or already occurring.[22] Six hundred painters affiliated with the AFL ended a month-long strike in Providence, Rhode Island, by accepting a raise in wages that would bring them $1.57 1/2 cents an hour. Five hundred employees walked the picket line at the Brooklyn Trust Company. A strike of 7,000 UAW-CIO-affiliates continued to drag along at Murray Corporation of America. Chicago railroads representatives were appearing before an arbitration board along with representatives of 17 brotherhoods of non-operating railroad workers. Power in-fighting among unions and brotherhoods was complicating the problems everywhere between workers and companies.

Regardless of difficulties with unionized workers, Woolworth finished the year 1947 with an improved net income of $41,913,414, highest in its history, as compared to the previous year's $39,930,684. These earnings did not include the Canadian subsidiary's 1947 earnings of $1,621,976.[23]

Princess Igor Troubetzkoy was having her own problems in early 1948. On January 23, Barbara underwent major surgery in a Berne, Switzerland, hospital for what was referred to as an intestinal problem. Five days later, she was released to recuperate at the Bellevue Palace Hotel where her husband had been staying. Her condition was "serious, but not dangerous," her doctors said. Still, when Barbara suffered a relapse the day after her release, she was taken back to the hospital where a second surgery was done on Sunday, leaving her in what doctors now said was "critical condition" after removal of an intestinal blockage and with a third operation under consideration.[24]

Her third husband, Cary Grant, would describe Barbara to a girl friend as being "heavily scarred" from her previous cesarean section when she had given birth to her son, and from the correcting of complications from the earlier cesarean section when she had nearly lost her life.[25] By this time, the scarring on her frail body had worsened.

While Barbara slowly recovered from her surgeries that spring, Woolworth President Cornwell announced that the company would spend $24 million on expansion in 1948 by constructing 16 stores and modernizing 87 older stores. The company's restaurant units, Cornwell added, made Woolworth "one of the biggest dispensers of food in the United States."

Cornwell's rosy expectations for the future of Woolworth were marred again, though, by division among its workers in two large warehouses—workers who were divided by allegiance to two different unions; Local 804 of the International Brotherhood of Teamsters, AFL, and Local 65 of the CIO. Local 65 already held the existing warehouse contract, but that contract would expire on July 8.

In a May 31 election, slated to determine whether more than 300 warehouse workers wished to transfer their representation to AFL Local 804, the results caused even more feuding between the two locals because CIO Local 65 claimed the election was rigged. Local 65 had been barred from the election by the National Labor Relations Board because of the refusal by some of the local's leaders to file non–Communist affidavits as required by the 1947 Taft-Hartley law, designed to curb the power of unions.[26]

In an attempt to calm union strife, the Woolworth Company posted notices in the two warehouses. The notices proclaimed that no union had, as yet, been certified, and that the company would authorize a 10-cent-an-hour pay raise as well as continuing the same insurance, holiday and vacation benefits as in the agreement.[27]

On July 14, warehouse employee-members of CIO Local 65 voted to ask the full membership of the local to vote for authorization of a strike against Woolworth, but the company refused to lie down and roll over despite the local's threat to picket Woolworth stores throughout the nation. A House subcommittee investigating Communist influences in the store-union field already had been roused to action by the "reciprocal discharge" clauses being sought in agreements by the "left-wing department-store locals," as termed by the subcommittee. Committee members were charging that left-wing union leaders could make use of the "reciprocal discharge" clause to get anti–Communists fired from their jobs.

"Not so," union leaders explained. The union would gain only the right to ask for dismissal of workers when their employment was causing overall "unharmonious relationships" in the workplace.

Even when four officers of Local 65 were listed among nine unionists facing prosecution for contempt of Congress because of their refusal to testify in regard to their membership in the Communist party or other so-called subversive organizations, members of Local 65 declared their overwhelming support for their officers. At a membership meeting of Local 65 on July 21, 1948, the members voted by secret ballot, 2,459 to 462, to back their union's policy of refusing to file non–Communist affidavits under the Taft-Hartley law.

At the same meeting, the union declared its support for the Henry Wallace-for-president Progressive Party in the upcoming election. It announced, also, that it would picket 200 New York Woolworth stores and 100 other stores in other parts of the country, using its more than one-half-million-dollar strike fund.[28] The strike fund had been built up by assessing its 13,000 members one week's salary (not a popular decision among the membership) to pay for a strike that, union officials estimated, would cost $25,000 a week.

In what was termed a "demonstration" preliminary to a strike, Local 65 picketed 500 Woolworth stores in the United States and Canada on July 31.[29] Supported by members of the Progressive Party, the demonstrators marched and handed out leaflets. However, the president of Local 65 made an announcement that slightly softened his union's stance. "If there is any reason to believe it is possible to find a solution, the strike will be postponed," he said.

The State Mediation Board of New York was experiencing the heaviest caseload in its decade-long history. By the end of June 1948, 1,022 cases had come before the board and the backlog of cases was growing. As yet, no new and definite date was set for the threatened Woolworth strike.

Before August 15, the trucking industry and the mechanics from American Airlines were threatening nation-wide strikes. Leaders of Local 65 Wholesale and Warehouse Union, affiliated with the Retail, Wholesale and Department Store Union, were ordered, again, by the international union to sign non–Communist affidavits of the Taft-Hartley law. If they refused to sign the affidavits, they faced removal and the international union could seize their organizations.

In-fighting among various unions was not helpful to locals struggling against what they saw as the ever-tightening noose of the Taft-Harley law. In September CIO-affiliated Local 65 Wholesale and Warehouse Union quit the CIO and formed an independent union, The Department Store Employees Union, Local 1250, and began negotiating with New York department stores to sign contracts with the new union. By the end of January, 1949, when the department store, Hearn's, signed a contract, the new union had reached agreement with a total of four large stores including Gimbel's and Saks Thirty-fourth Street.[30]

Battling among unions and locals continued, but on a much reduced scale by the time it was reported that Princess Barbara Troubetzkoy "of the Woolworth millions" was in the American Hospital in Paris after having had what was referred to as a "minor operation." "An abdominal operation" her husband elaborated, without relating it to the abdominal surgery his 36-year-old wife had a year previously.[31]

Her son, Lance, now attending St. George School in Newport, would, by agreement, be sent to Europe at the close of the school year to be with his mother for half of his summer vacation. At the approach of the end of July, when Lance was to be returned to his father, a petition was filed with the court to extend his visit with his ailing 88-pound mother, who was confined to her bed most of the time, the petition stated, and, under doctor's orders, was not permitted to take a sea voyage. Thirteen-year-old Lance wished to remain with his mother while she was ill, the boy said.

A Probate Court judge soon ruled that the boy's visit could be extended until September 7. Only a day after this ruling, Barbara was reported to be quietly vacationing in Venice and going by motorboat to Lido for lunch and a swim before returning to the Grand Hotel. When a photo of Barbara in a bathing suit was published in newspapers, her doctor reported that the swimming was recommended for health reasons because she was in pain and in fragile health.

Although Woolworth's board of directors had endured serious labor problems and strike threats during the year, the company opened an $8 million mega-store in downtown Houston, Texas, on November 16, 1949.[32] The three-story building contained more than a mile of counters, the company boasted, serviced by more than 700 employees. According to the company, the store would be "the largest and most impressive of the Woolworth chain." Profits for the year 1949 were impressive, too, amounting to $57,058,813, with net income, after taxes and all charges, racking up to $37,161,017 or $3.83 a share.

The new, independent Local 1250 of the Retail, Wholesale and Department Store Union, CIO, had turned its attention away from its stalemate with the flourishing Woolworth stores to picket New York department stores of Oppenheim, Collins & Company after that company refused to bargain with union representatives. While the company sought an injunction against the picketing, claiming that pickets were blocking entrances to the stores and jeering at company officials with shouts of "cutthroats, gangsters and fascists," the CIO local was barred from a ballot in a representation election held at the store. Again, the reason for barring the CIO local from the ballot was because its officers still refused to file anti–Communist declarations. Instead, the Retail Clerks International Association, AFL, was selected to represent

Oppenheim Collins employees. The in-fighting among unions and locals was almost as destructive as was big business-union confrontation.

Unions took renewed hope that the Taft-Hartley law would be repealed when President Harry Truman promised in his re-election campaign of 1948 to work for overturning that union-restraining legislation. The greatest advance in union power, however, would not occur for seven more years when the AFL and CIO finally merged into one powerful organization in December 1955. After that date, the organization began taking steps to try to eliminate racketeers from trade unions.

14

Approaching the Billion-dollar Sales Goal

The 1950s would remain in the minds of most Americans as a decade of prosperity, friendly neighborliness, innocence and peacefulness despite disturbing media reports of American troops battling North Korean troops who had invaded South Korea. The war had begun in June 1950 when North Korean soldiers, equipped for battle by the Soviet Union, pushed their way into South Korea and quickly captured Seoul. Soon afterwards, United States military forces joined those of South Korea and several United Nations contingents to push back the invaders.

For three years, young American soldiers faced the bitter cold of frigid Korean winters and the tough determination of North Korean troops (and sometimes Chinese troops) in vicious combat, even while peace negotiations were held. The negotiations dragged on, broke down, and began again later. Although a truce agreement was signed at Panmunjom on July 27, 1953, it would take another nine months until the ultimate peace settlement took effect. In the United States, a spokesman for the independent National Association of Variety Stores was predicting, as early as 1950, a revival of the market "for the old-fashioned dime-store merchandise." During recent years, the five-and-ten-cent stores "all but disappeared," he said, "because of the rush to sell high priced items such as trains for $100 a set." He pointed out that Japanese toy imports could not match the quality production of American toy manufacturers and that there would be greater use of plastics in toys and household goods in the 1950s.[1]

In the early part of 1950 and after a lengthy period during which the F. W. Woolworth Company had been conducting its own little war with the National Labor Relations Board, the company received a setback when it was ordered by the board to reinstate a female employee (fired because of her activity as a union member) to her previous job in a Cincinnati Woolworth store.[2] The Retail Clerks Union, AFL, had sought redress for the firing from the National Labor Relations Board. Along with its ruling regarding the reinstatement of the employee, the board cracked down on merchants and set up new and strict rules designating explicit dates and firm methods of making back-payments to re-hired workers. The rules also directed all companies to make available to the board, on request, all necessary payrolls, records of Social Security payments, time cards and personnel reports.

The board went further; it ordered the Woolworth Company to cease any practices (as determined by the board) to discourage a free choice in union elections. It set aside the election of June 7, 1949, that had been held at a New York Woolworth store and said a new election would be conducted when advised by the board's regional director that circumstances would permit a free choice of representatives by employees. The Retail Clerks Union AFL was strengthened considerably by these rulings.

Forced to accept the rulings, the Woolworth Company could only try to avoid running into any further trouble with the union as the year 1950 progressed with all signs pointing toward expanding sales volume for operations in the United States, Canada and Cuba. The company's expectations were met when 1950 turned out to be a record-breaking year with sales amounting to $632,135,790 and profits of $61,100,733.[3]

In Britain, the reports for 1950 were not as rosy. Governmental taxes had bitten heavily into 1950 profits from F.W. Woolworth & Co., Ltd., leaving a net income of only 5,355,272 pounds for the year.[4] But German Woolworth had opened new stores in Hanover, Kiel and Hamm, as well as renovating six stores damaged by wartime bombs, and making repairs to 17 others. With 41 stores now operating in Western Germany and the Western sector of Berlin, the accounting for the German stores showed steadily increasing sales and profits for 1950.

On the American side of the Atlantic, 21 new Woolworth stores had opened and 23 older stores closed during 1950, leaving 1,776 stores in the United States, 152 in Canada and eight in Cuba. By this time, the company was going ahead with plans for more expansion in 1951, leasing a space in the projected Herald Square shopping center in New York City and planning new stores in San Francisco and Fairlawn, New Jersey.

In these years of the early 1950s, large shopping centers already were causing complications to Woolworth's long-time policy of placing its Five and Ten Cent Stores on Main Streets, USA. Customer traffic was beginning to turn to shopping centers and, a bit later, to new and larger shopping malls already being constructed in burgeoning suburban areas, near freeway accesses, far removed from the Main Streets of America. Although the trend was only in its infancy at this point, Woolworth directors began to realize that the future for their stores might be in the new shopping centers and in outlying suburban malls.

For some time, Woolworth stores had carried "pop" recordings at price discounts. Only recently the company had inaugurated a trial merchandising of classical recordings in some of its stores in Massachusetts and Pennsylvania.[5] In early 1951, in a move that surely would have pleased the founder of the Woolworth chain, the company placed a large order with Remington Records for low-cost, long-playing classical records that would be available in all Woolworth record departments.

The Christmas-buying season officially opened for Woolworth stores, as in most other variety stores, on November 22. Woolworth directors were aware that the potential toy market was expanding since the country's population of children under ten years of age had increased approximately 40 percent since 1940, with the greatest increase occurring after the end of World War II.[6] In these prosperous post-war years, statistics proved that individual savings had risen and retailers knew that a substantial percentage of individual bank reserves was spent on holiday gifts, particularly for children. Plastic toys and inflated toys were big sellers in 1951, while inexpensive metal toy tractors, trucks and airplanes also sold well. During the 1950s and beyond, Woolworth would continue to sell large quantities of Silly Putty, which could provide hours of cheap entertainment for kids.

Among the memorabilia left over from the Woolworth heyday are various buttons and insignia worn by employees.

Silly Putty had derived from attempts by a General Electric engineer to make a synthetic rubber at a time when rubber products could not be obtained in the civilian market because of military demands during World War II. But when the combination of chemicals used in the attempts did not turn out well enough to satisfy the requirements for a synthetic rubber, the sticky product that resulted from the experiments was set aside. Later, after an enterprising fellow experienced in the advertising world thought that the substance might be marketed for children, he purchased the rights to the stuff and encased it in plastic egg-like containers. His Silly Putty made millions of dollars as it was sold at Woolworths and other variety stores. Some years later, Paul Harvey reported on his radio program that the putty was found to be a practical product used by astronauts in space who could temporarily prevent their tools from drifting away by attaching them to a blob of Silly Putty to hold them in place.[7]

Large maps of the United States, in puzzle form, were popular gifts purchased by customers who poured into Woolworth stores to buy Christmas cards, gift-wrappings and Christmas tree decorations in the early 1950s. Packets of baseball cards sold in quantity to schoolboys who hoarded and traded them in their fascination with the heroes of Yankee Stadium and Tiger Stadium and in their youthful yearnings to become great pitchers or first-basemen.

The old-fashioned children's game of Tiddlywinks would be brought back into Woolworth stores later in that decade when the game developed into a serious teen-and-adult competition with the adoption of a more sophisticated form of Tiddlywinks by several British universities, including Oxford. Groups of players, four in each group and each player equipped with colorful "winks," used "squidgers" to aim for a central pot located on a large mat. A new dictionary of words became known to serious players ("squopping," "potting out," "fluppet") as they took the game from

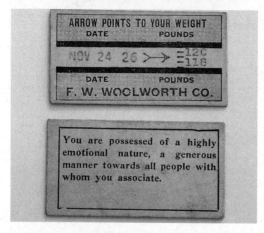

Top: "Hot Wheels" replicas, made by Mattel, of Woolworth delivery trucks.

　　Bottom: Weighing machines, often located near the front entrances, were one of the things most people remember about Woolworth stores. Customers loved the "fortune" cards that, along with their weight, could be obtained by dropping a penny into a slot many years ago.

the realm of a nursery toy into the higher echelons of Oxford and Harvard competitions.

　　Woolworth stores would satisfy an even greater demand, before the end of that decade, by piling high on their counters the new, inexpensive and so-called "most popular American toy ever made." Hula-Hoops. Made of brightly colored plastic (a plain black one could be bought slightly cheaper than the more colorful ones), the hoop was rotated around the body by the user's hula-movements of the hips. The goal? To keep the hoop circling longer than any other contestant. Although Japan refused to stock the item, evidently disapproving of the necessary hip movements, the Japanese censure was scarcely noticeable because a bonanza of Hula-Hoops — one hundred million of them — would be sold worldwide in 1958. Hula-Hoops sold for an average of 98 cents at Woolworth stores and, in a six-week period of 1958, Woolworth, alone, sold more than $3 million worth of the circular whirlers. For two more decades, Woolworth buyers hoped to find another toy that might match the popularity and profitability of the Hula-Hoop.[8]

　　Woolworth's Board of Directors had many changes to consider at their meetings in the early 1950s. Along with the trend toward shopping centers and suburban malls, the self-service trend had to be evaluated.

　　On August 22, 1952, the F. W. Woolworth Company launched its first experiment in this trend at its New York Fourteenth Street store in the Stuyvesant Town area by changing over three of its four departments to self-service. The company had been tentatively experimenting with what it called "self-selection" of merchandise by customers in some of its stores in other parts of the country, but the New York–based store would be the first to be almost totally involved in the new procedure, with checkouts situated at the front of the store for payment and wrapping. If the test-trial worked out well regarding customer satisfaction, the experiment would be expanded to other stores.[9]

　　At this same time in late summer, a new doll was patented and would be introduced to the public in time for the Christmas season. The rush to reality in dolls was originated by this product that actually burped by way of a flattened rubber tube that forced low-pressure air into the doll's head when the rubber body was squeezed. Did it say "pardon me?" was the question from quizzical potential buyers.[10] An infant doesn't say "pardon me," was the usual response. And as yet, there were no talking dolls. But it would not be long (1960) until the popular Chatty Cathy doll ("I love you," she chattered at the pull of a string) appeared on the market.

While hoping that Woolworth could stock the burping doll for Christmas of 1952, the company ordered a shipment of 127 dozen cocker spaniel earthenware figurines at 60 cents each, and sold them for $1.19, making a gross profit of $899.16. What was not known to the Woolworth Company was that these dogs had been copied from Contemporary Arts Products by the supplier that sold them to Wool-

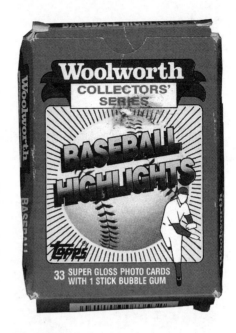

Boxes of Woolworth Collectors' Series Baseball Highlights cards were very popular.

worth. By marketing the dogs, Woolworth "became an infringer," and was assessed $5,000 plus attorneys' fees in the Circuit Court after Contemporary Arts sued Woolworth.[11]

The Woolworth Company pursued the case up to the U.S. Supreme Court. There, the Woolworth attorney insisted that the unsuspecting Woolworth Company could be liable only for the profit it had made on the sale. The trial judge, Justice Jackson, said that if an infringement of copyright was established, there was enough evidence upon which to assess damages up to $5,000. Although Justices Black and Frankfurter disagreed with the other members of the Court, saying that the damage-assessment "smacks of punitive qualities," the final judgment affirmed the decision by the earlier court.

The company finished the year 1952 with sales approximating $712 million, another record-breaking amount.[12] Twenty-four million dollars of that amount were distributed to stockholders in dividends. If that did not erase the sting of publicity surrounding the fining of the company by the U.S. Supreme Court, it may have been erased by the honor bestowed upon the company's founder in Chicago's Hall of Fame in 1953.

The deceased Frank Winfield Woolworth was one of four pioneer merchants honored for his accomplishments along with Marshall Field of Chicago, John Wanamaker of Philadelphia and George Huntington Hartford of New York. A four-foot bronze sculpture of each honoree was placed on permanent display at Merchandise Mart on a wall overlooking the Chicago River. Merchandise Mart had appropriated the title "the world's tallest office building," which had been held for 17 years by the

A Woolworth cosmetics ad, originally published in *Woman's Home Companion* magazine in
November 1952. (Author's Collection)

Woolworth Building in New York. (It had been the pride of its founder Frank W.
Woolworth until his death. Later, when the Chrysler Building in New York eclipsed
the vertical measurements of the Woolworth Building, the Chrysler edifice appropriated the title—in 1930.) The names of the four honorees were announced at the
lavish dinner given by Joseph P. Kennedy, former U.S. ambassador to Britain, for 375
guests. Held at a rooftop garden constructed at the Mart for the occasion, the dinner was highlighted when a letter to Joseph Kennedy from President Eisenhower was

read. In the letter, Eisenhower praised the "Hall of Fame" and said the observance was a "stimulus to progress in the nation's merchandising economics."[13]

Barbara Hutton, the so-called "Woolworth heiress," had not been as compliant regarding court rulings as her grandfather's company had been in accepting rulings of the National Labor Relations Board. After filing for a Mexican divorce in Cuernavaca from Prince Troubetzkoy in March 1951, a disgruntled Princess Barbara had returned to New York when Troubetzkoy blocked the divorce by claiming that he had not been notified properly. Deny, deny was Barbara's watchword on her arrival in New York. No, she had not made any offer of money to her fourth husband in an attempt to accomplish her divorce, she said. And no, she had no plans to remarry.[14] In additional comments, freely offered, she blamed "others" for her present predicament. She had listened to these anonymous "others" all her life, she pointed out. And following the advice of "others" had led her, almost without exception, into doing the "wrong thing." Now she had a new credo of independence. "I am going to do what I want to do," she announced.

When thwarted from doing what she wanted to do, she followed her customary practice. In April, she entered a hospital after what was referred to as a "virus attack." "Not serious," a hospital spokesman said.

Once again, the unpleasant publicity surrounding Princess Barbara was in sharp contrast to the publicity that appeared in late May 1951 when the Dionne quintuplets celebrated their seventeenth birthday. At the end of October, that same year, the five demure sisters were honored by their presentation to Queen Elizabeth as the Queen visited Canada.

Barbara's divorce remained in limbo for a while because of an injunction obtained by her husband. Four months later, the Mexican divorce was granted,[15] after Prince Troubetzkoy tried to effect reconciliation even though he knew of Barbara's discontent with their marriage.

Fifteen-year-old Lance was old enough now to be both bewildered and disturbed by his mother's marital problems. He had observed that the athletic Troubetzkoy, who had been a bicycle-racing champion in France, was very patient with his wife's health problems, her temperamental outbursts and even her flirtations with other men. Lance was old enough now, too, to have difficulty dealing with his domineering father, Count Haugwitz-Reventlow. Both parents were discovering that their son was becoming a strong-willed teenager.

Even before her divorce from Troubetzkoy became final late that summer, and before all the financial arrangements for paying off her husband had been worked out, the ex-princess moved back to Paris. She seemed happiest only when cousin Jimmy also came to Paris. But Jimmy was more independent these days, having received control of the millions in his trust fund at age 35. Even Jimmy had to have tired quickly of Barbara's fuzzy speech when she had been drinking—which was frequent, day or night. And he was only too well aware of her dependence on sleeping pills. It was no longer so much fun being with Barbara; in fact, it was kind of worrisome. And it was no longer quite so much fun for Jimmy when he was with "David and Wally" either, and bowing to every wish and whim of the imperious duchess. It would be only a short time before his break with the Windsors would occur in an ugly incident when Jimmy, once again, had been drinking too much.[16]

The Woolworth Building was back in the news as it celebrated its fortieth birth-day on April 14, 1953. The company had completed a thorough modernization of the building so that it could hold its foremost place in the office-skyscraper field with the help of 200 service employees taking care of nearly 30 acres of floor space. "Chilled" air-conditioning (as it was popularly called) now maintained the comfort-level in two new restaurants and offices within the building. Twenty-four new high-speed elevators swished passengers to upper levels. The current emphasis on natural light accented architect Cass Gilbert's foresight when he designed the Gothic build-ing as a U-shaped structure with corridors down the center of each wing so that every office had an "outside" view.[17]

In 1954, James T. Leftwich (a former company bookkeeper) assumed the pres-idency of the Woolworth Company at the retirement of A.L. Cornwell.[18] Leftwich soon acquired $110 million in loans to modernize a number of Woolworth stores and to build new stores in some of the shopping centers that were under construction in suburban areas. First, though, Leftwich was attracted to a 16-acre site in Dover, New Jersey. The Woolworth Company was among the first to lease in this center that was not on the outskirts of a town or city, but was planned to create a new "Main Street" in Dover with the additional advantage of parking available for 2,000 to 2,500 auto-mobiles. This fit Woolworth's policies very nicely, but the company still retained plans to locate in suburban malls as well and, in 1954, began setting up its own chain of cafeterias and restaurants, named Harvest House. Located near, usually adjoin-ing, Woolworth stores, the new Harvest House restaurants, with their cornucopia insignia, were not intended to take the place of the in-house lunch counters and soda fountains, but to supply more leisurely settings for customer dining.[19]

Such far-sighted planning was foreign to the impulsive Woolworth grand-daughter Barbara Hutton. She remained unsettled in 1953 — taking up one thing after the other (travels, a fling with Yoga and other exercise and diet fads and, of course, men) to try to escape her restlessness. After a less-than-serious attempt at suicide with a razor blade, she was taken to the hospital.[20] It was likely that Lance, who visited again that summer, also found his visit worrisome after he had learned of the suicide attempt. Other things annoyed him, too. His mother nagged at him. She worried about him getting hurt while playing polo. But she worried even more about the Hollywood starlets that she was certain were pursuing her tall, handsome, blonde only son.

In the fall of 1953, Barbara found something else to think about when she attended a polo tournament and kept her field glasses trained on a player who was easy to follow — his red helmet distinguished him from all the other players in white helmets. Certainly she had heard of the red-helmeted Porofino Rubirosa (known familiarly as "Rubi") because he traveled the same circuits that she had traveled for so long. She had heard, too, of his latest and ongoing love affair with Zsa Zsa Gabor, American actress, but that relationship mattered no more to Barbara than did Rubirosa's history of three previous marriages. If anything, he seemed more desir-able in Barbara's eyes, not only because of his highly publicized love affairs but also because of his reputation as a great lover.[21]

Born in the Dominican Republic, he had married President Trujillo's daughter for political advantage, then married a French actress, and, still later, married American tobacco heiress Doris Duke who, at the time of their divorce, gave him a house on the Rue Bellechasse.[22] The Parisian house soon became a rendezvous for him and Zsa Zsa Gabor, the flamboyant Hollywood actress married to actor George Sanders.

Rubirosa's love affair with Zsa Zsa was not terminated with his marriage to Barbara Hutton on December 30, 1953.[23] Barbara had gone ahead with wedding plans even though gossip reports, widely circulated in newspapers just previous to the wedding, had told of Rubirosa following his paramour, Zsa Zsa, from Paris to Los Angeles and Las Vegas where the two, in a jealous frenzy, had argued until the fiery Rubi rewarded Zsa Zsa with a black eye. Barbara surely had read the reports, including follow-up reports wherein the glamorous Zsa Zsa appeared on stage with an eye patch. Eye patches quickly became a fad adopted by hundreds of Zsa Zsa "wannabees" who bought black eye patches at a variety of specialty shops and sported them at parties and other events, trusting that the patches graced them with the glamor of Zsa Zsa rather than the fierce look of one-eyed pirates.

Very quickly after Rubirosa flew back to Paris after the black-eye incident, he and Barbara were married in the New York City apartment of the Dominican Consul General, who conducted the brief ceremony on December 30, 1953. The bride's son, Lance, was her only attendant. The groom's best man was his former brother-in-law, who was head of the Dominican Air Force. The newlyweds had not bothered with the formality of getting a marriage license, dismissing that procedure as "unnecessary." After all, Dominican property was considered a "foreign territory," the bride pointed out. Instead, Barbara had become a citizen of the Dominican Republic by way of a special decree issued by President Trujillo, who remained on good terms with Rubirosa (and continued to have him serve, also, as minister plenipotentiary) despite the latter's earlier divorce from Trujillo's daughter. The newlyweds would live in Paris, it was reported.[24] Apparently, it seemed unimportant to either bride or groom that their marriage was not recognized in New York State because of their failure to obtain a marriage license.

If that was not enough to get the marriage off to a rocky beginning, Barbara was unlucky enough to break her ankle the day after the wedding "in a slip in the living room," she said, at their New York hotel suite.[25] With her left ankle in a cast, she had to use a wheelchair from which she hobbled into the 88-passenger chartered airplane, which would take them to their honeymoon in Florida.

The honeymoon was short-lived. To Barbara, her new husband seemed to be obsessed with the telephone. She quickly discovered that his phone calls were being made to the Hollywood actress who was the actual source of his obsession.[26] By March 14, reports circulated that Barbara was separating from her husband of less than three months. Magazines reminded readers of the value of the Woolworth heiress' fortune and of the costly gifts she had bestowed on Rubirosa — polo ponies, an airplane and a sports car, plus a plantation in the Dominican Republic among other lavish presents.[27]

A mutual statement made confirmation of the separation to the press in which the couple emphasized that the separation was "entirely friendly." By June, Barbara was on her way from New York to her home in Tangier, traveling by plane on her

Danish passport under the name Princess Barbara Troubetzkoy. So quickly was the charming Rubirosa erased from her life as she denied to reporters that she was attempting to get a French divorce from her fifth husband.

Humiliated by her short-lived marriage to Rubirosa (most sources indicate it lasted 73 days), Barbara sought solace by phoning the German baron Gottfried von Cramm, with whom she had been in touch periodically for years. Another 13 months would pass, however, before her divorce from Rubirosa would become final.[28]

The Woolworth Company had spent $26 million in 1953 to build 44 new stores (many of them were the self-service type) and for improvements in others of its stores. Although sales that year had reached a record $713,870,367, earnings declined nearly $2 million from the previous year.[29] Salary increases for employees accounted for 86 percent of increased expenses, company officials explained. State laws had set both wages and hours that were being strictly enforced. Still, one of Woolworth's stores in New Jersey ran into trouble with the State Department of Labor and Industry when the store manager was charged with violating the maximum of ten work-hours a day and 54 work-hours a week for women and minors.

President Leftwich wanted 1954, the year in which the company celebrated its diamond anniversary, to reach new heights in both sales and profits, but not at the risk of violating any state labor laws. By March, he was busily planning for a Woolworth chain in Jamaica as the company bought two stores which would be converted into Woolworth stores in Kingston's central King Street. He announced impressive plans for opening two new stores in Mexico. Another plan was for opening what would be the company's largest store in New York City, on 34th Street. There were plans, too, for opening the first Woolworth's Hawaiian store in Honolulu. In Germany, Woolworth stores already had increased to 50 while British Woolworth now had 819 stores.[30]

In the spring of 1954, the Dionne sisters were back in the news in a disturbing way. Four of the sisters attended a ceremony at which the other sister, Marie, became a novice at a convent, but shortly afterwards, Marie left the convent for health reasons. Then, a newspaper report told of Emilie's bewilderment when she became lost and confused on her way to meet with Marie in Montreal. On the heels of this, Emilie, after entering a convent, died suddenly of what was described as accidental asphyxiation during an epileptic stroke.[31] Marie, too, became ill.[32] Still, the four remaining girls, including Marie, joined the rest of the Dionne family at Christmas, although the parents were to complain, later, that the four daughters largely ignored the rest of the family at that time. Soon, as the "quints" reached age 21, a million-dollar trust fund would be distributed to them, but their future would become much more clouded and their family relationships more strained.[33]

Woolworth's colorful 75th Anniversary Christmas Catalog of 1954 flaunted the name "America's Christmas Store." Its Christmas sales contributed heavily to sales of $721,312.990 and a net income of $26,948,193 in that anniversary year, with its stock equaling $2.78 a share.[34] Still, Leftwich was committed to expansion in his drive to increase both sales and profits for the following year. As a part of the expansion, he established Woolworth stores into two shopping centers in Long Island — a self-service, 30,000-square-feet unit in Valley Stream and another in Hempstead.

President Leftwich achieved his target when 1955 sales of $767,778,962 (including the United States, Canada, Cuba, Hawaii, plus earnings from the partially owned companies in England and Germany) climbed to the highest point in the company's 76-year-old history. Earnings had increased by $7,207,705 over the previous year and the value of Woolworth shares leaped up to $3.52.[35]

The Woolworth heiress' divorce from Rubirosa became final at the end of July 1955. Two months later the 42-year-old Barbara, who seemed unable to be without a husband, married Baron Gottfried von Cramm — a man she had met 18 years previously on a Cairo tennis court and, soon afterwards, had learned that von Cramm had been hauled into court and found guilty on a morals charge. Still, the two had remained friends. Now, as she married her sixth husband in a secret civil service at the Versailles Town Hall, she acquired another title: Baroness.[36]

In a burst of candor, Barbara confessed that she always had been afraid to be alone. Afraid or not, her marriage to von Cramm collapsed six months after the wedding date. Barbara found that the outwardly pleasant, impeccably mannered baron had a penchant for disappearing frequently to pursue his own entertainment with male acquaintances. Once again, Barbara was a divorcee after a short-lived marriage. Her earlier announced decision to "do what I want to do" had made her life no less muddled than it had been previously when, she said, she had followed the advice of "others."

It would seem, though, that Barbara no longer could envy the favorable publicity that the Dionne "quints" had attracted because the events in the lives of the sisters, now of fading fame, were changing drastically. Marie, who had returned to the convent, left once again when she became seriously ill with pernicious anemia. Both she and Annette were hospitalized in Montreal in the same hospital in which their two sisters were nursing students. A bit later, Marie suffered a nervous breakdown, and then married but the marriage failed. Annette and Cecile also married and their marriages failed as well. The events in their lives were duly reported, but without the fanfare that surrounded their early lives. It had become difficult for the sisters to adjust to being just ordinary people rather than celebrities. It seemed that after years of being "managed," the Dionne girls had no experience in managing their own lives or assets. Yvonne, who envisioned making a career for herself after taking art classes, suddenly entered a convent in 1961 — the same year that Marie died from a blood clot in the brain. Yvonne left the convent and the three surviving sisters continued to live together thereafter while they faded into obscurity.[37]

Forty-eight-year-old Winston Guest of Long Island (divorced first husband of Helena McCann of the Woolworth clan) appeared in court in August 1954 as he tried to revoke the terms of his $785,000 trust fund.[38] He told the judge that, without realizing it, he had signed away his rights to draw on the fund's capital five years previously. Now he needed $225,000 to continue operating his Mexican airline business — Aerovias Guest. But an attorney representing other heirs to the fund (including under-age grandchildren of Guest's mother, Amy Phipps Guest) contested the request to draw on the fund's capital as Guest admitted that he'd had to borrow money previously from his mother to help support his business. Nonetheless, by early 1959 a spokesman announced that the airline (under the name Guest Aerovias Mexico) would begin a weekly DC-4 Trans-Atlantic service from Mexico City to Paris.

In late fall of the same year, 86-year-old Amy Phipps Guest died, leaving two sons and one daughter — brothers Winston and Raymond and their sister, Countess Diana de la Valdeen — plus nine grandchildren. "Society Leader," her obituary said.[39] It was also disclosed that Mrs. Guest had been interested in air flights as early as 1928 when she had provided financial backing for Amelia Earhart's flight across the Atlantic when Earhart became the first woman to accomplish this feat.

In 1957, *Fortune* magazine had listed billionaire oil magnate Jean Paul Getty as the richest American, naming Mrs. Frederick Guest (the former Amy Phipps) third on the list of Americans worth $200 to $400 million and crediting inherited wealth as the source of her fortune. (Her grandfather had been a partner of Andrew Carnegie, steel magnate.) Howard Hughes and Joseph P. Kennedy were listed fourth and fifth below Mrs. Guest.[40] "I don't think there is any glory in being known as a money-bags," newspapers quoted Getty as saying.

At Amy Phipps Guest's death, her beautiful blonde daughter-in-law (Winston's second wife and mother of their five-year-old son) soon appropriated the "Society Leader" title. Ever since Winston's marriage to the former Boston debutante (turned Ziegfeld Follies' dancer) Lucy Douglas Cochrane, the young Mrs. Guest had climbed the society ladder by working tirelessly for charitable causes. She shared, with her husband, a passion for race horses, riding horses and foxhunting.

Barbara Hutton had not been listed in Fortune magazine's compilation of big-money people. Still, she was one of the foremost public figures and could have verified, if she chose to do so, that not only was there little glory in being a "money-bags," but that there could be plenty of ridicule.

By this time, Barbara's cousin Jimmy Donahue was on his way to satisfying a desire to re-invent himself as a serious figure in the world of established society. In August 1956 he bought the Alfred Gwynne Vanderbilt 108-acre estate in Brookville, Long Island, and paid $400,000 for it.[41] Still enamored of the stage and performers, he planned to entertain lavishly at his new home — to host parties, charity events and dinners with entertainment featuring operatic singers and performers from the concert stage. His North Shore estate, a 29-room mansion highlighted by an enormous living room with elaborate ceiling-moldings and a magnificent marble fireplace along with other features and accommodations, was admirably suited to entertaining. Summer guests could enjoy the bathing pavilion with a 61-foot swimming pool at the end of a sunken garden.

Woolworth's Mexico City Five and Ten on the Avenida Insurgentes (a main shopping thoroughfare) had its grand opening on a Thursday morning, April 5, 1956. Two hundred salesgirls (chosen from more than 2,000 applicants) eagerly awaited the flood of expected customers. This store would be the first of two Woolworths in the city — the other to open within two months while the company promised that 97 percent of the 2,500 items on sale would be manufactured in Mexico. Seventy-three percent of the merchandise was priced at less than 12.50 pesos — less than one dollar in American money.[42]

By December, however, the F. W. Woolworth Company was having a problem with the National Labor Relations Board regarding a Woolworth store in San Bernardino, California. Earlier, while the Retail Clerks Union, Local 1167, was negotiating with the store for a new contract, the union had requested payroll data. When the company refused the request, a lower court had ruled that the company could not be forced to furnish the union with a list of the store's employees, the number of hours they worked and their rates of pay. But in a December appeal to the Supreme Court by the National Labor Relations Board, the Supreme Court upheld unanimously the discretionary power of the NLRB to require an employer to provide a union with explicit information concerning individual rates of pay and working hours of its employees. Woolworth, of course, had to comply.[43]

In 1957, the National Retail Dry Goods Association reported that in the past ten years, only four department stores had been built in downtown areas. In February of that year, the State of New York increased the minimum wage for workers to one dollar an hour, and serious labor problems in retail stores shifted, temporarily at least and to the great relief of Woolworth, to Sears Roebuck and Montgomery Ward.

When a new president and chief executive, R. C. Kirkwood, was named to head the Woolworth Company in June 1958, the controversy over whether the New York State law prohibiting Sunday business should be changed was under heated discussion.[44] The Roman Catholic Archdiocese of New York opposed any change in the law, but the Union of Orthodox Rabbis was backing a bill to permit those who observe the Sabbath on a day other than Sunday to conduct business on Sunday. Catholic priests included warnings about "not shopping on Sundays" in their sermons to parishioners. So-called "blue laws" in cities, such as the law in Ocean Grove, New Jersey, which forbade any outdoor work or recreation (except walking) on Sunday, were resurrected and examined.

The debate continued to rage and to spread into other states. Still, an even bigger problem for merchants at this time was that of pilfering in their stores and the increasing loss of revenue it was causing — a problem that would only worsen in the hectic years of the 1960s.

The problems regarding Sunday openings — whether to open Woolworth stores or keep them closed in various communities — was overridden, though, by a larger problem facing Kirkwood in the late years of the 1950s. The problem was how to deal with the fact that Fidel Castro's revolutionary followers were threatening a takeover of all foreign businesses (which would include Woolworth's money-making stores) in the island-country that had been ruled for years by the dictator Batista. The threat soon became a reality, with many Americans and the Catholic Church, along with some other churches in the United States, cheering the downfall of Batista. Kirkwood's problem dissolved in futility as Castro's threat was carried out by the end of the decade. Batista was banished, foreign businesses fell into Castro's hands, and Cuba became an island fortress.

For the Woolworth Company, business went on as usual in other parts of the world in the late fifties. Its American stores were stocking quantities of Capri pants for women and girls and were catching up with the more exclusive stores by stocking the pink shirts that already had become popular for men in Fifth Avenue's fashionable shops. New stretch, one-size men's socks were another big item at Woolworths. Inventories of men's socks no longer needed to be so extensive since the stretch socks lessened the need for stocking many different sizes.

Play-Doh, now selling in packs of four colors, was a popular item in the toy department in the late 1950s, as was the game Scrabble. The very first of the Barbie dolls were produced in 1959. They would become wildly popular in the 1960s when Woolworths and all toy stores stocked them, as the Barbies of the early 1960s escalated into hippie versions of Barbie and her friends complete with changing hairstyles, designer wardrobes and fashionable accoutrements including a pink convertible car. Barbies retained their popularity and, in the early 1990s, Mattel would manufacture both a traditional blond Barbie and an African-American Barbie — both sold exclusively ("Special Expressions") at Woolworth stores.

On April 23, 1959, the American Newspaper Publishers' Association's Bureau of Advertising presented President Kirkwood of the F.W. Woolworth Company with an award — an engraved bronze plaque acknowledging the company's major use of newspaper advertising. The presenter pointed out that, in 1958, Woolworth had placed ten million lines of advertising in newspapers. It was, indeed, a long way from founder Frank W. Woolworth's firm belief that advertising by way of store show-windows was sufficient.

President Eisenhower came to New York City on May 14, 1959, to break ground for constructing the first building of the new Lincoln Center for Performing Arts. Since the first building would be the glass-walled Philharmonic Hall, which would open in 1961, Barbara Hutton contributed $100,000 toward the $75 million fund-raising campaign as a memorial to her music-loving grandfather.[45] Her cousin Jimmy Donahue would join her soon and would contribute an equal amount. Jimmy's gift would finance the orchestra pit and lift for the new Metropolitan Opera House to be

A Woolworth store in Alaska, where the company made plans to do business just months after Alaska entered the Union in 1959. (John Compton Collection)

completed in 1963 at Lincoln Center. His gift, too, was designated as a memorial to Frank W. Woolworth, who had occupied Box 50 in the Grand Tier at the "Met" in the late years of his life.[46]

The Woolworth Company issued a news release on May 1, 1959, that was captioned "Woolworth Five and Ten to Enter Alaska." The store was to be built in Anchorage, at Fourth Avenue and F Street. *The New York Times* pointed out that "only a few months ago," their headlines had read: "Alaska to Enter Union."[47]

Woolworth officials were pleased with sales reports at the end of 1959—$916,569,000. Sales for 1960 would be even higher, they predicted. Eager to leave his imprint of achievement on the company, President Kirkwood announced that Woolworth would invest approximately $35 million in 150 stores in the next year, and that 95 percent of the new stores would be self-service types.[48] Kirkwood was determined that the company would remain on the so-called "cutting edge" of what was happening and was eager to lead the company into the 1960s. He could not have guessed, at that point, that the "cutting edge" of the 1960s would prove to be both frustrating and threatening to the health and well-being of Woolworth stores.

15

Sit-ins Challenge Woolworth

In the 1960s increasing numbers of stores began opening for business on Sundays in states where Sunday "blue laws" against the sale of merchandise did not prevail. Woolworth policy became to "go with the flow." Although Woolworth stores on Main Street, USA, continued to observe Sunday closings, if most of the other stores in shopping centers and malls opened on Sunday, Woolworth stores opened their doors as well.

Woolworth's main rival, Kresge stores, refused to surrender to the pressure of competition and did not open their doors to Sunday customers until 1966, at which time the highly principled Detroit-area matriarch Mrs. S. S. Kresge protested the change by selling her personal stock in the company. Fifteen years later, when the Kmart discount chain began selling beer and wine, Mrs. S. S. Kresge's son would follow his mother's example by giving away most of his Kmart stock.[1]

The F. W. Woolworth Company had begun experimenting in the credit field before the arrival of the 1960s. But President Kirkwood admitted in May of 1960 that results from the introduction of credit plans for customers were not decisive as yet. He was quoted as saying that he did not expect credit to become a significant factor to the company "until our average sale has increased well above its present level of less than $1.00."

In reality, the F. W. Woolworth Company scarcely had time to savor the arrival of the new decade when it became more difficult to conduct experimentation of any kind. The company suddenly was thrust into the vortex of the very early and soon-to-be-even-more-turbulent 1960s. In the late afternoon of February 1, 1960, four black college students, all freshmen at North Carolina A&T State University, entered a downtown Greensboro, North Carolina, Woolworth store.[2] They made a few small purchases, then, much to the consternation of waitresses, they sat on stools at the lunch counter (customarily reserved for white people) and waited for service.

The manager, hastily summoned by a waitress, was not prepared for any such confrontation. It just wasn't done — that's all; black people never had sat at the lunch counter where whites were served. The unspoken ruling prevailed at all Southern variety stores that "Negroes" could receive stand-up service only in that area, and could not sit down with "white folks." The Greensboro waitresses were simply following orders and customs when they ignored the four blacks and their request for coffee and doughnuts.

These four young men — David Richmond, Franklin McCain, Ezell Blair, Jr., and Joseph McNeil — broke the rules when they sat down at the Woolworth store's lunch counter (where blacks received only stand-up service) in Greensboro, North Carolina, on February 1, 1960. "The Four Freshmen" started a series of sit-downs that quickly spread to variety stores in many Southern cities.

"They can just sit there. It's nothing to me," the frazzled manager would be quoted, later. Regardless of what he said, the manager did attempt to get help from the local police department but was told there was nothing the police could do about it as long as the would-be customers were quiet and polite. It was quite possible that had Frank Winfield Woolworth still been in charge of his Five and Tens, he might have been motivated to some degree (at least to feel some guilt) by the memory of his mother, Fanny Woolworth, and her active abolitionist views. But the year was 1960 and awkward and difficult changes lay ahead (quite unknown as yet and many of them uncomfortable and upsetting to the status quo).

At 5:30 p.m., the early closing time announced by the manager, the black students rose from the stools and left the store. At the same moment, a newspaper photographer (someone had made a telephone call to the *Greensboro News and Record*) arrived and snapped a photo of the four young men as they walked away.[3]

The hurried photo would be the only picture taken of David Richmond, Franklin McCain, Ezell Blair Jr. and Joseph McNeil (referred to in future stories as "The Four Freshmen") on that memorable February first. Questioned by reporters, the group's leader responded that more students would come to the counter the next day and that the sit-in, as the movement came to be known, would continue until the activists were served.

If company officials expected that the day's sit-in was just a blip that soon would dissipate, they were mistaken. Newspaper headlines across the country carried reports of the "Negro Sit-in" at Greensboro's Woolworth store. The sit-in continued for two days without many problems as shifts of college students sat, without service, at the lunch counter. The next day, the situation tightened when white youths came to the counter and sat on the available stools before the blacks arrived, the groups of white and black young people increasing until there were approximately 60 in each group, many simply observing. Still the scene remained relatively peaceful, although four of the white fellows had hunting knives strapped to their belts and one black protester carried a toy pistol. The white young men gave up their seats whenever regular patrons came to the counter, but hurriedly re-claimed them when the patrons departed.[4]

The following day, the protest moved a step forward when more white teenagers plus a splinter group from the Ku Klux Klan showed up to prevent blacks from sitting on the counter stools.[5] Black youths crowded into the store, too, telling reporters they were protesting Woolworth's policy of not serving food to "Negroes" sitting at the counter while permitting them to shop at the store. Soon, the protesters were joined by supportive white college students, some of them moving away from the Woolworth store to spread the protest into a downtown S.H. Kress & Co. variety store. The police, continuing to monitor the situation, ejected several of the teenagers from the Woolworth store.

In early afternoon on the following day, Woolworth management reported receiving a telephone call with the information that a bomb had been placed in the basement of the Greensboro store. The black students then moved away from Woolworth's to sit at stools in the Kress store while the Woolworth store closed. Kress closed its store too, though, as black and white teenagers contested for seats, pushing and shoving one another.[6]

A mass meeting took place that same night. Black young people agreed to halt their demonstrations for two weeks while officials of the two stores attempted to set up policies on food service to "Negroes." Two days later, both Woolworth and Kress stores reopened in Greensboro during the two weeks' "cooling-off" period, but kept their lunch counters closed.[7]

In the meantime, demonstrations against "stand-up service only" for blacks spread to Woolworth and Kress variety stores in Durham, North Carolina. Black students, accompanied by four white Duke University students, showed up, first, at a Woolworth lunch counter in Durham. But they had to get up from their stools when a bomb threat forced the manager to close the store. The 40 demonstrators quickly moved on to a Kress store that closed immediately without explanation from anyone. A Walgreen drug store across the street took hurried precautions by roping off the dining area of the store and closing its lunch counter before the protesters might arrive.[8]

The sit-ins moved on to Fayetteville, Winston-Salem, Charlotte and then to Raleigh. But despite fears of violence, the worst incidents were egg throwing and rougher pushing and shoving. A Woolworth official was quoted: "Local discretion is governing the question of closing the lunch counters. We cannot interfere with local customs."[9] However, the American Civil Liberties Union in New York backed the black students by saying they were within their rights in staging the protests.

The protests spread farther, into Virginia and South Carolina, soon gaining the support of the National Association for the Advancement of Colored People. Although some of the protests were held at drug stores and variety stores other than Woolworth and Kress, the latter two remained the major targets. Forty-one black students were arrested on a sidewalk outside an F. W. Woolworth store in a Raleigh, North Carolina, shopping center on charges of trespassing.[10] Reports of the sit-ins stirred fears, now, of wider unrest in the South. No longer did citizens think of the demonstrations as a passing fad by teenagers. Black professional people began expressing their support for the demonstrations, as did some human-relations organizations and councils.

There was no doubt that Woolworth and Kress were embarrassed by the continuing protests and publicity. One Kress store removed all stools at its lunch counter and "desegregated" by observing a standing-only policy for all. Both companies realized that allowing blacks to sit and eat at the same counters as whites would bring protests by many white Southerners to their stores. Southern city officials expressed dismay at what was taking place — after all, hadn't they already observed the 1954 desegregation of their schools (at least a token desegregation) after the Supreme Court had so ordered?[11]

Dangers generated by the sit-ins, quickly spreading into Tennessee and Alabama, were emphasized by newspaper headlines: "Negro Sit-down Ends in Fist Fight"; in growing threats of boycotts in the South against Woolworth and Kress; in a heated civil rights debate that was beginning in the U.S. Senate.[12] At the same time, in an attempt to minimize the effect of sit-ins, Woolworth President Kirkwood confidently re-emphasized that the company's goal of $1 billion in sales for the year 1960 would be accomplished.

Different tactics were tried in different cities to discourage sit-ins. At one Hampton, Virginia, lunch counter (not Woolworth's) "Negroes" were served, to their surprise, only to find that prices for their food had been raised to outrageous amounts on their bills. Police began making arrests at sit-ins of blacks who refused to leave the counters when ordered to do so. The Virginia Assembly hurriedly approved three trespass bills proposed by the governor, making it possible for police to legally break up demonstrations.

But it seemed that all the "tactics" introduced only increased the determination of demonstrators as the sit-ins began spreading into Alabama and the Deep South. More northerly cities also were experiencing increasing numbers of sympathy demonstrations, marked by skirmishes and fights as students picketed Woolworth stores in Madison, Wisconsin. In an early March session of the House of Representatives, black Congressman Adam Powell of Harlem was forced to admit that he had used his franking privileges to back picketing of Woolworth stores. Three days later, an apparently unabashed Powell urged a national boycott of both Woolworth and Kresge stores by black people and their sympathizers.[13]

In that same month, both the Woolworth and Kress company chains, along with S. S. Kresge and W. T. Grant Company chains, plainly stated their policies regarding the sit-ins. The policies were identical. They would respect local customs by continuing segregation or, if necessary, would close their lunch counters until Southern public opinion agreed to a change.

On April 2, as if in response to the policy statement, about 2,500 people picketed 100 Woolworth stores in sympathy protests in New York City and suburbs. At the Herald Square Woolworth, both black and white demonstrators walked into the store and sat at the lunch counter, quietly reading newspapers and working crossword puzzles.[14]

The F. W. Woolworth Company clung grimly to its position while, on April 20, the pressure intensified as George Meany, Walter P. Reuther and other influential union leaders pledged to boycott F. W. Woolworth stores and other chains that refused to serve "Negroes" at Southern lunch counters.[15] Reuther ridiculed former President Harry S. Truman for his statement that the student sit-ins were inspired by Communists.

While the garment worker's Union picketed three Woolworth stores in New York, the American Jewish Congress also picketed Woolworth. Other picketers turned their attention to bus-station lunch counters and then to segregated libraries. Still, Woolworth remained the main target. In Florida, the St. Petersburg Improvement Association warned the company to make its facilities available to all or face a "Negro" boycott. By this time, students were being expelled from colleges for sit-in and demonstration participation. Woolworth closed its lunch counter in Greensboro, but opened its lunch counter in Suffolk, Virginia, on a service-to-all stand-up basis. Although it may have been doubtful how many customers cared to remain standing while trying to relax with coffee and a sandwich, the service-for-all might have been considered a frail kind of breakthrough.

On April 13, Governor Rockefeller of New York hailed the demonstrations and Dr. Martin Luther King expressed his favor of a national boycott of companies that were making use of segregation policies. Dr. King also appealed to other countries with Woolworth stores to back similar boycotts and demonstrations. In another response to former President Truman's statement that he thought Communists were influencing the boycotts and picketing, Walter Reuther supported Eleanor Roosevelt, who said that it was "almost impossible" that Communists could have organized so many demonstrations.

Pressures continued to build. When the Woolworth Company's annual meeting in Watertown, New York, was picketed in May, some stockholders urged the company to take the lead in integrating its lunch counters according to local custom, which left Woolworth in much the same position that it already had taken. Five days later, when Winston-Salem citizens voted in favor of desegregating lunch counters, Woolworth quickly agreed to take part in the movement — after all, the voters had spoken. But desegregating all Woolworth lunch counters was not a simple matter. Woolworth officials realized only too well that such decisions could bring about boycotts — even silent ones — by many white people who might refuse to sit down at lunch counters with blacks.

The picketing continued. The Miss America of 1951 joined others, including a number of ministers, in symbolic picketing (since there was no segregation at its lunch counter) of a New York City Woolworth. Great numbers of "Negro" children picketed in Rock Hill, South Carolina. By June 23, Woolworth desegregated its lunch counters in Arlington, Virginia, and one month later, along with Kress, made history (and headlines) by desegregating its lunch counter at the site of the very first sit-in at Greensboro, North Carolina.[16]

Still, problems escalated in many cities. In late August, 50 people were hurt and 62 held by police after whites and blacks clashed in Jacksonville, Florida. The unrest was attributed to the frequency of demonstrations and the resulting tie-ups of traffic and business activities. In late August, the mayor of Jacksonville ordered emergency police measures put into effect because, he claimed, gun-firing "Negroes" were spreading terror through suburban streets.

In a reverse tactic, though, Judge Grayson of Tampa urged whites to boycott 18 stores that had integrated their lunch counters. By this time, the sit-ins were making headway by accomplishing the desegregation of lunch counters in at least 14 Southern cities in North Carolina, Tennessee, Texas and Virginia. But as was the case in Greensboro, few blacks entered the stores in the 14 cities to order something to eat at the integrated counters in the first days or weeks of the new policy of accommodation.

An October report from several chains—Woolworth, Kress, W.T. Grant and McCrory McClennan—was a positive one, claiming that the chains had integrated lunch counters in 112 cities during the past eight months.[17] Gradually, the problems with sit-ins, boycotts, jailings and fines lessened as many more lunch counters and restaurants were integrated. In March 1961, blacks tested 36 white restaurants in Dallas, Texas, and were served, along with white diners, without incident. At the same time, Leggett's Department Store in Lynchburg, Virginia, began hiring blacks after a pre–Easter boycott had begun of stores practicing discrimination in employment.

Despite their problems with sit-ins, Woolworth officials expressed their faith in the American economy in 1961 by announcing plans to enter the discount market. Much of their faith in the 1960s decade must have stemmed from the release of a rosy financial report at the beginning of 1961, which disclosed that President Kirkwood's 1959 prediction (that sales for the year 1960 would hit the one-billion-dollar mark) was reached.[18] Sales for 1960 had amounted to $1,035,292,793. The year's earnings (including, for the first time, income from Mexican, British and German subsidiaries) amounted to $46,927,512. With these figures as an incentive, Woolworth officials announced that they were planning to build 150 new discount stores called Woolco Department Stores, most of which would be the self-service type.

Store officials could not have guessed at this point that the 1960s would bring a host of other problems to America. Integration problems moved on from lunch counters at Woolworth and other variety stores into many other areas until, in June, 1963, Governor George Wallace stood firmly in the doorway of the University of Alabama in a symbolic move to block integration of the university and moved aside only at the imperative order of federal troops under the directives of President John F. Kennedy. Only five months later, the assassination of President Kennedy threw the nation into turmoil—turmoil that was further inflamed later in the decade by destructive race riots, the Vietnam War and the assassinations of Martin Luther King, Jr. and presidential candidate Robert Kennedy. An overwhelming change was taking place in American society, including the rise of the hippies and "flower children" and their communes and marijuana along with their disdain of the so-called "establishment," expressed in their rock music and choices of sexual "freedom," rag-bag clothing, long hair and whatever else most people found bizarre.

Largely untouched by the societal changes, wealthy gadabouts such as Barbara Hutton went on with their self-indulgent lives, now viewed as meaningless even by many of the "establishment." On March 23, 1960, Barbara had arrived at San Francisco from her home in Mexico, her bachelor cousin Jimmy Donahue at her side. On the following day, Donahue was slated to be the best man at the wedding of Barbara's son, 24-year-old Lance, to movie starlet Jill St. John, already divorced from a first husband.[19] In a civil ceremony performed by a California Supreme Court justice in the Royal Suite at the Mark Hopkins Hotel, the couple spoke their vows.

Despite her misgivings, Barbara had dared to hope that Lance would become more settled after his marriage and might put aside his aspirations to achieve star status in sport-car racing. But he had been encouraged a few years previously when, in a 40-lap race with 60 competitors at New Smryna Beach, he drove his Maserati to third place after a pull-out because of engine trouble removed one of the leaders. Carroll Shelby won the Sports Illustrated Trophy that day but Lance was awarded special recognition for outstanding young driver.

Marriage to a Hollywood actress brought more publicity into Lance's life—the kind of publicity that he always had attempted to avoid because he had seen so much of it in his mother's life. Four months after his marriage, Lance was on his way to Rheims, France, to compete in the French Grand Prix with his two Scarab race cars. For the past two years he had poured money into planning, building and rebuilding the perfect American race car—a car that he hoped would overpower and overtake the best of cars on European race tracks. Until this July he'd had little success in racing his Scarabs; the inside front wheels would lift off the road in a right-hand bend. But he put his staff back to work and had not allowed the failures to dim his faith in his Scarabs and winning the big one—the Grand Prix at Rheims.

The practice run at Rheims ended in failure for Lance; both Scarabs (the one driven by Lance and the other by his hired driver) broke down and needed major overhauling. Racing the next day was out of the question. Despairing at the collapse of his aspirations, Lance sent his cars, workers and gear back across the ocean to the California quarters of Reventlow Automobiles, Inc.[20]

His marriage to Jill St. John broke down just one year later. At that time the Hollywood actress, charging mental cruelty, sued for separate maintenance after the couple had been separated for ten days.[21] In Lance's dedication to becoming a winning race car driver, he had pared down his drinking, carefully watched his diet and given up partying to get long hours of sleep at night. His wife had remained decidedly unconvinced about his dedication to his marriage.

Despite Barbara's earlier efforts to keep in close touch with her Aunt Jessie Donahue and Jessie's two sons, she was not on hand to witness the second wedding of her cousin, Woolworth Donahue, later that year. Woolworth, who had been divorced fourteen years earlier from his first wife, Gretchen Hearst, married divorcee Judith Claire Church on November 4, 1960, at his large home (which he referred to as his hunting lodge) at Manorville, New York.[22] The marriage, once again, made him a stepfather to a young boy — his new wife's son. His bachelor brother, Jimmy, who could be depended upon to appear at all such family functions, was in Manorville for the wedding as was Jessie Donahue, doting mother of the two brothers, to observe the quiet ceremony conducted by a Justice of the Peace. Cousin Barbara, who was having her own problems in her sixth marriage at this time, did not attend the ceremony, having gradually withdrawn from most family functions as her interests and reflections turned further inward. Her pending divorce from Baron Gottfried von Cramm, which was kept a secret for a year after it occurred in very early 1961, became public knowledge only in 1962 after Von Cramm himself divulged the divorce in Vienna.[23]

In the spring of 1961 President Kirkwood announced that, in addition to the company's 2,075 stores in the U.S., its 1,053 stores in the United Kingdom, 248 in Canada, 99 in West Germany and eight in Mexico, Woolworth's new chain of Woolco stores (the name evidently taken from the long-time supplier of the popular crochet cotton sold at Woolworths) would begin operating before the end of the year.[24] The new chain was to have its own director and would not conflict with Woolworth variety stores in any way, Kirkwood added quickly, nor would there be any conversion of present Woolworth stores. Some departments for the new chain, such as appliances and footwear, might be leased to concessionaires, he said. At this announcement, Woolworth stock soared more than six points to a high of 74 3/8 on the New York Stock Exchange.

The following month, Kirkwood expanded on his forecast to inform the public that each new Woolco was to have a minimum of 60,000 square feet of floor space, twice the space in the largest of the company's variety stores. Woolco was slated to offer credit and some delivery services to its customers, but experienced Woolworth buyers (some 35 of them working out of the Woolworth Building) would also order all the merchandise for Woolco Department Stores.

By the end of September, the public was informed that the first Woolco discount store would be ready to open in Columbus, Ohio, in the spring of 1962, selling appliances, floor coverings, furniture and other major items not available in Woolworth's variety stores.

At the other end of the spectrum, relatively inexpensive women's apparel, such as the new and popular muu-muu and the so-called "short nightie" that resembled a shirt, became big sellers at Woolworth variety stores in late 1961. Plastic yo-yos, produced first in 1960 by the Duncan Company which previously had produced wooden yo-yos, became such a craze in 1962 that 45 million of them were sold that year to F. W. Woolworth and other companies so that kids could learn the language and practice the toys' tricks: walk the dog, loop-de-loop, hop the fence.

During 1961, the Woolworth Company had opened 120 new variety stores, operating a total of 3,570 in both the United States and in seven foreign nations. It had chalked up record sales of $1,861,401,832 that year, but income dropped slightly. For

One of the Woolco stores. The Woolco chain began in the 1960s and offered appliances, floor coverings, furniture and other major items not available in Woolworth variety stores. (John Compton Collection)

the following year, it planned to open 100 new variety stores, mostly the self-service type, emphasizing its continuing commitment to that side of its business. Company officials were certain that with the opening of Woolco discount department stores in 1962 and 1963, gross sales and net income would zoom much higher in 1964.

Opening for business in a Columbus, Ohio, shopping center on June 6, 1962, the company's first Woolco discount store was jammed with 40,000 people that day.[25] The store was heralded by President Kirkwood as one of three monumental milestones in the company's history along with the founding of Woolworth's first "The Great Five Cent Store" in 1879 (which quickly converted into a Five and Ten) and the gradual lifting of price limitations from 1932 to 1935. Kirkwood described the company's objective as that of making Woolco "as pre-dominant in the low-margin, mass-merchandising field as Woolworth's is in the variety store field."

Long lines of basket-pushing customers kept cashiers busily occupied at the 18 checkout counters in the Ohio store's 106,000-square-foot building. (Predictions regarding the size of the typical Woolco had grown considerably from the first forecasts made by spokespersons.) "Looking good," was the consensus among Woolworth officials who would be opening a second Woolco in another large shopping center ten miles north of the first store, with 16 more Woolcos slated to open in the United States and Canada within a year.

Unlike the great numbers of stores that were relying on the popularity of trading stamps to increase their volume of business, the F.W. Woolworth Company never had succumbed to the lure of these colorful stamps to promote its business. Instead, Woolworth stores had become redemption centers for the International Merchandising Corporation's clown coupons or trading stamps in May 1962.

Plaid stamps, green or gold stamps, and stamps of various colors were treasured by shoppers who pasted them into the appropriate books and then traded them in for gifts selected from a catalog — three books for a set of pots and pans for the kitchen, four books for a wool blanket. Few shoppers concerned themselves with surveys which claimed that many stores (largely supermarkets) giving trading stamps were charging slightly more for purchases because of the expense of dealing with stamps.

The Woolco venture was not the only major action taken by Woolworth officials to promote growth in the early 1960s. In 1963 the company acquired the Kinney Shoe Corporation as a subsidiary. It also declared a three-for-one stock split that reduced its common shares to $1.75 a share, but the Woolworth Board of Directors was certain that the share value would improve quickly.[26]

Frasier W. McCann and his sister Helena (the latter now married to a second husband, Richard Charleton) adhered to the McCann-Woolworth traditions in March 1964 by making a gift of $600,000 through the Winfield Foundation to Princeton University. The gift would benefit the Woolworth Center of Musical Studies in honor of their grandfather, Frank Winfield Woolworth.[27]

In less admirable tradition, Woolworth family members were continuing to collect husbands or wives as casually as ordinary shoppers collected and redeemed trading stamps. By February 1964 Judith Claire Donahue was in Reno, Nevada, seeking a divorce from her husband of three years, Woolworth Donahue.

Shortly after the April divorce of the Woolworth Donahues, Woolworth mar-

Union picketers in front of the New York Woolworth in 1963. Their signs tell passersby not to buy at Woolworth and to "support Martin Luther King in the fight for human rights." In the early 1960s such demonstrations were spreading across the country. (Walter P. Reuther Library, Wayne State University. Photograph by Sam Reiss, deceased labor photographer, permission for use granted by Helen H. (Mrs. Sam) Reiss

ried for a third time to the twice-divorced and once-widowed radio and television performer Mary Hartline.[28] The blonde and attractive Mary, elected "Queen of Love and Beauty" in her Illinois high school days, had achieved queen status again in the late 1940s (rivaling Woolworth's cousin Barbara in her acquisitions of royal titles) by being introduced as "our Queen" of the televised-live show *Super Circus* and, later, "Princess Mary" of the *Magic Castle*. A toy company produced Mary Hartline dolls, and Woolworth stores sold cutout books of Mary Hartline paper dolls.

In the same year, 1964, of the Woolworth Donahue–Mary Hartline marriage, Barbara Hutton acquired still another "princess" title as she married for a seventh time in the lush Japanese gardens at her Cuernavaca, Mexico, home. Mayor Celso Castrejon performed the civil ceremony uniting Barbara and her Vietnamese husband, Prince Pierre Raymond Doan Vinh.[29] C. David Heymann's biography of Hutton, *Poor Little Rich Girl*, claimed that Barbara purchased the title for her husband in Laos. In any case, once again she had become a princess, or possibly a pseudo-princess—but one who was practical enough to see to it that her prospective hus-

A Woolworth ad featuring radio and television performer Mary Hartline, published in Life magazine February 18, 1952. More than a decade later Hartline would be the bride of Woolworth Donahue. (Author's Collection)

band (professing to be a writer and painter) signed a separation-of-property agreement before the ceremony.

Six months later, Princess Doan de Champassak (as Barbara was now deigned) received a high honor during a reception at the Laotian embassy in Paris.[30] The honor made her an officer of the Laotian order of the Million Elephants and the White Parasol. The prince and princess were guests, in Paris, of Prince Doan's uncle, the head (in name only) of the Laotian right-wing faction.

Since the reception honoring Barbara took place on November 7, 1964, it is possible that conflicting dates could have prevented Barbara from attending the wedding of her son, 28-year-old Lance, to Cheryl Holdridge, a former Disney Mouseketeer.[31] The wedding ceremony was held at the Westwood Community Methodist Church in Hollywood on November 8 and was attended by some 600 guests, but Barbara was not among them. From her Paris hotel, she claimed that illness had prevented her from attending. But Cary Grant, whom Lance considered his "father," was present at the church.

By this time, the Woolworth Company was discouraging the use of the description "discount stores" or even "low margin stores" for its Woolco division. Instead the company chose to refer to them as "mass merchandise, competitively priced units," which was quite a mouthful for most people to handle. In line with its promise that Woolworth variety stores were not being neglected in the shadow of Woolcos, the company expanded its downtown Denver store to 174,000 square feet. The company called the store the largest Woolworth variety store in the world.

In contrast, Woolworth officials decided, in November 1964, to build Woolco units that would be much smaller than the average 130,000 square feet that had been deployed. The smaller units— 70,000 to 80,000 square feet — were designed for less populated areas such as the Sault Ste. Marie, Ontario, Canada, site where construction of the first smaller Woolco already had begun. These smaller units were intended for inclusion in 20-acre shopping centers, largely in the South, with parking facilities for at least 1,200 cars. Expansion of its larger Woolcos was to proceed as planned, officials explained, with 11 more department stores scheduled for 1965, some as large as 100,000 square feet.

With the larger Woolcos averaging sales of more than $5 million a year, and some of them as much as $7 million, and the smaller Woolcos expected to make sales in the $2.5 million to $3 million range, the Woolworth Company was looking forward to tallying up a most profitable year for 1964 and in the remaining years of the 1960s.[32]

16

Expansion Becomes the Byword

At the beginning of the year 1965, Walter C. Luy was named director of Worth Mart operations for the Woolworth Company.[1] President Burcham explained that Worth Mart was "the name selected for a new and promotional discount mass-volume chain of stores being developed by Woolworth." It seemed that the earlier confusion created by Woolworth's resistance to labeling Woolcos as discount stores might have added to the confusion of newspaper readers as, now, they saw the new announcement including the words "discount mass-volume chain" applied to the name Worth Mart.

As Woolworth officials had anticipated, February 1965 sales reports for the previous year, (including sales by the company's subsidiary (the Kinney Shoe Corporation purchased in 1963 for $39 million in cash and the assumption of a $6 million obligation), had resulted in a 13.13 percent rise in 1964 sales over those of 1963 to a total $1,338,365,954. Net profits had amounted to $57,793,490 and common stock shares had risen from $1.75 in 1963 to $1.99 in 1964, both figures reflecting the Woolworth three-for-one stock split in May 1963. The company had optimistic expectations that profits for 1965 would match or surpass those of 1964.[2]

The 1964 tally listed 2,106 Woolworth variety stores operating in the United States and Puerto Rico, 277 in Canada, 113 in West Germany and ten in Mexico. Sixteen Woolcos flourished in the United States and Canada, and 620 Kinney stores were doing business in the United States. In Britain, F.W. Woolworth & Co., Ltd., now had a total of 1,110 stores.

For Princess Barbara Doan Vinh de Champassak, there was little optimism in her outlook at this time. She was experiencing discomfort and then increasing pain in the early part of 1965. On February eighth, she and her husband flew from Mexico to San Francisco. That night she entered the Presbyterian Medical Center where she spent several days undergoing diagnostic testing and treatment of the intestinal ailment for which she had undergone several bouts of surgery in previous years.[3]

In May, another tragedy touched the lives of the Woolworths when the lifeless body of the second daughter of Helena Woolworth and Charles McCann was found in the bedroom of a San Francisco hotel suite.[4] This daughter (named Helena for her mother) had been divorced from Winston Frederick Churchill Guest years earlier, after a picture-perfect wedding uniting two super-wealthy families and after the birth of two sons, Winston Jr. and Frederick, both adults now.

The McCanns' only son, Frasier, also was divorced from his first wife. Only two years previously, the brother and sister, Frasier McCann and Helena, had donated $600,000 to Princeton University (Helena's earlier marriage to Guest had taken place in the chapel at Princeton) through the Winfield Foundation for the Woolworth Center of Musical Study in honor of their late grandfather, Frank Winfield Woolworth. Designed by Spanish architect Juan Navarro, the new building for musical studies featured a three-story atrium and library with two skylights.

After Helena's divorce from Guest and marriage to Richard Charleton, the Charletons lived in Phoenix where Richard became the director of the Sombrero Playhouse and his wife owned the Galaxy Art Gallery. When a maid discovered Helena's body in a San Francisco hotel suite in 1965, the coroner noted that a variety of prescription-drug bottles and several empty liquor bottles were found nearby — all indicating another shocking tragedy to contribute to the Woolworth legacy.

In the same month of Helena Charleton's death, Woolworth opened its first gallery of fine art at its Fifth Avenue store at 39th Street, New York. On May 7 and until the eight p.m. closing time, 6,000 people came up to the second floor to survey the collection of paintings, prints, posters and engravings offered on a 10 percent layaway plan for purchasers and a seven-day money-back guarantee for dissatisfied customers. A $24,000 Gainsborough painting was one of the more expensive pieces of art. At the other end of the spectrum, various prints were on sale at $19.95 each.[5]

Until the profitability of the art gallery was established, Woolworth did not plan to open additional art galleries at other stores. "We want to wait two or three months and see what happens here," the company's art buyer said. It soon became apparent that the idea of expanding this type of Woolworth art galleries had been dropped. There was no further ballyhoo concerning the placement of expensive Gainsborough or Da Vinci paintings in other stores.

In October, the Woolworth Company, the largest variety chain in the United States, demonstrated its renewed optimism in the resurgence of a New York City area that the company had deserted seven to ten years previously. In that three-year period, Woolworth had closed two of its East Fourteenth Street stores. Now it was opening a new two-level variety store that would stretch from 13th to 14th Street, accessible to both streets with an entrance on each and featuring a restaurant that would seat 275 diners.[6]

Once again, Barbara Hutton had demonstrated very clearly her attachment to France and to the trappings of royalty when she responded to the plea for donations to refurbish the palace at Versailles in the elaborate style that had distinguished it previous to the time of the French Revolution. In 1794 the furnishings had been stripped from the chateau and sold at public auction after King Louis XVI was guillotined, followed shortly thereafter by the beheading of his wife, the proud and haughty Marie Antoinette. When the French Minister of Cultural Affairs, Andre Malraux, conducted a tour of the partly refurbished palace in June 1965, he paid tribute to the various donors and their gifts, including a red and gold brocade tapestry donated by Barbara and displayed in the king's bedroom.[7]

Later in the year, reports surfaced that Barbara was seeking a divorce from Prince

Vinh, but when she arrived in New York City in December, Barbara denied the divorce rumors and said that her husband would join her soon in Mexico City. In the following month of January 1966, Princess Barbara reported a theft from her Cuernavaca, Mexico, home. Gems worth $100,000 were missing, she said, along with $14,000 in cash.[8] The theft remained unsolved.

By the end of the year the theft was relegated to the area of trifling matters, as far as Barbara was concerned, in contrast with the stunning news she received in December of the death of the man who, except for her son, Lance, had provided her with the most supportive love and friendship of her life — her cousin Jimmy Donahue.[9] Jimmy's mother, Jessie, was distraught. She could not imagine what devastating twists of her son's mind had bedeviled him to the point where he had consumed so much alcohol and so many sleeping pills that she had found the body of 51-year-old Jimmy in the bedroom of her Fifth Avenue apartment (where he sometimes spent the night) sprawled motionless on the bed. And no matter what the coroner said, she could not have entertained a doubt that Jimmy had committed suicide, just as his father had done 35 years ago at age 44. Each of them had been the light of her life. And each had cruelly extinguished that light without a thought, apparently, for her misery as she wept in the lonely void of her bereavement. Was it true, she must have wondered, that there was a terrible curse on the Woolworth family?

Ever since Jimmy had gained control of his $15 million Woolworth inheritance in 1950, he had been receiving favorable publicity for his activities in charitable causes and promotion of the arts. Jessie knew that he had been pleased with that. These press notices seemed to have overshadowed his earlier misadventures in the years that he had been dependent upon the largesse of his mother and, often, gifts from his cousin Barbara. For Jessie, there were no answers to the puzzle of why he had ended his life.

In a preliminary autopsy report, the medical examiner attributed the death to "visceral congestion," explaining that there were no signs of foul play or heart failure. He added, however, that the results of tests, both microscopic and toxicological, would be known the following week. Nonetheless, most newspaper reports reminded readers that the senior James P. Donahue had committed suicide by drinking poison in 1931.[10]

Jimmy's body was interred in the Woolworth family mausoleum on December 9 following a requiem mass in Mater Dei Roman Catholic Chapel of the New York Foundling Hospital that had been one of the charities to which Jimmy contributed. Four days later, the Medical Examiner's office issued a report indicating that Donahue had died of acute alcohol and barbiturate intoxication.

Following the funeral, Jimmy's older brother, Woolworth, soon returned to his home in Florida, and Jessie was alone in the large apartment that had been her home for many years. The days, years, of travels and parties were no longer a part of her life. With Jimmy's death, her life became intensely confined to the apartment, kept darkened against any intrusion of sunlight and with minimal, shaded artificial light. Without Jimmy's lighthearted presence, silence prevailed throughout the rooms most of the time.

For 54 years the Woolworth building in Watertown, New York, had served as the Mecca for the corporation's annual meeting, but the decision was made to hold the 1966 yearly meeting in San Francisco, and thereafter in different cities in various sections of the country. One thing remained the same, as defined by Frank Winfield Woolworth: each annual meeting would begin at high noon on the third Wednesday of May.[11]

Even before the meeting was held in San Francisco, the dynamic team of President Burcham and Chairman Kirkwood took pride in its announcement that 1965 had been a year of record sales and earnings, consolidated sales rising to $1,443,322,466 and profits crowning at $73,001,321.[12] Its 632 Kinney Shoe stores, plus 30 leased departments, and its British Woolworth stores (the latter affected favorably by new changes in English tax laws) had made important contributions to overall profits. The conversion of 27 of the company's variety stores into Worth Marts during 1965 was being carefully evaluated as to their performance to determine whether more such conversions would be scheduled.

In still another move toward diversification in June 1966, Woolworth made an agreement with Gateway Sporting Goods Company (operators of retail stores dealing in photographic supplies, toys and luggage in addition to sporting goods) to purchase Gateway for $14.7 million.[13] For Chairman Kirkwood and President Burcham, the purchase was one more step in their major policy of expansion as the two officials worked in tandem to distinguish the imprint of their leadership roles upon the company.

Their goal for the near future was an ambitious one: to attain a sales volume of $2.5 billion by 1975. This would entail changes, which the enterprising team of policy makers was ready to introduce. The first change suggested was setting up a franchise system in which small, independent stores in various communities would be licensed by Woolworth to make use of the Woolworth name and to display and sell merchandise purchased in mass quantities by Woolworth buyers. The selected franchisees would be required to pay a yearly charge plus a fee on purchases from Woolworth.[14]

In a new Woolworth store slated to open in Marshfield, Wisconsin, in October, the chairman-president team planned to expand its junior department in line with the company's new emphasis on junior departments in towns similar to Marshfield — each with populations between 10,000 to 25,000. Woolworth officials also planned to open 30 Woolco stores each year to add to the 32 Woolcos already operational, as a part of the company's goal of operating the biggest department store chain in the United States.

In January 1967 a Woolworth announcement informed the public that the company would open its first variety store in Madrid, Spain, in the near future.[15] The two-level store of 35,000 square feet was to feature an outdoor sidewalk cafe; all operations would be handled by the company's Spanish subsidiary. Before the end of the year, the Woolworth leadership team pointed out the impact that the company was presently making on the international scene. In early October, Chairman Kirkwood informed the public that the British subsidiary's Woolco division was now opening its first Woolco store at Oadby, a suburb of Leicester.[16] At 91,000 square feet, the store was planned to be the largest one-floor department store in England outside of metropolitan London, bringing the company's British operations up to 1,127 stores. In 1968, two more Woolco stores would open in England.

Although admitting that the company had no plans to open Woolworth stores in Japan, Chairman Kirkwood pointed out that Woolworth had its own export-import company in that country whereby goods were exported to the United States and manufactured goods from the United States were furnished to 12 Japanese department stores. However, all this discussion concerning foreign countries had not detracted from Woolworth's goal of expanding both Woolco stores and variety stores within the United States.

In another major development, the Woolworth Company undertook a $2 million enlargement and modernization program in November 1967 for its existing Harlem store at West 125th Street just west of Seventh Avenue.[17] Still smarting from the public-relations sting the company had experienced with the sit-ins in the early 1960s and concerned with repairing its image, Woolworth signed a $1 million contract with the "Negro-owned" Winston A. Burnett Construction Company to do the work on a greatly expanded store, which was scheduled to open with all modern accoutrements in 1968. The store would require 150 additional employees, the company pointed out, hired largely from within the Harlem area.

One year later, the Woolworth Company sold the land and the building to the Harlem Freedom Associates under terms that would make it possible for the purchasing association to pay off the $1,885,000 mortgage within 25 years from the annual $157,000 that Woolworth would pay for rental. To Woolworth, it seemed a significant move on its part to spur black ownership of Harlem business property as well as an important action to help remove the stain of the bad publicity of Woolworth's experience when it had become the major target for sit-ins. At the same time, there would be tax benefits for the Woolworth Company in the form of rental deductions amounting to a larger amount than those permitted for depreciation subtractions if the company had retained ownership of the building.

By October 1968, Woolworth had another announcement regarding its investments for expansion in Harlem. The company was planning to start construction of a new Harlem store with 23,000 square feet of space at the northwest corner of Lenox Avenue and 116th Street.

Before the end of 1967, Winston F. C. Guest (who had only tenuous ties to the Woolworths now by way of his two sons born to his first wife, Helena, who had committed suicide long after their divorce) was having serious financial problems. His stunning second wife, a former Ziegfeld Follies entertainer, was now widely known among socialites as "CZ" Guest — mother of son Eric and a younger daughter, Cornelia, whose godparents were the Duke and Duchess of Windsor. Some years later, the gifted "CZ," now listed among the "best-dressed women in the world," would write her first book on horticulture, with an introduction by her friend Truman Capote. Others of her close friends were Lee Radziwill, Michael Butler (Producer of *Hair* and the controversial *Pope Joan*) and, of course the Windsors.[18]

But at this earlier point in the Guests' lives, Winston's Mexican airline had been taken over by the Mexican government. In 1963, the Civil Aeronautics Board canceled the airline's permit to operate. Guest, and the fashionable "CZ," had been sued in previous years for payment of personal debts owed to various companies, but a large debt of a half-million dollars was owed now to the Universal Trading Corporation of Florida for second-hand airplanes that had been leased by a Panamanian airline controlled by Guest.[19]

Eventually, a bankruptcy referee in Federal Court in Brooklyn set a date for payment of the debt. Guest made arrangements to satisfy payment by the deadline, selling an antique collection at auction for a half-million dollars.[20] At the same time, his annual income was made public — $600,000 yearly from trusts set up by his mother. The Guests also owned 30 racehorses at their Templeton Stables and they took great pleasure in having their prized racers compete in this country and abroad. Unfortunately, the stables had not made a profit in several years, an attorney stated.

The F.W. Woolworth Company had no financial problems with its acquisitions. In 1968 it announced plans for acquiring Richman Brothers Company, producer and retailer of men's wear. One share of a new Woolworth preferred stock, at $2.20, was to be given for each Richman common share with the provision that each new share could be converted into a $1.42 share of Woolworth common.[21]

Rumors of another divorce for Barbara Hutton no longer drew as much attention from the public that her previous marriages and divorces had attracted, possibly because her increasingly poor health restrained her, at least in part, from continuing the frantically paced, exaggerated lifestyle of earlier years. At age 56, she filed for divorce from her seventh husband, Prince Raymond Doan Vinh Champassak of Laos, in Cuernavaca, Mexico.[22] The January 1969 official notice confirming the pending divorce was published in a Tangier, Morocco, legal notice, which was necessary under Moroccan law because Tangier was, legally, her home.

Her grandfather's company no longer concerned itself with any notoriety stemming from the excesses or tribulations of Barbara Hutton or any of the other remaining Woolworth descendants. Decades had passed since the Great Depression of the 1930s had contrasted so strongly with the excessive expenditures of the Five and Dime–financed Woolworth heiress. The 1960s had propelled the Woolworth Company into working out other, much more important problems dealing with the strong forces of the rising civil-rights demands. Woolworth had been thrust, at that time, into the embarrassing position of becoming a symbol as the enemy of the downtrodden seekers of justice. Throughout the sixties, Woolworth officials had attempted to repair its image and now, with the approach of the 1970s, began to think that it was achieving its goal.

The fading 1960s had still another blow to direct at the Woolworth Company, though, as an incendiary device exploded in a Brooklyn Woolworth store on June 30, 1969.[23] Although only minor damage was done and no one was injured, Woolworth officials were concerned that their company might be the selected target for destructive tactics — this time by political malcontents. Still, it was only one incident of minor proportions, and it could have happened to any company.

In September a major fire erupted in a Woolworth variety store in downtown San Juan, Puerto Rico, shortly before midnight. Firemen battled the flames all night but could not contain the blaze until more than $1 million in damages had taken their toll.[24] The fire set off an investigation at other American-owned stores in the city, resulting in the discovery of incendiary devices in a Lerner shop and a Kresge variety store.

The Woolworth Company was informed that there had been a celebration on that same day of the fire — a celebration that was reputed to be one of the outstanding holidays of many Puerto Ricans who were advocating independence from the United States. When another bomb exploded on December 21 in front of the large Woolworth store at New York's Fifth Avenue and 14th Street, it blew out several windows. Since there were two other such incidents (one in a Puerto Rican bank) that same day in New York City, detectives expressed their thoughts that the bombings might have been a part of a Puerto Rican terrorist campaign for independence.[25] Their suspicions were verified two months later when an underground Puerto Rican revolutionary movement that called itself "Mira" admitted it had carried out 19 terrorist acts since December, including seven in New York City.[26] Still, other rumors were spreading also — rumors alleging that the bombing of department stores was part of a plot by the Black Panthers.

Because of the economic slowdown that had persisted throughout 1968 and 1969, the country's financial markets were under heavy pressures. Per capita personal income in 1969 was estimated at $3,687, inflation was increasing and prices rising. With the approach of 1970, uncertainty prevailed regarding the outlook for economic conditions.

Woolworth Chairman Robert C. Kirkwood, who already had announced his resignation as chairman and chief executive officer, effective January 1, 1970, passed on his duties (and worries) of chairman to the former president, Lester A. Burcham, while the executive vice president, John S. Roberts, became the new Woolworth president. Before leaving office, Kirkwood claimed that Woolworth now headed the biggest international operations of any American retailer, with annual worldwide sales adding up to more than $3 billion. In an expansive mood, he added that the British chain, popularly known as "Woolies" in Britain, had some 1,138 stores with annual sales equaling approximately $1 billion.[27]

At the beginning of the new decade (1970s) the Woolworth Company suddenly experienced a flashback into the early 1960s when, at the beginning of February, the Greensboro, North Carolina, newspapers reminded readers that exactly ten years ago demonstrations at the local Woolworth store had begun a period marking great changes in race relations. Hot coffee was served now, without incident, at Woolworth lunch counters to both black and white customers, and the city boasted of a black councilman, legislator and judge among other integration improvements. And it all had started with Woolworth. Cultural patterns and attitudes between the races, however, were a different matter that would take much longer to improve. At the next annual meeting of Woolworth's British subsidiary in London on March 7, 1970, it was disclosed that although Britain's 1,140 stores had sales for 1969 of $748 million, net income had fallen $2 million from the $50 million income of the previous year. Of the 700 stockholders attending the London meeting, more than a dozen were openly dissatisfied and scrappy regarding "Woolies'" performance, which they called stagnant. Still, the British company had a 22 percent return on net capital and a 12 percent pre-tax return on sales in 1969.[28]

Two days later, a Woolworth employee found an incendiary bomb in the basement of the company's Fulton Street store in Brooklyn. When deactivated by the police bomb squad, it was discovered that this bomb was similar to the bomb that had exploded in the same store the previous June 30. Woolworth officials were not particularly willing to talk about bombs— their policy now seemed to be to give out as little information as possible on this subject to reporters.

Keeping quiet about incendiary devices did not appear to be a helpful policy

Top: "Woolies" was the nickname used by most British people for their Woolco stores. *Woolies News* was the employee newsletter. (John Compton Collection)

Bottom: Woolies customers voted for a year after the installation of buttons at each cash register. They would vote yes ("Smiley") if they were satisfied with the service, or no ("Frowny") if they weren't. (John Compton Collection)

because on Saturday, June 6, 1970, when Woolworth's Broadway and 44th Street store remained open until 8:45 p.m., a series of explosions occurred after 9:30 p.m. when only a few employees remained inside the store. Within 45 minutes, five incendiary devices exploded inside the store's street-level floor, followed by four more explosions on the lower level. Police and fire investigators found that the nine devices (small cubes containing sulfuric acid and other chemicals) had been hidden in clothing, under stationery, in stacks of underwear and behind toys. The entire store had filled with smoke and the odor of burned clothing. The few employees who had remained in the store were interviewed in a nearby building, but none had observed anything unusual prior to the explosions.[29]

Less than a month later, bombs exploded in three Manhattan Woolworth stores. In the 34th Street store, just west of Broadway, smoke billowed through the building at seven p.m. as incendiary devices ignited on counters where the devices had been hidden in clothing. Shaken customers dashed out of the store into the street, but there were no injuries. In two other Woolworths— one at 86th Street and Third Avenue and the other on Broadway between 79th and 80th Streets—fires broke out at approximately the same time that evening. Large crowds gathered outside the stores when fire engines responded to the three fires, snarling traffic.[30] Was it safe to continue shopping at Woolworths, people must have wondered as firemen quickly brought the fires under control with only a small amount of damage to each store.

After an August report from a community center official stated that several elderly New Yorkers had died from malnutrition, Woolworth officials decided to set up a program to try to prevent such tragedies and to help improve the company's community relations. They announced that 400 of their stores would provide nutritious meals, priced at only one dollar, for senior citizens.

Although malnutrition of old people was a problem about which Woolworth officials could do something to alleviate, merchants' growing problems with both shop-lifting and other forms of lawlessness rising out of the 1960s and spreading into the 1970s were lessened only slightly by the increased hiring of guards and store-detectives and installation of hidden cameras and mirrors. As a Woolworth manager and employee left the Fifth Avenue store on their way to take $13,000 to a night depository on September 13, the date turned out to be an unlucky one for the two men. They were shot and wounded by three gunmen who fled with the money.[31]

Such were the swelling problems of big-city merchants, but Woolworth officials had not been unduly hesitant to proceed with plans to build its largest variety store in a return to downtown Boston and to open the nine-floor, 133,000 square-foot building on September 11, 1970. Almost twice as many items as were sold in other Woolworths would be stocked on the four selling floors of the Boston store, with four of the five upper floors making up a ramp-connected parking complex for as many as 1,000 cars.[32]

The winter of 1970-1971 brought bitterly cold weather to New York. The cold and wind gusts worsened in late January and early February when, on the afternoon of February 1, neighboring two- and three-story homes in the Bronx caught fire and forced 91 people to flee their burning residences.

Shortly after six p.m. the next day, a fire was discovered by a Woolworth employee in the West 125th Street store, which was in the process of being renovated. Customers and employees fled the store as quickly as possible as flames and smoke spread. A dispatcher at the Fire Department sounded a "fifth alarm," which meant that the department's resources were already so depleted that a fourth-alarm call would not bring the necessary 160 firemen and 29 pieces of equipment to the burning store. As the Woolworth fire blew out a wall and one building collapsed, flames, fanned by the wind, engulfed two other buildings and moved toward Eighth Avenue. At that point, the wind shifted and the fire moved south to burn a building on 124th Street.[33]

At the same time, fire fighters and equipment were hard pressed to keep up with responses to multi-alarm blazes breaking out near the same area. Spray from the firemen's hoses froze into ice pellets before the pellets hit the ice-covered streets. It was, the Fire Department reported, one of the roughest nights the department ever had encountered. Investigators at the Woolworth store could find no clues as to the origin of the fire but company officials had to have been concerned about sabotage.

Still, when the annual meeting of Woolworth shareholders was held in May 1971, Chairman Burcham's report was a glowing one. Again, he stressed expansion plans: the addition of more than 60 new Woolworth and Woolco stores along with the remodeling of 56 other Woolworth stores, plus three new Woolworth stores and seven Woolcos for Canada. Food service, he announced, would be enhanced by 43 new dining facilities for the variety stores and 35 for Woolcos, which would guarantee that Woolworth would remain the world's largest food handler. The company's subsidiary, Kinney Shoes, would add 100 new units to hit the 1,200 mark. And plans had been made to add six Woolworth stores in Mexico, five in Germany, five in Great Britain and one in Spain. The company looked forward to a 10 percent increase in sales for 1971 despite continuing inflation, and uncertainty in the stock market.[34]

Barbara Hutton had escaped part of the fierce, early 1971 winter weather by going to Palm Beach and enjoying the company of her cousin Woolworth Donahue and his wife, Mary, at their invitation to be their house-guest. Mary, a charming hostess, also entertained the Duke and Duchess of Windsor and other prestigious house guests at various periods that winter.

Vacationing in Rome the following spring, Barbara fell and fractured her femur in May. Flown back to Los Angeles where she was hospitalized in June, she underwent still another surgical procedure; a "serious" surgery, her doctor said.[35] She was slowly recovering from the thighbone surgery when she was shaken by news that her 85-year-old, reclusive Aunt Jessie (who had been a mother-figure to the motherless Barbara as a child) had died at home.[36] The body of this last and youngest daughter of Frank Woolworth was placed in the Woolworth family mausoleum on November 3, 1971. Her estate, the bulk of which already had been distributed to her two sons, was now turned over to the surviving son, 58-year-old Woolworth Donahue.

For Barbara, who observed her 59th birthday anniversary only two weeks after her Aunt Jessie's death, connections to Woolworth family members now had been reduced to two—her cousin, Woolworth Donahue, and her son, Lance. Lance, of course, had come to be with his mother at the time of her surgery but often he was not in the Los Angeles area. Since abandoning his interest in race cars and turning instead to skiing and playing polo, he spent much of his time in Aspen, Colorado, where he was planning to buy some property.

In December, the Woolworth Company took a loss of almost $5.5 million, as well as a 19 cents per-share decrease in stock value, with the sale of Top Form–Yolande and Sherman–Underwear Mills. Both of these enterprises had been subsidiaries of Kinney Shoe Corporation which had been acquired by Woolworth in its drive for what the company termed "diversity." Nonetheless, the company completed the year 1971 with total consolidated sales of $2,801,012,539 — an increase of $273,047,834 from 1970 sales, but total earnings of $76,580,850 in 1971 were slightly reduced ($43,220) from the previous year.[37]

More than 2,000 Woolworth stores and some 200 Woolco stores were operating now, and expansion remained the primary goal in the minds of Woolworth officials.

17

Struggles with the Economy

Although American businessmen were concerned about a lagging economy plagued with escalating prices and increasing unemployment in 1971, Woolworth officials followed through with their prepared plans for expansion. The company opened 15 new Woolworth and Woolco stores across the country in the first quarter of 1972.

In August 1971, President Nixon had announced a 90-day wage- and price-freeze program that continued and extended into 1972 at a time when Americans were complaining about the 3.5 percent rise in the cost of living.[1] The Price Commission cracked down on the Woolworth Company on April 26, 1972, claiming that the company was violating freeze regulations by raising prices in its restaurants and lunch counters.[2] In an attempt to pin the word "greed" on Woolworth, the commission chairman pointed out that the company's total sales in 1971 had climbed to $2.8 billion and that five to ten percent of these revenues were generated by its food operations.

Woolworth officials voiced a quick defense. They pointed out that the chain increased its prices only within the last month and then, only because of increasing costs of supplies—foods purchased in categories that were no longer covered by price restrictions. Woolworth had filed papers for such increases in December 1971, in line with commission rules that permitted retailers to raise prices based on increased costs of their food supplies. When there was no response from the commission for three months, the company raised its prices for meals. But as soon as the Commission protested in April, Woolworth quickly responded that its chain would restore pre-freeze prices immediately—unaware, as yet, that price-ceilings would remain in place on beef, lamb and pork for most of the time until September 30, 1973.

On April fifth, 1972, 59-year-old Woolworth Donahue—the last Donahue heir to the Woolworth fortune—died of a heart attack at his Palm Beach home while watching television with his wife, Mary Hartline Donahue.[3] After a private service took place in Palm Beach, his coffin was taken to New York and placed in the Woolworth mausoleum, whereupon his wife, Mary, became a very wealthy widow.

Even though Barbara Hutton had visited her cousin Woolworth during his illness and had known that that he was battling cancer, she was shocked at the abruptness of his death. Always, there had been at least one of the Donahues ready to offer solace and comfort to her in the troubled times of her life. Now her son, Lance, was the only one on whom she could depend to care about her.

Reports estimated that Lance's wealth approached $50 million at this time — a fortune that allowed him to continue indulging his passion for skiing and playing polo. However he was not skiing in the mountains on July 24, 1972, but flying with friends as a passenger in a single-engine Cessna in the Colorado Rockies near Aspen, Colorado when a sudden heavy thunderstorm broke. As hail pelted the Cessna, the small plane wobbled and cracked into the side of a wooded mountain with a terrible crash that none of the four shattered occupants could have heard for more than a fragment of time before they were lost to eternity. The will of 36-year-old Lance was filed in Probate Court two days later. The bulk of his fortune was left to his wife, Cheryl.[4]

At the loss of her son, Barbara was overcome with grief and with guilt concerning her role as a mother. Surely she, too, must have wondered if it was a curse on the Woolworths that had claimed Lance's life. Doctors visited her hotel suite, meting out tranquilizers and writing prescriptions for stronger drugs. Nurses followed their patient's querulous commands — keep their voices subdued to low whispers, draw the drapes all the way, day and night, and dim the lamps to their lowest wattage. Consciously or unconsciously, Barbara Hutton was gradually sinking into the life-stifling formula for deadening any stimulus that might rouse her from her insulated cocoon — just as her once-vibrant Aunt Jessie had done after the suicide of her adored son, Jimmy Donahue.

There was good news for the country that year with the winding-down of the lengthy Vietnam War. But Woolworth officials were concerned with an August report of a second-quarter decline in earnings from the matching date of the previous year. Even allowing for the current 5.5 percent of unemployment and a rising national deficit, which would amount to $23 billion by the end of the 1972 fiscal year, Woolworth directors were alerted and alarmed by any such quarterly decline.

To add to their concerns, two fires erupted in a New York Woolworth store at East 44th Street in the early morning of August 18. Investigators concluded that incendiary bombs had been planted in the store the previous evening before closing time. They discovered that explosions of Ping Pong balls filled with inflammable liquids and equipped with timing devices had triggered both fires. Damages at Woolworth, though, were considerably less than damages at a midtown Lerner Shop, where the second floor was gutted by explosions of the same kind of bombs on the same date. An S.H. Kress & Co. store also suffered fire damage, as did a Fifth Avenue E.J. Korvette store.[5]

The previous afternoon, both Cuban and Puerto Rican groups had demonstrated outside the United Nations building on behalf of Puerto Rican independence from the United States. That same day, Cuba submitted a proposal to the United Nations Special Committee on Colonialism asking that Puerto Rico be listed among territories victimized by colonialism. But investigators could prove no connection between the demonstrations and the incendiary devices.

At the end of 1972, Woolworth board members had to face the unpleasant fact that domestic income of both Woolworth and Woolco Department Store operations had declined from the previous year. But including the company's 52.7 percent equity in its British subsidiary, Woolworth's 1972 consolidated net income amounted to $79.1 million — a healthy increase from the 1971 net income of $76.5 million.[6]

As the stock market perked up in January 1973, President Nixon initiated the third phase of his economic stabilization program, which ended wage and price controls except for controls on food, health care and construction. Still, interest rates began to rise again and stock market prices declined.

As early as January 20, Gateway Sporting Goods Company announced the termination of its leased operations in chain discount stores (88 of these leases were in Woolco department stores), acknowledging that Gateway would accumulate a $7 million loss for the fiscal year ending February 28. At the same time, the F. W. Woolworth Company agreed to buy the Gateway inventory in the 88 Woolcos, which would turn out to be only a first step in what would, a decade later, become Woolworth's revolutionary change into a major sporting goods outlet.[7]

Keeping in tune with the times, Woolworth officials appointed the company's first black female store manager. Mrs. A. Wells, in June.[8] The store, located in San Diego, played its part in the policy that soon would be referred to as "diversity"— not in expanding into new locations at this point, but in managerial appointments. The following year, the company's first black district manager, Walter Granison, would be appointed to oversee all the Woolworth stores in Philadelphia.

For most of 1973, profits would continue to be erratic in retail businesses and, near the end of the year, there were gloomy forecasts of a recession in 1974, occasioned in part by an anticipated Arabian oil embargo. Still, before the end of 1973 the Woolworth Company went ahead with an investment of $35 million to purchase 10,000 cash registers equipped with computer systems. By way of the computer systems the new "point-of sale" registers would handle a myriad of tasks that could have befuddled counter clerks. The machines not only read price tags, added up sales and counted change, but also checked credit cards and tracked inventories.[9]

Retail chain stores were encouraged when year-end reports showed that sales (including those of Woolworth) had improved an average 14.1 percent for 1973 above sales for 1972. Woolworth's net income for the year (including income from the British stores) was raised to $93.5 million from the preceding year's net income of $79.3 million.[10] Another lift for retail chains occurred in March 1974 as, with the easing of gasoline shortages, retail sales turned out to be more than ten percent higher than those in February of the previous year. Still, it was not easy for chain retailers to stay ahead of rising inflation. By the end of April, S.S. Kresge was the envy of the competing chains with a 25.5 percent gain in sales for the year to date. Woolworth, still frantically checking out its quarterly reports, had to settle for a 12.4 percent gain, only slightly above 50 percent of sales accumulated by the Kresge chain — its chief competitor since before the turn of the century.[11]

The gains evened out, though, and dropped as a sluggish economy persisted throughout the year while a disgraced President Nixon, under pressure, resigned his office in August and Vice President Gerald Ford took the presidential oath of office. Christmas shoppers found Woolworth's prices reduced 10 to 20 percent below those of the previous year, but rising unemployment contributed to a disappointing holiday selling season for the retail chains.

Edward F. Gibbons, who had become a Woolworth board member in 1973, was named to succeed John S. Roberts as Woolworth President in 1975 while Roberts became vice president of the board of directors. Gibbons, viewed as a particularly enterprising man to meet the challenges of a difficult financial period, surprised everyone when he resigned, citing illness, within a few months of his appointment.[12] Chairman Burcham had to take over the presidency until a new president could be appointed.

In June there were extensive layoffs throughout the country, even while inflation continued. The toll the economy was taking on the retail chains became clear in October 1975 when a longtime Woolworth competitor, W.T. Grant Company, filed for Chapter II bankruptcy, sending a chill through the boardrooms of retail chains. W. T. Grant closed the doors to 712 of its variety stores, adding many hundreds of dismissed employees to the rolls of the unemployed.[13] More drastic economy changes followed — reducing executives to a skeleton number and selling leases, fixtures and equipment to raise money. Even so, the beleaguered company anticipated losses of another $24 million for October. Regardless of the company's attempts to re-structure and continue business, a federal court handed down an order to liquidate the entire business.

When Woolworth reported its net income for 1975, however, it amounted to $93.1 million, a $24 million increase from the previous year. By July 1976 another shifting of officers took place as Woolworth officials re-elected Edward Gibbons to return as president and chief executive, while Burcham continued as chairman of the board.[14]

Two months later, under Gibbons' firm direction, a major change was initiated when Woolworth officials decided to sell, for cash, its customer credit programs to General Electric Credit. This involved some 1.1 million Woolworth and Woolco credit customer accounts, which were reported to be operating at a loss. Woolworth would continue to offer the programs in 300 stores, which were presently involved with the credit operation, but General Electric Credit would be in charge of operations. The $185 million received for the sale of the accounts could be used by Woolworth for debt reduction.[15]

A suit filed by the Beverly Hills Hotel in late November in Superior Court was concerned with the bad credit of none of the Woolworth or Woolco customers, but rather of the Woolworth heiress Barbara Hutton, who had been holed up in her plush hotel suite for a considerable length of time. The hotel wanted reimbursement for some $7,000 in unpaid bills. Moreover, it also wanted to be reimbursed for $500 worth of hotel property that, the suit claimed, the heiress had removed from the suite when she had left the hotel recently without notification and moved into another hotel.[16]

At this point in her life, Barbara (who held a long-time suspicion that people always tried to take advantage of her because of her fortune) had developed a paranoid belief that her employees, including her nurses, were secretly gossiping about her and conspiring to steal from her. She was especially suspicious of theft from her prized jewelry collection which, periodically, she inspected from her bed.[17]

Only six months later, she would become the defendant in another suit — this one filed by her former chauffeur, Thomas Creech. Creech, who now had his own business, running a limousine service, had worked for Barbara for six years until she fired him without paying the $32,290 he claimed she owed for back wages. He also sued for civil penalties of $3,360.[18] One year later, Barbara was ordered to pay $12,000 to Creech for duties performed "unrelated to driving" since 1976.[19]

Barbara also had problems with maids who made claims for payment against her. Most of all, she felt that she was taken advantage of by over-priced lawyers she was forced to hire to work out settlements for her many legal problems.

Although economic uncertainty lingered throughout January 1977, shoppers braved bitterly cold weather in the East, Midwest and even the South to shop at retail chains, boosting their sales well above those of the previous January. Again, the S. S. Kresge Company had double the sales gain of Woolworth's 10.5 percent, but this seemed only to spur Gibbons and his aides to begin what they called a "refurbishment and expansion program" with capital expenditures requiring approximately $107 million to build 240 new outlets, not only in the United States but also in Canada and three other countries. The outlets would consist of Woolworth, Woolco, Richman and Kinney stores to add to its present roster of 4,460 stores and leased departments.[20]

This seemed to be a bold move at a time when the worldwide recession was continuing, the cost of oil still rising, and President Carter was appealing to the richer industrial and oil-producing countries to contribute to the International Monetary Fund to assist poorer nations.

By this time, Woolworth already had relocated in what company officials said were 25 "re-cycled" W.T. Grant stores. At the end of March it opened five Woolcos in the rapidly growing Suffolk County, New York, area. These locations, too, were former W.T. Grant properties, and Woolco arranged to employ 500 former Grant employees in the new stores.[21]

Once again a store in a foreign land brought the Woolworth name into the national news in July 1977 when a Woolworth store in Salisbury, Rhodesia, was bombed in an act of violence by black guerrillas. The attack resulted in 11 people killed and 76 injured, most of them blacks.[22] The fact that the store was locally owned did not seem to matter in the guerrillas' war against the white government of the country. Motivation for the attack on shoppers and clerks who were, largely, black seemed to stem from the choice this independent store had made — keeping the name of the internationally recognized Woolworth chain.

Woolworth directors were elated when profits for the fiscal year of 1977 rose to $108.2 million. But they were not so happy with the $21 million drop in profits for its Woolco division.[23]

They were concerned, too by a new ruling by the Financial Accounting Standards Board that would take effect when company accountants prepared their balance sheets in December 1978. Woolworth, like other chains, leased a great number of the buildings in which its stores were located. In fact, many of these leased buildings had been built to the leasees' exact specifications. These leases, formerly shown only as footnotes on balance sheets, now would be treated as debt, reducing the income of retailers who relied heavily on lease arrangements (as F. W. Woolworth certainly did.) The Woolworth Company would be forced to take another look at leasing to see if outright purchase would be more attractive in the future.[24]

Nonetheless, encouraged by increased sales in the first quarter of 1978, Woolworth entered into acquisition talks with Rockower Brothers, a retailer of men's and boys' apparel that had 147 Woolco men's and boys' departments. Woolworth made an offer of $32.2 million for Rockower stock at $14 a share. The talks went on for two months, but collapsed in May. By the (following spring, circumstances had changed completely as Rockower faced complete and voluntary liquidation and Woolworth had agreed to purchase Rockower's store fixtures and inventory and to pay $7 million following the Rockower closing.[25]

By the end of the third quarter, 1978, Chairman Gibbons had announced with pride that earnings for the first nine months of the year, including the equity of the British stores, had doubled from those of the previous year to $50.4 million. When tallied on January 31, 1979, at the end of its 1978 fiscal year, corporate sales for the Woolworth empire (its 5,600 retail stores in various countries—1,800 of them flaunting the Woolworth name, and including its other divisions— Woolco, Richman, Kinney) were anticipated to pass the $6 billion mark. The Woolworth empire was a survivor, still flexing its muscle in a swiftly changing world, while many other similar companies that had originated at or before the turn of the century had folded— S.H. Kress and McCrory among them. W.T. Grant (at least its remnants) was still hanging on the ropes. S.S. Kresge had already phased out most of its variety stores to concentrate on its flourishing Kmart operations. In contrast, Woolworth's net income for 1978 pumped up the company's biceps' measurements with a bulging net profit of $130.3 million — up 52 percent from the previous year.[26]

For Woolworth, it was party time in February 1979. Although the Woolworth store in Lancaster, Pennsylvania, always had been acclaimed as the "first" of Frank W. Woolworth's stores, the century celebration was held in the same month that Woolworth had opened "The Great Five-Cent Store" in Utica that had failed so dismally.

No matter. Failure was not in the vocabulary of current Woolworth Chief Executive Edward F. Gibbons, who partied at the century observance along with other officials and invited guests in the great marble lobby of New York's Woolworth Building. In an entertaining *New York Times* story, Ron Alexander described Bee Walker sitting at an upright piano and jazzing up tunes that were popular some fifty and sixty years previously. Ms. Walker was right at home with the sheet music in front of her, rattling off the same melodies that she had performed decades earlier in a Woolworth store music department. It was there that Ms. Walker had been "discovered," she told Alexander, by a talent agent after which she hit the "big time" as accompanist to such stars as Eddie Cantor and Bob Hope.[27]

Then it was back to work for Woolworth officials, buyers and department heads —all of them under the gun to keep profits flowing. In the company's fiscal first quarter for 1979, however, a 19.3 percent decline in earnings reflected a currency loss and drop in income from its British subsidiary. The strengthening of the British pound had reduced the equity in earnings of the British company to $2.4 million for the quarter, in contrast to the $5.5 million in the same period, 1978.[28]

By this time, the Woolworth Company had larger concerns with a greater problem. On April 9, Branscan Ltd. of Toronto, Canada, tendered a $1.1 billion bid for a takeover of the F. W. Woolworth Company.[29] In the following seven weeks of stubborn resistance from Woolworth and persistent pressure from Branscan (a holding company with interests in oil and gas explorations), Woolworth accused Branscan of having had access to confidential Woolworth bank records. At a public hearing presided over by the New York State Attorney General, Branscan denied the charge while admitting that its chairman and three of its directors were board members of the Canadian Imperial Bank of Canada.

The fight wore on, complicated by the fact that Branscan itself admitted to expenditures of $5 million to try to prevent its own takeover by Edper Equities Ltd. of Toronto after Edper acquired more than 6 1/2 million shares of Branscan stocks. The Branscan attempt at a takeover of Woolworth faded within days after Federal Judge Pierre N. Levan lifted a temporary restraining order that had blocked Edper from voting its millions of shares it had acquired in Branscan.[30] Since Edper's powerful votes would have been negative on Branscan's acquisition efforts, Woolworth was able to slip out of the Branscan noose.

Then it was back to the planning boards as Woolworth announced it was preparing to enter the apparel discounting area with a new retail specialty-store chain that would sell both women's and men's clothing. The new subsidiary would aid Woolworth, Chairman Gibbons stated, in achieving its goal to become "a more diversified, more aggressive company" alert to resisting any takeover attempts.

All the while the Branscan-Woolworth power struggles had been continuing, the 66-year-old, severely emaciated and haggard Barbara Hutton was enduring her own fight for life. The years of spa and rejuvenation treatments, cosmetic surgeries, kneadings and pattings by masseurs and manipulations by famed European make-up artists seemed only to have contributed to the premature aging process of the heiress. In late March an extremely weakened Barbara, suffering from pneumonia, was taken to Cedars-Sinai Hospital where she was received into the intensive care unit.

Weeks later and weighing only 80 pounds, she was removed from intensive care and taken to an intermediate-care private room where she insisted on leaving the hospital, against doctors' advice, and returning to her Beverly Wilshire Hotel penthouse. There, her condition deteriorated for eight days until she simply stopped breathing on May 3. Despite attempts by paramedics to revive her, she was pronounced dead of a heart attack when the ambulance arrived at the hospital.[31]

Barbara had left instructions that she wanted only a small and private funeral service. The mortuary held the body, listed as "Barbara Doan," for several days. When her casket was shipped to New York, there were no reporters at the May 25, 1979, brief service at Woodlawn Cemetery. There were only a few mourners and no minister in attendance. Placed in the Woolworth mausoleum, next to her mother and her son, the so-called richest girl in the world had passed out of this world as quietly as if she were an unknown pauper.

18

Ups and Downs of the 1980s

In 1979, the year in which Barbara Hutton died, the Woolworth empire flourished again as net income rose to $180 million. The $180 million, however, set a record that would not be matched for a few years despite Chairman Gibbons' five-year forecast of "growth through new formats" such as the company's new subsidiary, Woolco Fashion Corporation. This new subsidiary was slated to enter the field of discounted brand-name apparel to compete with T.J. Maxx–type stores by taking over all buying and merchandising of women's and children's clothing for Woolworth and Woolco stores.[1]

While planning intensified for "growth through new formats," British Woolworth's reports for the first fiscal half of 1980 were disappointing. Great Britain's 1,000 Woolworth-Woolco stores, employing 40,000 full-time sales and support personnel, had reported a business volume of $2.1 billion in 1979. Now, for the first fiscal half of 1980, British Woolworth's profits were in free-fall, amounting to only $700,000 compared with a 1979 profit of $38 million for the same period.[2] This was bad news for the parent company which depended heavily on its majority share of the proceeds from the British subsidiary.

The decline of British Woolworth was matched by a general major decline that year in other British stores, including the largest retailer, Marks and Spencer. British Chairman Geoffrey Rodgers quickly announced a Woolworth- Woolco price-cut of ten percent for three weeks, beginning September 14, in all 1,000 stores.

Abandoning its customary caution in early August 1980, British Woolworth became more adventuresome when it invested $40 million to buy the year-old B&Q group of do-it-yourself stores. The British also planned a new venture for 1981, announcing its intention to open six units as a part of its proposed string of Foot-Locker stores, selling a full range of foremost brand-name athletic footwear and sports clothing.[3] In another bold move a year later, British subsidiary B&Q would expand by investing $38.1 million in the purchase of Dodge City Ltd., another chain of do-it-yourself stores which would total 80 stores run by B&Q.

At the American parent company headquarters, Chairman Gibbons was disturbed by the third-quarter 1980 financial report; net income had fallen 44.9 percent ($24.8 million) from the previous year's third-quarter period, as the continuing recession battered Gibbons' earlier predictions of growth. End-of-year reports were not entirely unexpected. The 1980 profits had amounted to $161 million, but U.S. Woolco's pre-tax losses had taken a big bite of $72 million from those profits.

Woolworth's Chief Executive Gibbons, on his election as chairman of the National Retail Merchants' Association in January 1981, admitted to the association's members that he did not anticipate a strong first half-year ahead. He was aware that although Woolworth's annual financial reports in previous years had tallied up to a comfortable growth in dollars, high inflation had cut sharply into the value of those dollars. Rising interest rates paid by the company were another problem — interest that had amounted to nearly $185 million in 1980, up from an approximate $78 million in 1979.[4]

Throughout the Great Depression of the 1930s, the Woolworth Company had thrived by attracting customers with its lower prices on goods considered essential to day-to-day life of average families. But over the decades, especially during the recession years of the 1970s, and now inflation, again, in the 1980s, the company gradually had raised its prices for a cup of coffee to 50 cents. And by this time, Woolworth had attained its goal of diversification so well that it no longer had such a strong and singular pull for the blue-collar families who had been its biggest customers. The company's delineation had become blurred.

During 1981, the economy in Mexico had greatly improved. Emboldened by its prosperity, the Mexican Woolworth subsidiary forcefully pressed the American company to sell its majority holdings to the subsidiary company which then would hold the controlling interest.[5] The sell-off agreement was accomplished in July 1981 when the Mexican subsidiary paid American Woolworth $13 million, after which American Woolworth owned only a 49 percent interest, duly reported in the *New York Times*.

While Mexico planned to expand its Woolworth outlets, American Woolworth was tightening its budget and cutting way back on its former program of opening new stores. The variety stores were to have less than ten new units in 1982, Chief Executive Gibbons announced. Woolco would have none.

In an effort to restore Woolco to profitable discount sales, Bruce G. Allbright, former president of Target Stores (the most thriving division of Dayton-Hudson Corporation), was brought into Woolworth to fill the new position of chairman and chief executive officer of United States Woolworth and Woolco divisions. Gibbons, of course, remained as overall chairman and chief executive of the entire company. Allbright took up his duties on January 1, 1982, shortly before a loss of $15 million for the first quarter was announced, then a loss of $9 million for the second quarter.

Whatever the future of the Woolworth Company might be, its concern for the soaring 68-year-old Woolworth Building that housed the company's New York headquarters, as well as offices of many other companies, had resulted in a four-year restoration of the landmark edifice. The $22 million renovation, being completed at the end of 1981, had consisted of cleaning the entire structure and replacing some of the terra cotta surface as well as all of the 2,843 windows.[6] A tax abatement of $11.4 million (spread over 19 years) reimbursed Woolworth for a part of its expenses, and the 792-foot skyscraper, across Broadway from City Hall, still proudly bore the name

Woolworth as its tower soared high near the taller and towering towers of the World Trade Center. No one could have guessed that on September 11, 2001, hijackers would seize control of four American commercial airplanes and that two of the planes would explode as they smashed into the World Trade towers, killing and maiming thousands of people and leaving only rubble in their wake.

At the end of the fiscal year 1981, Woolworth reported that net income had dropped again — this time to $82 million.[7] Making the financial picture much worse were figures showing that the company was "in the red" because Woolco's losses amounted to $125 million.[8]

However, President Ronald Reagan's new programs, first enacted in 1982, would begin to show positive results very soon — results that gradually would bring the country out of its lingering recession and into a period of business expansion. Woolworth officials were hopeful that, in the improved climate that seemed to lie ahead, their chain of stores could arrest the decline that gripped the company's economic growth so tightly. Still, most of the country's retailers were running scared at this point because they were operating at such small profit margins. Woolworth's profit margins had dropped to a minuscule 0.7 percent. Strengthening of the U.S. dollar had further reduced the "income received from foreign countries in which we participate," Edward F. Gibbons reported. A Paine-Webber executive pointed out that Woolworth's big problem had been "the Woolco division which has never made any money...."[9]

By the end of March 1982 a Woolworth public announcement seemed to bear out the fact that Woolco was losing a lot of money. Thirteen Woolco stores in three states (seven of the stores located in Chicago) were to close and 900 employees would be let go.[10]

Earlier, Bruce Allbright had mapped out plans for an entire reorganization of Woolco stores to make them profitable, but the Woolworth Company had been unwilling to go through two more years of high Woolco losses to carry out Allbright's plans. By this time, Woolworth had decided to concentrate on its variety stores in the United States and on its Woolworth and Woolco operations in Canada plus its Richman Brothers chain, its Kinney Shoe Corporation and several small apparel businesses.

Kinney Shoes, which was operating 315 Foot Locker Stores, was the subsidiary on which Woolworth focused the most enthusiasm for reasons regarding its potential for great growth and success. Fitness was an in-thing. Millions of Americans in all age groups were taking up jogging, trotting, running and exercising on treadmills. Shopping malls opened their doors early in the mornings to accommodate senior citizens, dressed in sweats, who set out on long walks through wide, no-traffic corridors before shopping sieges began. Foot Locker stores, selling various name-brand athletic shoes, tennis racquets and related sports equipment, were expected to expand to 700 units in the near future.[11]

Despite Allbright's detailed long-term plans to return the Woolco division to profitability, the parent Woolworth Company entered into discussions with Sheik Mohammed al-Fasi, who wanted to buy the Woolco discount chain of stores. The talks broke down and in late September 1982 Woolworth announced the closing of the 336 Woolco stores remaining in the United States "to eliminate persistent losses." Canadian Woolcos remained open.[12]

There was another surprise announcement from Woolworth the following month. The parent company was going to sell its majority interest in Britain's Woolworth chain. The price tag — $279 million. The purchaser turned out to be Britain's Paternoster stores, which now would become Woolworth Holdings P.L.C. British stockholders were paid $248 million for their shares.[13]

In this same month of October, Woolworth's chief executive, Edward F. Gibbons, died of a heart attack.[14] John W. Lynn, former chairman of domestic Woolworth's variety stores and Woolco units, took Gibbons' place as chief executive.

Woolworth's fiscal-year earnings for 1982 had slipped down to $66 million. But with discontinued operations amounting to a staggering $435 million, the 1982 earnings report skidded down from profits to $353 million in losses.[15]

By January 1983, retail businesses were perking up. Woolworth reported nicely increased sales for January to a total $440.4 million as compared to $332.7 million the previous January. Of course, the sales figures included close-out sales at the Woolco stores. Still, the net increase for the month was 14.2 percent and Woolworth and other skittish retailers were heartened by the gains.

The first nine months of 1983 brought more changes to Woolworth as Burger Kings replaced some of the stores' longtime lunch counters as a part of Chairman Lynn's renovation program for the variety stores. There were 5,300 variety and specialty stores now making up the Woolworth chain in the United States, and according to the chairman's plans, the purchase of more specialty stores lay ahead.[16]

The latest purchase of a specialty chain in August 1983 was the acquiring of Holtzman's Little Folk Shop, its 110 stores adding up to the largest children's clothing chain in the country. Woolworth paid $25 million for the acquisition. Chairman Lynn planned to spend another $25 million to update Woolworth variety stores, with an equal amount of money scheduled for more variety store renovations in 1984.

The chairman was energized by sales reports for 1983 arriving at headquarters. They showed first-quarter earnings of $1 million, compared to a loss of $16 million for the first quarter of 1982. Second quarter earnings of $16 million compared with $9 million lost in the same quarter of the previous year. Fourth-quarter net income zoomed up to $100 million from the $58 million of fourth quarter 1982. Still, 240 Canadian Woolworths closed that year. But for the fiscal year 1983, results were encouraging at American Woolworth headquarters after the rough going of the past two years. Total 1983 sales amounted to $5.5 billion with net income reaching a $118 million figure.[17]

But was the 1983-84 F. W. Woolworth Company still a variety-store chain? Not exactly. The company was investing heavily in the acquisition of stores selling a single range of products. The costume jewelry store — Afterthoughts. Frame Scene, specializing in frames and posters. Rx Place — discount drugs. And others — many of them, each contributing in some degree (and with Kinney Stores and Richman Brothers contributing in a major degree) to what Chairman John W. Lynn hoped would be banner years in 1984-85. Other Woolworth acquisitions were operating in West Germany and Canada.

Income for the fiscal year 1984 amounted to $141 million on sales of $5.7 million — a 5.6 percent sales gain. The gain was overshadowed, though, by Kmart's sales gain of 11.8 percent.[18]

Still, the sales gain encouraged Woolworth to purchase more acquisitions. In April 1985 a Woolworth announcement informed the public that the company was to open 548 specialty stores worldwide, at which time Woolworth would have a total of 4,557 specialty stores in contrast with only 1,194 of its hallmark variety stores. Woolworth officials also explained that approximately 300 of the new specialty stores would be in 15 chains already introduced into the Woolworth line, including the popular Kids Mart and the Athletic Shoe Factory. In the past year, a Woolworth spokesperson pointed out, 33 percent of total sales was attributed to the specialty stores.[19]

Expansion of the specialty stores and ongoing renovation of variety stores were going to cost Woolworth $225 million in 1986. The cost would be financed, Chairman Lynn said, entirely from internally generated funds. His expectations were, he stated, that the specialty stores should produce at least 56 percent of the parent company's operating income within two years. At the end of 1986, plans were already made to spend the larger part of $212 million on expansion of specialty stores.

Three months later, *Crain's Detroit Business* reported that Woolworth had been negotiating with Kmart to buy 116 Kresge stores.[20] The talks ended, though, when no agreement was reached.

The turnaround in Woolworth's fortunes had attracted the attention of the powerful Dart Group Corporation. Acquisition games took on a new aspect that frightened Woolworth in March 1988 when the Dart Group chairman notified the government that an investment partnership controlled by the Dart chairman might buy up to 15 percent of Woolworth stock.[21] The next day the news of Dart's intention pushed Woolworth stock up $8.875 to $54.125. Woolworth quickly took action against a possible takeover by putting a "poison pill" plan into action, giving shareholders an opportunity to purchase additional Woolworth shares at half price.

Within a short time, the Dart threat disappeared as had many similar takeover attempts made by Dart. The Woolworth Company boasted of its second-quarter 1988 sales and earnings. Sales had risen from $1.63 billion in the same period of 1987 to $1.84 billion in 1988; income rose $37 million to $43 million.[22]

At age 65, Chairman John W. Lynn retired with plaudits for revitalizing the fortunes of the formerly lagging Woolworth Company. The younger Robert G. Lynn became president and chief executive of the company's U.S. Woolworth division on February 1, 1989. The following April, Lynn and the rest of the executive board approved a plan that would set up a new holding company, the Woolworth Corporation, with its seven retail entities becoming subsidiaries. Each subsidiary was to be totally responsible for its own operations. The corporate office was to be committed to long-range financial goals.

Under the new plan, expansion continued. In the late months of 1989 there were major acquisitions.[23] Woolworth and Kaufhof applied to purchase most of the Bilka discount stores in West Germany. The acquisitions expanded in 1990 when Woolworth's thriving FootLocker B.V. unit purchased Profoot Nederlander B.V. — a Netherlands athletic retailer.

Woolworth Corporation now owned 6,400 specialty stores in addition to 1,600 variety stores. It planned to make a capital outlay of $325 million by the end of the fiscal year 1991. At the same time, Woolworth was edging into the area of closures for some of its older variety stores as leases expired and, for various reasons, were not renewed. Such were the circumstances for the announced closing of the 61-year-old Woolworth store in the upscale community of Rye, New York.

What about the Rye citizens, especially the seniors, who could not afford to shop in the high-priced, Fifth Avenue-type stores that edged the sidewalks of downtown Rye? Variety-store customers demanded to know this as they undertook a petition drive to save their beloved Woolworth store. Women, mostly grandmothers, gathered at the luncheonette counter and sipped coffee as they complained about the proposed closing of the store where they liked to chat with friends as they shopped.[24]

The Woolworth Corporation, though, had much larger visions for its future. Now that the divided sections of Germany had been reunited, Woolworth officials were preparing for a move into former East Germany, where the company would set up stores in some of the same locations where its stores had flourished before World War II. At this time, approximately 15 percent of Woolworth's revenues was coming from countries outside of North America. Harold Sells, promoted to Woolworth Corporation's chairman and chief executive in October 1986, was particularly enthusiastic about setting up a store in Halle (in former East Germany), where a Woolworth store had flourished before the 1940s. Sells said that he saw the North American retailing economy as "sluggish" at this time.

Recessions in the United States, Canada and Australia resulted in a downturn for Woolworth profits in the fourth quarter of 1990 as both the recession and the crisis in the Persian Gulf affected the spending habits of consumers and occasioned a 15 percent drop in earnings for Woolworth. For the full year 1990, profits amounted to $317 million—a loss of $12 million from the previous year. When the financial reports were made public, the New York Stock Exchange showed a fall of $1.25 for the corporation's stock, now listed at $33.25.[25] Still, there was little expectation at this point that the comparatively minor decrease in earnings might be the beginning of Woolworth's downfall.

19

Nobody's Store

Company executives, reacting nervously at any annual loss, closely examined quarterly reports for the following year. The first quarter 1991 drop in net income to $13 million (a 65.8 percent dip from that of the previous year) shook the confidence of board members. Nonetheless, confidence seemed to flow from the Woolworth spokesman who announced in June that the corporation would open 4,500 to 4,900 new Foot Lockers, Lady Foot Lockers and Champs Stores within the 1990s decade. This would expand revenue to $5 billion by the end of the decade, the spokesman predicted.[1]

In line with the expansion plan, the corporation had acquired two athletic footwear and apparel outlets early in the year: Freedom Sportsline Ltd. of England and five stores operated by a Dutch company — Sportsworld B.V.

Second quarter earnings were worse than those of the first quarter, falling 58 percent to $21 million, followed by another depressing report in the third quarter — a decrease of 49 percent.[2] Regardless of the losses, Woolworth acquired 25 Lamston general merchandise stores to add to the Woolworth roster during that third quarter.

Recessions in the United States and Canada had taken their toll on the economy, Chairman Sells stated. The invasion of Kuwait by Iraq on August 2 to seize control of Kuwait's oil wells, followed by the arrival of United States troops to turn back the invaders, had further diminished oil supplies and eroded the American economy. December sales were disappointing for most retailers, except for the giant discounter Wal-Mart.

After Woolworth's major losses of $166 million for the 1991 fiscal year,[3] officials announced in January 1992 that approximately 500 of their clothing stores would be closed along with 300 Kinney Family Shoe stores and 90 under-performing Woolworths. Some of the company's popular Lady Foot Lockers would move into several of the closing locations.

In April, even after earning $17 million in the first quarter of 1992, Woolworth decided to close its 260 Richman Brothers stores. Still, it planned to spend $390 million in 1992 to expand its specialty stores— mainly Foot Locker, Lady Foot Locker, Northern Reflections and Champs Sports. After Thoughts and Carimar boutiques, acquired from Edison Brothers Stores, also would be expanded.

189

Despite business analysts' encouraging predictions of major gains for Woolworth Corporation because of its ambitious modernization of its dated chain of stores and its closing of under-performing units, fiscal-year earnings for 1992 were disappointing. The earnings amounted to $280 million, but with stores abroad accounting for 40 percent of company sales.[4]

In the upper echelons of Woolworth, the days when company officials were comfortably secure in lifetime appointments were disappearing quickly. The chase was on for profitability. The bugle had blared — a warning to lagging runners with "Profits" emblazoned on their sweatbands. The profit race became a relay, with newly appointed, more competitive runners stepping in to replace those who stumbled. Old loyalties became cutthroat rivalries.

In July 1993, Woolworth's chief financial officer, William K. Lavin, was named the corporation's chairman and chief executive at the retirement of Harold E. Sells.[5] When it became clear that second-quarter earnings for 1993 had fallen well below the 1992 amount, it also became clear that drastic steps had to be taken for the company to recover from its decline. Drastic steps appeared to mean even more expansion. In early March, Woolworth had widened its holdings, which now included the Champs Sports chain of 400 stores, with plans to open eight new Rx Place Drug Marts in New York City.[6] Shortly afterwards, the company divulged plans to expand its nearly 9,000 specialty stores, worldwide, to 11,000 by 1997.

The Woolworth store at Broadway and 145th Street in Harlem was totally gutted by fire in September 1993. When firemen arrived at the scene, flames were shooting from the building from the basement to the second floor. Additional fire trucks arrived and 200 firemen fought the blaze for more than five hours. Investigators reached the conclusion that arson was a good possibility.[7]

The shifting about of executives by Chief Executive Lavin in the short time that he had been at the helm of Woolworth Corporation had not seemed to help the downward slide reported in sales. A September Standard & Poors report was discouraging when it showed a downgrade for Woolworth from stable to negative.

In October the company closed the historic Greensboro, North Carolina, Woolworth store — the site of the first sit-ins some thirty years earlier. At the closing, the lunch counter was removed from the store along with stools, the soda fountain and several accessories, all of which soon would be set up at the Smithsonian Institution in Washington, D.C. The tableau, named "Sitting for Justice," became a tribute to the history-making civil rights protests at Woolworth's Greensboro store that had set in motion a great chain of civil rights struggles.[8]

The Greensboro store's closing preceded an announcement that Woolworth would close 37 of its 103 variety stores in New York City. The closings were only a small part of the company's nationwide retrenchment policy planned for the next several months— a retrenchment that would include shutting down half of its surviving Five & Dimes.[9] Decisions on the future of the remaining 450 Five & Dimes had not yet been made, but Woolworth officials felt that their variety stores were being squeezed into extinction by the giant discounters, Wal-Mart and Kmart.

Additional Woolworth stores also were included in the present retrenchment — 400 of its discount stores and 330 Kinney shoe stores. Woolworth's Foot Locker stores and Bargain Shop stores (the Canadian chain of low-price clothing and household merchandise) would take over some 250 of the stores that were closing.

Along with the moves for closure of so many stores owned by Woolworth, a third quarter report for 1993 showed that the company would have earned $28 million for the quarter except for its previously announced restructuring charge of $480 million, which reduced the $28 million profit to a $452 million loss. Financial reports for the fiscal year 1993 (including sales throughout the Christmas-holiday season) showed a total loss of $104 million — a loss of $3.76 a stock share.[10]

The press of financial affairs had prodded Woolworth into selling its 142 Woolco stores in Canada for an approximate $300 million (in United States funds) from which the company was able to take a charge of about $45 million to allow for currency-exchange losses. The buyer was Wal-Mart, making its first move into Canada. After that announcement Woolworth stock rose 50 cents to $25.625 a share.[11]

Gloom over the financial mess that gripped the company continued to deepen in 1994. The depth of the gloom was disclosed to the public, in part, with an announcement by the Woolworth Corporation in March 1994 that its financial reports had been falsely adjusted to show less unfavorable quarterly results in 1993.[12] Some employees involved in the deception blamed the "profits at any cost" atmosphere created by their superiors for spurring the deception. In May, a special board committee announced its findings. It had found no wrongdoing but pointed its collective finger at top management for hard-nosed pressure and aggressiveness in pursuing profits. A financial analyst, reporting that the company had charged $5 million for bad checks during the second quarter of 1993, questioned the reliability of the huge charge. Others, who believed firmly in the century-old trustworthiness of the company with its Grandma Moses kind of image, blamed the problems on errors in the evaluation of inventories at a time of such rapid and overwhelming changes in company holdings. In any case, the financial statements for the fiscal year had to be reviewed and restated. A so-called whistle-blower resigned from the finance department but Chief Executive Lavin temporarily retained his executive position while receiving a demotion from chairman to vice chairman.

Behind the scenes, Woolworth officials searched desperately for a new chief executive — a man who could take over the company and lead it in more productive directions with a disciplined approach to solving deep financial problems. (The company did not yet know that a few of its present financial officers would get into more serious trouble four years later when the United States Securities and Exchange Commission would charge them — and fine them — for having filed quarterly reports for 1993 that inflated Woolworth Corporation earnings[13]).

By the end of March 1994, Woolworth Corporation announced more bold plans for expansion of its new discount drugstore chain in the Northeast. Ten more Rx Place Drug Marts were expected to open by fall.[14] New specialty stores numbering 470 (largely sports equipment units) also would be opened throughout the year 1994.

In the interim, Woolworth's stock had slipped to $15.125 a share. But the stock jumped up by two dollars after an April statement by Woolworth that the company planned to maintain its previous 29-cents-a-quarter dividend.[15] Still, suppliers were edgy about Woolworth's credit orders. The company stated that although it would adjust its quarterly statements of dividends for 1992–1993, its annual figures remained unchanged by its auditors.

Three months after announcing that the corporation's stock dividend would be maintained, the dividend was cut nearly in half to 15 cents. The cut reflected the company's concerns regarding the slowing of sales in its FootLocker division.[16]

Shortly before the end of 1994, Woolworth Corporation hired a new chairman and chief executive and a different figure finally was settled upon to establish how much money had been lost in the fiscal year 1993 — a net loss of $495 million on revenue of $9.6 billion.

The new 44-year-old executive, Roger Farah, was thought to be the youngest corporate executive in the country. Moreover, he had come from the "outside" rather than from within the Woolworth Corporation.[17] A graduate of the University of Pennsylvania's Wharton Business School, Farah had gained a good reputation serving as president of R.H. Macy & Co. of New York with previous experience at Saks Fifth Avenue and as head of merchandising at Federated Department Stores, Inc.

No one realized more clearly than Roger Farah that Woolworth Corporation and its 8,500 stores scattered through many countries needed a tough turnabout by a firm hand. Within a week of Farah's arrival in the plush office of what had once been the domain of F.W. Woolworth, the new chairman had to deal with bad financial news. The Mexican peso had been devalued by 50 percent, which meant that American Woolworth's minority interests in Mexico had dropped by 50 percent.

Farah reacted to this development as quickly as he could. Within three years of his arrival he had closed out Woolworth's Mexican interests and pulled out of Hong Kong because of an embargo on goods made in China (the source of many athletic products).

There were difficulties at home as well, including an antiquated inventory system that demanded, and received, Farah's immediate attention. In the re-inventing of the inventory process, he made many changes in personnel and, on a three-year basis, reduced expenses by $314 million.

Farah ordered sell-offs also, including the sale of 24 Rx Place discount drugstores to Pharmhouse in 1995 for more than $50 million. (A year later the remaining 14 Rx Place discount drugstores were closed.) Still, by February 1995 with the company facing a debt of $935 million, Farah decided to cut 2,000 jobs from the corporation's work force and he considered selling the poorly performing After Thoughts, Carimar and Accessory Lady Stores.[18] Eliminating payment of the corporation's quarterly dividends on stocks was another move by Farah to build up the cash flow so desperately needed.

The sell-off continued; several costume jewelry stores were sold in Germany as well as the corporation's Lady Plus large-size clothing stores. But there was an acquisition by Woolworth of a direct marketer of athletic equipment, Eastbay, in December 1996 for approximately $146 million in cash. At this point Woolworth shares were selling for $24.

Despite the major reduction of expenses at Woolworth in the three years that Roger Farah had held the executive position, there was a blow for the corporation when its stock was removed (along with Texaco, Westinghouse and Bethlehem Steel) from the Dow Jones listing.[19] Four months later, the corporation announced the forth-coming closing of all 400 of its remaining Five & Dime Stores.[20] Customers who had frequented the Woolworth stores, many of them senior citizens who gathered at the lunch counters at noon or later for afternoon coffee, were depressed by the closing announcement. Where else could they go to chat and linger over coffee and dough-nuts? Where else could they go to buy bobby pins, clear plastic rain bonnets, cap guns and slingshots for grandchildren, little notebooks with carbon paper between the small pages—again, so the grandchildren could play "waitress" or corner-gro-cery store owner? Where else were yards of red-and-white checked plastic (unrolled from large spools) so accessible for table-coverings at a church bazaar or ice-cream social; crepe paper and trimmings for a child's bike in a Fourth of July parade, embroi-dery thread to decorate a small apron? (Yes, some people still tied on aprons—June Cleaver style.) Colorful skeins of wool? Iron-on hemming tape? And all under one roof on Main Street, without walking the long corridors at a mall. To the loyal cus-tomers of Main Street's "Dime Stores," the final closing announcement sounded like a dirge—a melancholy reminder that perhaps there was no room for them in the 1990s era of fast-paced progress toward the millennium and a frightening, computerized "World Without Woolworth."

A Las Vegas newspaper ran an article bewailing the dazzling gaming city's loss of its two Woolworth Five & Tens.[21] The article was a poignant reminder to readers that ordinary working people and Vegas homeowners subsisting on middle-class retirees' pensions shopped for bargains at Five & Tens even while big spenders occu-pied lavish rooms at high-rise hotels and placed bets at the roulette wheels at all hours of the night.

The remaining Woolworth stores were to be closed in stages—with liquidation sales, advertising sizeable discounts on merchandise, drawing both bargain-hunters and teary-eyed people searching for souvenirs from the Five & Tens. At the same time, the corporation continued its acquisitions, paying some $10 million for 27 Koenig Sporting Goods stores in August 1997. These stores were scheduled for con-version into the Champs Sports format even while Woolworth's Foot Locker divi-sion was facing tough competition from Finish Line and Footaction with their larger mall-based stores. By the end of the fiscal year 1997, Woolworth's sales had fallen 4.3 percent from the previous year, a decrease due, in part, to Nike's flagging sales.

Still, Roger Farah continued reducing expenses to the point where the corpora-tion's debt had fallen to a near-zero level. Its stock in the first quarter of 1998 returned to a $26.625 level after the acquisition of Athletic Fitters and Eastbay, Inc., the lat-ter a catalog sales business. A rumor was persisting, though, that the Woolworth name would be abandoned for a new corporation name.

The following month, the corporation closed the last 82 of its Kinney Shoe stores in Canada. In May, Woolworth acquired the Sports Authority Inc., chain in a stock swap and an assumption, by Woolworth, of a debt of $179 million. In June, Wool-worth stockholders approved the name Venator Group for the corporation. Wool-worth was no more.[22] "Everybody's Store," as the Five and Tens had been referred to by the company in the early 1900s, had turned into nobody's store.

On the heels of the name change, Venator sold the New York City landmark office building bearing the name Woolworth to the Witkoff Group for $155 million.[23] Soon afterward, Venator placed furnishings from the Woolworth offices for sale at a New York auction by the venerable Christie's. [24] Frank Woolworth's 24th floor Empire Room furnishings were among the ornate pieces sold, some at prices well above their estimated value as catalogued by Christie's.

Frank Woolworth's magnificent, Empire-style, ormolu-mounted desk, its estimated value at $12,000 to $18,000, sold for $17,625. His swiveling desk chair, richly gilt-tooled and set on four scrolled legs with lion-paw feet, was estimated at $2,000 to $3,000 but sold at $23,500. His large ormolu-mounted, mahogany wastebasket, estimated at $1,000 to $1,500, was purchased for $3,055. Frank Woolworth's prized oil painting of Napoleon I in coronation robe (which had been displayed on the wall just opposite the dime-store owner's desk) was estimated at $5,000 to $7,000 but sold for $15,275.[25]

At approximately the same time, Venator would take the final step in exiting the entire general merchandise business by selling the 357 Woolworth stores in Germany — a buyout financed by Electra Fleming, a British investment firm. On November 1, 2001, Venator Group announced a name-change to Foot Locker, Inc. and quickly implemented "its divestiture strategy" by selling off the remnants of its remaining interests in all non-athletic businesses.

On a nostalgic visit to Watertown, New York, in late October 1997, this author and two companions visited the Watertown Woolworth store, not the one located on the first floor of the 6-story Woolworth Building (this store appeared to have been changed into a bargain "dollar" store with "offices for lease" signs at the upper-floor windows) but the more modern Woolworth, back of the Public Square. We saw the cornucopia emblem on the adjoining closed Harvest Restaurant, and then spotted the large banner in front of the store: "CLOSING AFTER 118 YEARS."

The store was spacious, with an escalator (shut off) descending to what once had been a busy lower level. Only a few potential customers wandered about, looking for close-out bargains among the displays of coffee mugs, piles of notebooks, cards for various occasions — most of them without envelopes, paperback books, combs of all sizes and colors, piles of bedroom slippers and canvas running shoes, and odd-lot assortments of various things. Large spiral notebooks were a bargain (I bought several of them plus a "Mr. Muggs" and two other mugs that I hoped would remind me of the Watertown Woolworth because of the Woolworth name stamped on their bottoms).

We left the store with a feeling of loss that the Woolworth stores (and the "soda-fountain era" as one woman phrased it) were quickly vanishing from the American scene. The great problem for many small towns was that the disappearance of Woolworth stores from Main Streets removed the mainstay of the central shopping blocks, after which other stores — including small theaters — closed, too. Most shopping was done now at malls that had sprung up along highways (most movie-viewing was done there, too, in large theaters where patrons could choose among three or four films showing at each mall-based cinema) while small town Main Streets became desolate, nearly deserted places — miniature core-cities from which once-bustling department stores had fled, leaving decay in their wake.

In some small towns, independent business entrepreneurs opened their own Dime Stores. If there were a senior-citizen complex nearby, an independent Dime Store might survive, at least for a while. But the Woolworth era of more than a century has been obliterated from the American scene. Forever.

Notes

Abbreviations

FML Gen   Genealogy Department. Flower Memorial Library. Watertown, N.Y.
FML Hist   Historical Department. Flower Memorial Library. Watertown, N.Y.
JCHSM   Jefferson County Historical Society Museum, Watertown, N.Y.
NYT   *New York Times*
Wool. Bldg.   Woolworth Building (New York City)
Wool. Co.   Woolworth Company
obit   obituary

Chapter 1

1. From a newspaper clipping in the collection of clippings on local businesses and buildings (1860s–early 1900s), Carnegie Library, Ishpeming MI.

2. "Demented Wife Gets All," *New York Times*, p. 11, April 15, 1919.

3. "The Romance of a Business," *NYT*, part 5, p. 6, January 1, 1911.

4. Woolworth booklet, "100th Anniversary" p. 30.

5. Woolworth booklet, "Fortieth Anniversary Souvenir," p. 2.

6. *Ibid.*

7. FML Hist.

8. FML Gen., F.W. Woolworth family file.

9. John Truslow Adams, *The Epic of America* (New York: Blue Ribbon Books, 1941, p. 136.

10. *Ibid.*

11. "The Romance of a Business," *NYT*, part 5, pp. 5–6, January 1, 1911.

12. Woolworth booklet, "Fortieth Anniversary Souvenir," p. 2.

13. FML Gen., F.W. Woolworth family file.

14. Adams, p.247; J.C. Furnas, *The Americans: A Social History of the United States, 1587–1914* (New York: G.P. Putnam's Sons, 1969), p. 530.

15. Woolworth booklet, "Fortieth Anniversary Souvenir," p. 2.

16. "The Romance of a Business," *NYT*, part 5, p.p. 5–6, January 1, 1911.

17. FML Hist., Scrapbook of North Jefferson County.

18. "The Romance of a Business," *NYT*, part 5, p.p. 5–6, January 1, 1911.

19. Woolworth booklet, "75th Anniversary."

20. Woolworth booklet, "Fortieth Anniversary Souvenir."

21. *Ibid.*

22. *Ibid.*

Chapter 2

1. FML Hist., Scrapbook of North Jefferson County.

2. *Ibid.*

3. Woolworth booklet, "Fortieth Anniversary Souvenir," p. 14.

4. James Brough, *The Woolworths* (New York: McGraw-Hill, 1982), p. 42.

5. Woolworth booklet, Fortieth Anniversary Souvenir," p. 3.

6. FML Gen., F.W. Woolworth family file.

7. FML Hist., Scrapbook of North Jefferson County.

8. John K. Winkler, *Five and Ten: The Fabulous Life of F.W. Woolworth* (Freeport, New York: Books for Libraries, 1940), p. 37.

9. *Ibid.*

10. Woolworth booklet, "Fortieth Anniversary Souvenir," p. 4.

11. *Ibid.*

12. "The Romance of a Business," *NYT*, part 5, pp. 5–6, January 1, 1911.

13. *Ibid.*

14. "Woolworth Held Friends," *NYT*, p. 14, May 9, 1913.

15. *Ibid.*

16. "Woolworth Skyscraper Lights Up and Big Dinner Starts on Signal from White House," *NYT*, p. 20, April 25, 1913.

17. FML Hist.

18. *Ibid.*

19. Woolworth booklet, "Fortieth Anniversary Souvenir," p. 5.

20. FML Gen., F.W. Woolworth family file.

21. Jefferson County Historical Society Museum, listings of Woolworth executives and achievements.

22. Woolworth booklet, "Fortieth Anniversary Souvenir," p. 6.

23. *Ibid.*

24. *Ibid*, p. 7.

25. Winkler, p. 77.

26. "The Romance of a Business," *NYT*, part 5, pp. 5–6, January 1, 1911.

27. FML Gen., F.W. Woolworth family file.

28. FML Hist.

29. Woolworth booklet, "75th Anniversary."

30. Winkler, pp. 75–76.

31. *Ibid.*

32. John P. Nichols, *The Skyline Queen and the Merchant Prince* (New York: Trident Press, 1973), p. 108.

Chapter 3

1. John Truslow Adams, *The Epic of America* (New York Blue Ribbon Books, 1941), pp. 313–314; J.C. Furnas, *The Americans* (New York: G.P. Putnam's Sons, 1969), p. 837.

2. Adams, p. 313.

3. John P. Nichols, *The Skyline Queen and the Merchant Prince* (New York: Trident Press, 1973), p. 52.

4. "Woolworth Died with Will Unsigned," *NYT*, p. 11, April 15, 1919.

5. John K. Winkler, *Five and Ten: The Fabulous Life of F.W. Woolworth* (Freeport, New York: Books for Libraries, 1940), p. 81.

6. Adams, pp. 319–320.

7. Detroit Public Library, Burton Historical Collection.

8. Woolworth booklet, "Fortieth Anniversary Souvenir," p. 19.

9. Walter Lord, *The Good Years* (New York: Harper & Brothers, 1960), p. 69.

10. From the collection of travel letters written by F. W. Woolworth, FML Hist., Scrapbook of North Jefferson County.

11. Winkler, p. 105.

12. *Ibid.*, p. 117.

13. *U.S. News & World Report*, January 28, 1991.

14. FML Hist.

15. "President McKinley and the Pan American Exposition of 1901," Internet.

16. "The Trial and Execution of Leon Czolgosz," Internet.

17. Lord, p. 63.

18. Detroit Library, Burton Historical Collection, S.S. Kresge file.

19. Winkler, p. 133.

20. *Ibid.*, p. 128.

21. "Coal Scarcity," *NYT*, p. 3, June 26, 1903, and a series of following articles.

22 "Arbitrator Rules in Favor of Miners," *NYT*, p. 1, September 29, 1904.

23. Winkler, p. 143.

Chapter 4

1. Walter Lord, *The Good Years* (New York: Harper & Brothers, 1960), p. 321.

2. *Ibid.*

3. Jefferson County Historical Society Museum.

4. "Mrs. Charles McCann, Woolworth Daughter, Dies," *NYT*, p. 23, March 16, 1938.

5. "Woolworth Co. Christmas Catalog," JCHSM.

6. John K. Winkler, *Five and Ten: The Fabulous Life of F.W. Woolworth* (Freeport, New York: Books for Libraries, 1940), pp. 143–144.

7. "The Romance of a Business," *NYT*, pp. 5–6, January 1, 1911.

8. Telephone interview with Helen Fargo, historian for Woolworth Memorial Methodist Church, Great Bend, N.Y.

9. "Treasured Aisles," *Ann Arbor News*, part B, p. 4, November 3, 1997.

10. Helen Fargo telephone interview.

11. James Brough, *The Woolworths* (New York: McGraw- Hill, 1982), p. 15.

12. "Mrs. Franklyn Hutton Found Dead," *NYT*, p. 15, May 3, 1917.

13. John P. Nichols, *The Skyline Queen and the Merchant Prince* (New York: Trident Press, 1973), p. 67.

14. James Truslow Adams, *Epic of America* (New York: Blue Ribbon Books, 1941), p. 355.

15. "Leading Business Queried on Economy," *NYT*, p. 22, March 22, 1909.

16. "Hat Ablaze at Waldorf Tea," *NYT*, p. 4, March 21, 1909.

17. "Women Madly Riot at Bargain Sales," *NYT*, p. 4, April 25, 1909.

18. FML Hist., Scrapbook of North Jefferson County.

19. Nichols, p. 71.

20. "Six-Cent Stores in England," *NYT*, p. 4, June 5, 1910.

21. "30–Story Woolworth Building to Be Erected at Broadway and Park," *NYT*, part 6, p. 9, July 10, 1910.

22. "Derrick Boom Falls: Man Dead; Boy Hurt," *NYT*, pp. 8 and 10, December 14, 1910.

23. ""F.W. Woolworth Will Erect World's Tallest Office Building," *NYT*, p. 5, January 20, 1911.

24. *Ibid.*

Chapter 5

1. "The Romance of a Business," *NYT*, part 5, pp. 5–6, January 1, 1911.

2. *Ibid.*

3. *Ibid.*

4. John K. Winkler, *Five and Ten: The Fabulous Life of F.W. Woolworth* (New York: Books for Libraries Press, 1940), p. 171.

5. "Col. Astor to Wed Madeleine Force," *NYT*, p. 1, August 2, 1911.

6. "Obtains $8,000,000 for Big Skyscraper," *Ibid.*

7. Woolworth booklet, "Fortieth Anniversary Souvenir," pp. 11 and 12.

8. *Ibid.*, p. 11.

9. "Incorporation Planned; All Stores in U.S., Canada and Great Britain to Be Amalgamated Under Same Management," *NYT*, p. 3, November 4, 1911.

10. *People*, August 4, 1997.

11. "Jessie Woolworth a Bride," *NYT*, p. 9, February 2, 1912.

12. Winkler, pp. 174–175.

13. Walter Lord, *The Good Years* (New York: Harper & Brothers, 1960), p. 269.

14. James Truslow Adams, *Epic of America* (New York: Blue Ribbon Books, 1941), p. 366.

15. "A Perilous Crossing," *NYT*, editorial page, June 5, 1913.

16. "Architect C. Gilbert to Set Up Model of Building in Munich," *NYT*, part 3, p. 4, October 20, 1912.

17. Winkler, p. 209.

18. "Woolworth Skyscraper Lights Up and Big Dinner Starts on Signal from White House," *NYT*, p. 20, April 25, 1913.

19. Woolworth booklet, "Cathedral of Commerce," 3rd from last page.

20. "Obtains $8,000,000 for Big Skyscraper," *NYT*, p. 1, August 2, 1911.

21. Woolworth booklet, "Fortieth Anniversary Souvenir," p. 13.

22. Woolworth booklet, "Cathedral of Commerce."

23. "Thunderbolt Hits the France in Bay: Woolworth Tower Hit," *NYT*, p. 1, June 21, 1913.

Chapter 6

1. FML Hist., Wool. Bldg. Safe Deposit Co.

2. "Bomb Damages St. Patrick's Cathedral" *NYT*, p. 1, October 10, 1914.

3. Woolworth booklet, "Fortieth Anniversary Souvenir," p. 13.

4. *Ibid.*, pp. 14 and 15.

5. Telephone interview with Helen Fargo, historian for Woolworth Memorial Methodist Church, Great Bend, N.Y.

6. "Woolworth Building Wins," *NYT*, p. 6, July 7, 1915.

7. John K. Winkler, *Five and Ten: The Fabulous Life of F.W. Woolworth* (Freeport, New York: Books for Libraries, 1940), p. 204.

8. "Dr. M.M. Crawford Marries: Uses Maiden Name," *NYT*, p. 11, December 2, 1915.

9. Woolworth booklet, "100th Anniversary," p. 27.

10. Winkler, p. 221.

11. *Ibid.*, p. 228.

12. "Woolworth Store to Open on 5th Avenue," *NYT*, p. 9, January 31, 1917.

13. *Ibid.*

14. *Ibid.*

15. "Astor Baby Spends $86,034 in 3 Years," *NYT*, p. 1, January 31, 1917.

16. Robert Lacey, *Ford: The Men and the Machine* (Boston: Little, Brown, 1986), P. 155.

17. "Has Plans to Call a Million Men," *NYT*, p. 3, March 22, 1917.

18. "Mrs. Franklyn Hutton Found Dead," *NYT*, p. 15, May 3, 1917.

19. James Brough, *The Woolworths* (New York: McGraw-Hill, 1982), pp. 161–162.

20. "Coroner's report," *NYT*, part 1, p. 15, May 3, 1917.

21. Winkler, p. 229.

22. "Holiday Fails to Halt Liberty Loan Efforts Here," *NYT*, p. 3, October 13, 1917.

23. Winkler, pp. 224–226.

24. *Ibid.*, p. 213.

25. Woolworth booklet, "Fortieth Anniversary Souvenir," p. 12.

Chapter 7

1. Woolworth booklet, "Fortieth Anniversary Souvenir," p. 22.

2. JCHSM, Woolworth 40th Anniversary Sale brochure.

3. "Upholds Vagaries in Women's Attire," *NYT*, p. 15, December 4, 1919.

4. "F.W. Woolworth Leaves $65,000.000: Owner of 1,050 Five and Ten Cent Stores Dies Suddenly," *NYT*, p. 11, April 9, 1919.

5. *Ibid.*

6. *Ibid.*

7. "F.W. Woolworth Buried," *NYT*, p. 11, April 11, 1919.

8. "Woolworth Died with Will Unsigned," *NYT*, p. 11, April 15, 1919.

9. *Ibid.*

10. Woolworth booklet, "100th Anniversary," p. 27.

11. "Mrs. Woolworth Ill," *NYT*, p. 14, May 25, 1919.

12. "J.S. Bache Buys Fifth Avenue Home," *NYT*, p. 17, December 19, 1919.

13. "Bache Sues to Recover $20,000 Deposit," *NYT*, p. 25, March 12, 1920.

14. "Women on Board," *NYT*, p. 22, May 20, 1920.

15. "Hold Man in Threat to Bomb Building," *NYT*, p. 11, November 2, 1920.

16. FML Hist.

17. "Woolworth Earns $20.04 a Share in '21," *NYT*, p. 22, February 7, 1922.

18. Winkler, p. 124.

19. "Supreme Court Decision of Encroachment on Street of Property Sold to J.S. Bache," *NYT*, p. 31, March 17, 1922.

Chapter 8

1. "Woolworth Sales on Dec. 23 Were $3,119,645; Company's Record for One Day's Business," *NYT*, p. 15, December 30, 1922.

2. "Woolworth Stock Exchange Approved," *NYT*, p. 24, December 29, 1922.

3. Woolworth booklet, "100th Anniversary," p. 28.

4. FML Gen.

5. C. David Heymann, *Poor Little Rich Girl: The Life and Legend of Barbara Hutton* (New York: Random House, 1983), p. 17.

6. "Winfield Hall at Glen Cove Sold to C.D.F. McCann, Son-In-Law," *NYT*, p. 3, June 7, 1925.

7. "Woolworth Drops $50,000,000 Asset," *NYT*, p. 25, October 15, 1925.

8. "Barbara Hutton Sells 50,000 Shares of Stock Inherited from Grandmother," *NYT*, p. 1, January 9, 1926.

9. Heymann, p. 22.

10. "Income Tax Refunds," *NYT*, p. 27, January 1, 1926.

11. James Brough, *The Woolworths* (New York: McGraw-Hill, 1982), p. 173.

12. "Woolworth Co. Report for 1926," *NYT*, p. 24, January 7, 1927.

13. "Mrs. James P. Donahue's Jewel Robbery," *NYT*, p. 20, March 14, 1926.

14. "Constance Woolworth McCann Marries Wyllys Rosseter Betts Jr. at St. Patrick's," *NYT*, p. 21, October 20, 1926.

15. "Scaffa on Trial in Gem Theft Case," *NYT*, pp. 8–9, November 9, 1926.

16. "Scaffa Trial Ends in a Disagreement," *NYT*, pp. 1, 2, and 11, November 10, 1926.

17. Woolworth booklet, "100th Anniversary," p. 28.

18. "Lady Astor Defends Women's Right to Wed During Debate in House of Commons," *NYT*, p. 21, April 30, 1927.

19. John P. Nichols, *The Skyline Queen and the Merchant Prince* (New York: Trident Press, 1973), p. 101.

20. John K. Winkler, *Five and Ten: The Fabulous Life of F.W. Woolworth* (Freeport, New York: Books for Libraries, 1940), p. 242.

21. "Palm Beach Greets Geraldine Farrar," *NYT*, p. 17, February 21, 1928.

22. Ronald Kessler, *The Season: Inside Palm Beach and America's Richest City* (New York: Harper Collins, 1999), p. 41.

23. "$100,000 Given in Frank Woolworth's Memory by Daughters Mrs. Donahue and Mrs. McCann to Museum of City of New York," *NYT*, p. 12, May 1, 1928.

24. "Scaffa Acquitted," *NYT*, p. 4, May 15, 1928.

25. "Woolworth to Adopt $50 Million Group Life Insurance for Employees," *NYT*, p. 6, April 27, 1929.

26. Gordon Thomas and Max Morgan-Witts, *The Day the Bubble Burst* (New York: Doubleday, 1979), p. 21.

27. Woolworth booklet, "Fiftieth Anniversary."

28. "10–cent Monthlies — New Magazines to Be Sold at Woolworth's," *NYT*, p. 14, November 4, 1929.

29. "Woolworth Orders 1930 Stock Despite Tariff Uncertainty," *NYT*, part II, p. 6, November 10, 1929.

30. Woolworth booklet, "Fiftieth Anniversary."

Chapter 9

1. "Cheney Lays Crash in Stocks to Banks," *NYT*, p. 25, March 21, 1930.

2. "No Basis for Undue Pessimism on Fall and Winter Sales, Mr. Parson Says," *NYT*, part II, p. 18, August 24, 1930.

3. "J.P. Donahue Dies; Poison Kills Broker," *NYT*, p. 2, April 24, 1931.

4. *Ibid.*, pp. 1, 2 and 19.

5. "Donahue Poisoned, Toxicologists Say," *NYT*, p. 12, April 25, 1931.

6. "Throng at Funeral of J.P. Donahue," *NYT*, p. 29, April 26, 1931.

7. James Brough, *The Woolworths* (New York: McGraw-Hill, 1982), p. 178.

8. "$100,000 Slander Suit Up," *NYT*, p. 34, April 16, 1932.

9. "Actress Wins $25,000 Suit," *NYT*, p. 18, July 22, 1932.

10. "Wyllys R. Betts Have Son," *NYT*, p. 25, October 31, 1933.

11. *Dublin Gazette*, June 2, 1931, reported in *NYT*, p. 38, June 3, 1931.

12. John K. Winkler, *Five and Ten: The Fabulous Life of F.W. Woolworth* (Freeport, New York: Books for Libraries, 1940), p. 241.

13. Woolworth booklet, "100th Anniversary," p. 28.

14. JCHSM, listings of Woolworth executives.

15. "Woolworth Gains in Year's Earnings," *NYT*, p. 29, January 31, 1934.

16. "Woolworth Heiress Leaves Count Borromeo-D'Adda on Pier," *NYT*, part II, p. 3, January 29, 1934.

17. "Stench Bombs Hurled in Halle, Germany," *NYT*, p. 10, March 25, 1933.

18. "Close Woolworth Shops," *NYT*, p. 8, March 29, 1933.

19. "Nazis Close 6 German Stores; Woolworth Co. Officials Announce Original Woolworth Was Not a Jew," *NYT*, p. 12, March 30, 1933.

20. *Ibid.*

21. Waiters & Waitresses' Union, Detroit headquarters, Historical Library.

22. "I.T. & T. and Woolworth Stores, Employing Thousands, Join the NRA Movement," *NYT*, p. 17, July 16, 1933.

23. "American Stores Bombed in Cuba," *NYT*, p. 7, October 18, 1933.

24. "Business Protests in Cuba on Labor," *NYT*, p. 18, December 29, 1933.

Chapter 10

1. Elsa Maxwell, *R.S.V.P.: Elsa Maxwell's Own Story* (Boston: Little, Brown, 1954), p. 200.

2. "Barbara Hutton Is Wed to Prince" *NYT*, p. 21, June 21, 1933; "Mob Balks Police at Hutton Bridal Rites," *NYT*, p. 14, June 23, 1933.

3. Maxwell, p. 204.

4. *Ibid.*, p. 205.

5. "Woolworth Donahue, 59, Heir to Chain Store Fortune, Dies," *NYT*, p. 46, April 6, 1972.

6. "Mayor Tells Reds They Prey on Poor," *NYT*, p. 1, June 3, 1934.

7. "Welfare Council Reports on Hospital Cases and Deaths," *NYT*, p. 25, June 1, 1934.

8. "Woolworth's Bans All German Goods," *NYT*, p. 11, March 21, 1934.

9. "West German Observer Asks Nazis Boycott Woolworth Stores," *NYT*, p. 28, June 4, 1934; a series continuing from June 6 through June 9, 1934.

10. "Miss Helena McCann Wed to Winston F.C. Guest at Oyster Bay," *NYT*, Part II, p. 5, June 3, 1934.

11. Maxwell, p. 204.

12. "Franklyn Hutton Visits Daughter in London Clinic," *NYT*, p. 7, June 2, 1934.

13. "Woolworth Co. Financial Report, 1933," *NYT*, p. 35, January 29, 1934.

14. "Quintuplets Born to Mrs. E. Dionne, Corbeil, Can.," *Toronto Daily Star*, p. 21, May 28, 1934.

15. Pierre Berton, *The Dionne Years: A Thirties Melodrama* (New York: W.W. Norton, 1977), pp. 37–38.

16. "Father Crawls Through Drainpipe for Visit," *NYT*, p. 23, June 28, 1936.

17. "Case Over Dionnes Opens," *NYT*, p. 1, September 28, 1938.

18. "Dr. Dafoe Wins Suit," *NYT*, p. 38, November 26, 1938.

19. Woolworth booklet, "100th Anniversary," p. 28.

20. Woolworth booklet, "100th Anniversary," p. 30.

21. "Barbara Hutton Gets Reno Decree on Extreme Cruelty Charge in 10 Minutes," *NYT*, p. 22, May 14, 1935.

22. "Princess Mdivani Weds Danish Count," *NYT*, p. 23, May 16, 1935.

23. "Count Haugwitz-Reventlow Says 'It's A Relief to Be Abroad,'" *NYT*, p. 23, June 6, 1935.

24. James Brough, *The Woolworths* (New York: McGraw-Hill, 1982), p. 192.

25. "Mdivani Is Killed in His Auto in Spain," *NYT*, p. 3, August 2, 1935.

26. "Countess Shows Grief" *NYT*, p. 2, August 9, 1935.

27. "Reventlow Stirs Romans by Cheering for Ethiopia," *NYT*, p. 2, September 26, 1935.

28. "Jimmy Donahue Is Forced to Leave Italy; Shouted 'Viva Ethiopia' at Rome Fascisti," *NYT*, p. 12, October 2, 1935.

29. Ronald Kessler, *The Season: Inside Palm Beach and America's Richest Society* (New York: Harper Collins, 1999), p. 45.

30. "Sale of Goods Up to 40 Cents Extended," *NYT*, p. 34, February 5, 1936.

31. "Woolworth Extends Merchandise Price to One Dollar," *NYT*, part III, p. 9, June 14, 1936.

32. "Serge Mdivani Is Killed Playing Polo in Florida," *NYT*, pp. 1 and 3, March 16, 1936.

33. "Woolworth Heir Is Born in London," *NYT*, p. 21, February 25, 1936.

34. "Countess Reventlow Seriously Ill," *NYT*, p. 14, March 3, 1936.

35. "Heir to Woolworth Fortune Christened," *NYT*, p. 9, June 20, 1936.

36. "History of Trade Traced in Exhibit," *NYT*, p. 19, March 3, 1936.

37. "Frasier W. McCann Weds Carol Ware," *NYT*, part 2, p. 3, August 23, 1936.

38. "Pay Row in London Menaces U.S. Play," *NYT*, p. 16, October 2, 1936.

39. "Ruth Etting Leaves U.S. Revue in London," *NYT*, p. 30, October 3, 1936.

40. "J.P. Donahue Here After Backing Play," *NYT*, p. 30, October 13, 1936.

Chapter 11

1. "Dionnes' Earnings Are Near Million," *NYT*, p. 23, March 26, 1937.

2. "Woolworth Shares Up 3 percent for 1936," *NYT*, part III, p. 9, February 7, 1937.

3. William Cahn, *A Pictorial History of American Labor* (New York: Crown, 1972), p. 263.

4. *Ibid.*, p. 264.

5. All information regarding a Detroit Woolworth store becoming first department store in the nation hit by a sit-down strike was acquired from the Historical Library files at the Waiters and Waitresses Union Headquarters, Detroit, and from interviews with Floyd Loew, Union organizer.

6. "Woolworth Girls Strike in 2 Stores," *NYT*, p. 1, March 18, 1937.

7. "Girls Scream, Weep As They Are Ousted from Woolworth Branch," *NYT*, p. 1, March 19, 1937.

8. "Woolworth Strikers Win Tentative Pact; Pay Rise Granted; Workers to Be Rehired," *NYT*, p. 17, March 30, 1937.

9. "Retailers, Wholesalers Form Group to Combat Chain Store Competition," *NYT*, part A, p. 10, July 27, 1937.

10. James Brough, *The Woolworths* (New York: McGraw-Hill, 1982), p. 189.

11. "Fact Finding Committee Appointed to Study Conditions for Workers in All 5–and–10 Shops," *NYT*, p. 17, December 17, 1937.

12. "Countess Haugwitz-Reventlow Renounces American Citizenship in Favor of Denmark," *NYT*, p. 3, December 17, 1937.

13. "Countess's Move to Benefit Heirs," *NYT*, p. 17, December 19, 1937.

14. "Haugwitz-Reventlows Visit India," *NYT*, p. 3, February 1, 1938.

15. "Lance Has Own Apartment in Parents' Winfield Home," *NYT*, part VI, p. 7, November 7, 1937.

16. "Count Freed in 2,000 Pounds Bail on Wife's Threat," *NYT*, p. 1, July 2, 1938.

17. "Woolworth Earns $33,176,509 in Year," *NYT*, p. 27, February 2, 1938.

18. Doris Kearns Goodwin, *The Fitzgeralds and the Kennedys* (New York: Simon and Schuster, 1987), p. 550.

19. "Buys Woolworth Loan," *NYT*, p. 35, August 12, 1937.

20. FML Hist.

21. "Realism in the Playroom," *NYT*, part IV, p. 9, February 19, 1939.

22. "Dr. Dafoe Wins Suit on Dionnes' Contract," *NYT*, p. 23, September 30, 1938.

23. John K. Winkler, *Five and Ten: The Fabulous Life of F. W. Woolworth* (Freeport, New York: Books for Libraries, 1940), p. 242.

24. "Haugwitz Dispute Rises Over Child," *NYT*, pp. 1 and 4, June 23, 1938.

25. "Haugwitz Reunion Believed Unlikely," *NYT*, p. 15, June 19, 1938.

26. "F.L. Hutton Attempts Reconciliation," *NYT*, p. 17, June 25, 1938.

27. "Reconciliation Believed Impossible," *NYT*, p. 13, June 27, 1938.

28. "Wife Gave 2 Millions to Alexis Mdivani," *NYT*, p. 23, May 6, 1938.

29. "Dispute Over Child," *NYT*, pp. 1 and 4, July 23, 1938.

30. "Haugwitzes Part, Both Sign a Deed," *NYT*, p. 15, July 30, 1938.

31. "Mrs. Charles McCann, Woolworth Daughter, Dies," *NYT*, p. 23, March 16, 1938.

32. Goodwin, p. 592.

33. *Ibid.*, p. 568.

34. *The Dionnes*, p. 184.

35. Alan Jenkins, *The Forties* (New York: Universe Books, 1977), p. 16.

36. "Barbara Hutton Sails," *NYT*, p. 2, October 14, 1939.

37. "Hutton Renounces Wife," *NYT*, p. 16, October 19, 1939.

38. "Hutton Recalls Statement," *NYT*, p. 23, November 22, 1939.

39. Woolworth booklet, "100th Anniversary," p. 52.

Chapter 12

1. "Woolworth Donahue, Store Heir, Weds Ex-Wife of John Hearst in Palm Beach," *NYT*, p. 1, January 28, 1940.

2. "Countess Denies She Will Wed," *NYT*, p. 16, February 9, 1940.

3. "Mdivani Estate Settled," *NYT*, p. 25, March 7, 1940.

4. Maureen Donaldson and William Royce, *An Affair to Remember: My life with Cary Grant* (New York: Putnam, 1989), p. 204.

5. "Countess's $10,000 Assists Red Cross," *NYT*, p. 31, June 11, 1940; "Gives Pay to Red Cross," p. 4, October 5, 1940.

6. "Barbara Hutton Files as Alien," *NYT*, p. 3, September 8, 1940.

7. "Count Seeking News of Divorce," *NYT*, p. 12, August 1, 1940.

8. "Mrs. Gompers in C.I.O. Job," *NYT*, p. 3, July 8, 1940.

9. "Toy Show Previews," *NYT*, p. 20, October 22, 1940; p. 34, October 23, 1940.

10. "Woolworth 1940 Financial Reports," *NYT*, p. 28, January 29, 1941.

11. "Franklyn Hutton, Retired Broker, 63; Father of Woolworth Heiress, Former Barbara Hutton, Dies on Estate in South," *NYT*, p. 23, December 6, 1940.

12. "F.L. Hutton Estate Is Left to Widow," *NYT*, p. 38, December 15, 1940.

13. C. David Heymann, *Poor Little Rich Girl: Life and Legend of Barbara Hutton* (New York: Random House, 1983), p. 173.

14. "Haugwitz Reventlows' Divorce Decree Final," *NYT*, p. 23, March 6, 1941.

15. "Woolworth Cuts Quarterly Dividend to 40c; Directors Act to Meet Heavier Tax Burden," *NYT*, p. 29, July 10, 1941.

16. "Woolworth Tower Closed," *NYT*, p. 29, July 10, 1941.

17. "$26,114,372 Net for Woolworth," *NYT*, p. 36, February 2, 1942.

18. "British Subsidiary's Income 6,404.759 Pounds Before Taxes— German Losses Set," *NYT*, p. 36, February 2, 1942.

19. "Blackout Doll Patented," *NYT*, Part II, p. 7, December 28, 1941.

20. "Cary Grant Becomes American Citizen," *NYT*, p. 9, June 27, 1942.

21. "Barbara Hutton, Former Bride of Prince and then of Count, Is Bride at Secret Ceremony in California Mountains," *NYT*, p. 23, July 9, 1942.

22. "HaugwitzReventlow Weds Astor Kin in West," *NYT*, p. 12, July 30, 1942.

23. "M'Cann Art Sale Realizes $266,382," *NYT*, p. 55, November 22, 1942.

24. *People*, August 4, 1997.

25. FML Hist.

26. "Fined for Blackout Violations," *NYT*, p. 37, April 23, 1943.

27. "OPA Charges Chains Exceeded Ceilings," *NYT*, p. 39, September 9, 1943.

28. "American Toy Fair," *NYT*, p. 27, March 7, 1944.

29. "Ex-Husband Sues Barbara Hutton," *NYT*, p. 30, May 27, 1944.

30. "Court Order Issued Restraining Barbara's Language in Presence of Son," *NYT*, p. 22, June 8, 1944.

31. "Miss Hutton's Plea Fails; Coast District Attorney Refuses to Accuse Count of Child-stealing," *NYT*, p. 21, July 20, 1944.

32. "Miss Hutton Gave Count 3 Millions," *NYT*, p. 21, July 25, 1944.

33. "Grants Make Reconciliation Statement," *NYT*, p. 15, October 3, 1944.

34. "War Toys Give Way to Those of Peace," *NYT*, p. 16, October 31, 1944.

35. "OPA Pricing Process on Toys," *NYT*, p. 17, October 17, 1944.

36. "James Paul Donahue Classified 1A in Draft," *NYT*, p. 23, November 3, 1944.

37. "Woolworth Heir Drafted; Donahue, Barbara Hutton's Cousin, Is Inducted into Army," *NYT*, p. 36, November 10, 1944.

38. "Pvt. James P. Donahue Charges in G.H. Williams Injury Dismissed," *NYT*, p. 21, April 20, 1945.

39. Charles Higham, *The Duchess of Windsor: The Secret Life* (New York: McGraw-Hill, 1988), p. 371.

40. "Cary Grant Separates from Wife, 2nd Time," *NYT*, p. 25, February 27, 1945.

41. "Radar Factory Has All of Stamford's Marbles," *NYT*, p. 11, July 28, 1945.

42. "U.S. Lists Seizures by Soviet in Berlin," *NYT*, p. 8, August 17, 1945.

43. Woolworth booklet,"100th Anniversary," p. 30.

44. "Capt. Winston F.C. Guest Gets Soldier's Medal," p. 4, *NYT*, December 27, 1945.

45. "Barbara Hutton Sues for Third Divorce; Charges Grant Caused 'Mental Anguish'," *NYT*, p. 34, September 1, 1946.

46. "Woolworth booklet, "75th Anniversary.""

Chapter 13

1. Woolworth booklet, "100th Anniversary," p. 30.

2. FML Hist., Scrapbook of N. Jefferson County.

3. "U.S. Accepts Mrs. Barbara Hutton's Offer of London Residence as Home of Embassy," *NYT*, p. 6, August 2, 1946.

4. "Painting Presented to the National Gallery in Washington," *NYT*, p. 42, February 24, 1946.

5. Marion Coburn Standish interview.

6. *Ibid.*

7. Ralph G. Martin, *The Woman He Loved* (New York: Simon and Schuster, 1973), p. 515.

8. "Mrs. James P. Donahue Sells Florida Home," *NYT*, p. 46, April 11, 1946.

9. "Woolworth Attorney Opposes NYS Minimum Wage Order," *NYT*, p. 16, May 2, 1946.

10. Woolworth booklet, "100th Anniversary," p. 20.

11. "Barbara Hutton Buys Home in Tangier," *NYT*, p. 4, September 3, 1946.

12. *U.S. News & World Report*, November 29, 1999.

13. "*Salute* Magazine Purchase Reported," *NYT*, p. 17, June 15, 1946.

14. "Imports to U.S. of German Toys for Christmas," *NYT*, p. 23, July 3, 1946.

15. Woolworth booklet, "100th Anniversary," p. 30.

16. "Woolworth NYC Store Fined for Sanitary Code Violations," *NYT*, p. 14, August 12, 1946; p. 4, September 2, 1946.

17. "Labor Strikes Spread," *NYT*, p. 14, August 12; p. 4, September 27, 1946.

18. "British Woolworth Report," *NYT*, p. 22, February 10, 1946.

19. "Barbara Hutton to Wed," *NYT*, p. 21, February 21, 1947.

20. "Barbara Hutton Marries Prince Igor Troubetzkoy in Zurich, Switzerland," *NYT*, p. 27, March 4, 1947.

21. "Negotiations with Wholesale and Warehouse Workers Union 65 Break," *NYT*, p. 4, June 22, 1947.

22. William Cahn, *A Pictorial History of American Labor* (New York: Crown, 1972), pp. 281–282.

23. "Woolworth's 1947 Income Highest in History," *NYT*, p. 18, February 14, 1948.

24. "Barbara Hutton Undergoes 2nd Operation," *NYT*, p. 21, February 2, 1948.

25. Maureen Donaldson and William Royce, *An Affair to Remember: My Life With Cary Grant* (New York: Putnam, 1989), p. 204.

26. "Store Union Backs Congress Defiers," *NYT*, p. 15, July 22, 1948.

27. "Employees of 2 Woolworth Warehouses to Take Strike Vote," *NYT*, p. 46, July 13, 1948.

28. "Warfare Flares in Unions' Disputes," *NYT*, p. 6, August 14, 1948.

29. "500 Woolworth Stores Picketed in Union's Drive in U.S., Canada," *NYT*, p. 1, August 1, 1948.

30. "Dave Beck of Seattle Is the Moving Spirit in Merging Warehouse and Store Workers into Own Unit of About 1,000," *NYT*, p. 14, January 27, 1949.

31. "Mrs. Barbara Hutton Troubetzkoy Undergoes Operation," *NYT*, p. 28, February 8, 1949.

32. "Two National Chains to Open Texas Units," *NYT*, p. 33, November 14, 1949.

Chapter 14

1. "National Association of Variety Stores Convention in New York" *NYT*, p. 40, March 15, 1950.

2. "NLRB Rules Against Woolworth; Sets Aside June 7 Election," *NYT*, p. 28, June 14, 1950.

3. "Woolworth 1950 Financial Report," *NYT*, p. 35, February 16, 1951.

4. "British-Woolworth Financial Report," *NYT*, p. 35, February 16, 1951.

5. "Woolworth to Sell New Records," *NYT*, p. 34, February 2, 1951.

6. "Christmas Sales Expected to Surpass Last Year's Volume," *NYT*, p. 48, November 22, 1951.

7. Paul Harvey's radio show and Internet.

8. Joyce Hawkins interview.

9. "Woolworth's to Try Out Self-Service Store Here," *NYT*, p. 31, August 23, 1952.

10. "New Doll Does What Babies Do When Basic Trick Is Applied," *NYT*, p. 19, August 16, 1952.

11. *F.W. Woolworth Co.* v. *Contemporary Arts Inc.*, U.S. Supreme Court, Nov.17, 1952; Decided December 23, 1952.

12. "Woolworth 1952 Annual Report," *NYT*, p. 30, February 13, 1953.

13. FML Hist., Scrapbook of N. Jefferson County; Woolworth booklet, "100th Anniversary," pp. 27–28.

14. "Princess Troubetzkoy Denies Offering Husband Money for Divorce," *NYT*, p. 35, March 18, 1951.

15. "Mexican Court Upholds Divorce," *NYT*, p. 8, August 23, 1951.

16. Charles Higham, *The Duchess of Windsor: The Secret Life* (New York: McGraw-Hill, 1988), pp. 394–395.

17. "Woolworth Building Observes 40th Year As City Landmark," *NYT*, part VIII, p. 1, April 12, 1953.

18. Woolworth booklet, "100th Anniversary," p. 30.

19. *Ibid.*, p. 31.

20. "Barbara Hutton in Hospital for Checkup," *NYT*, p. 50, January 25, 1953.

21. James Brough, *The Woolworths* (New York: McGraw-Hill, 1982), p. 180.

22. Pony Duke and Jason Thomas, *Too Rich: The Family Secrets of Doris Duke* (New York: Harper Collins, 1996), p. 139.

23. Zsa Zsa Gabor and Wendy Leigh, *One Lifetime Is Not Enough* (New York: Delacorte, 1981), p. 126.

24. "Barbara Hutton Wed to Rubirosa; Heiress Becomes the Bride of Dominican Envoy — Nuptials Not Recognized by State," *NYT*, p. 9, December 31, 1953.

25. "Mrs. Rubirosa Breaks Ankle," *NYT*, p. 42, January 8, 1954.

26. Gabor and Leigh, p. 127.

27. *Fortune* magazine, February 1954.

28. "Barbara Hutton Denies Seeking French Divorce," *NYT*, p. 22, June 25, 1954.

29. "Sales Record Set by Woolworth Company," *NYT*, p. 45, February 11, 1954.

30. Woolworth booklet, "100th Anniversary," p. 31.

31. "Emily Dionne Dies of Stroke at Age 20," *NYT*, p. 1, August 7, 1954.

32. "Frailest Quintuplet Is Ill," *NYT*, p. 21, December 1, 1954.

33. "Dionne Sisters' Trust Fund," *NYT*, p. 9, May 29, 1955.

34. "Woolworth Annual Report, 1954," *NYT*, p. 14, February 10, 1955.

35. "F.W. Woolworth Sets Sales Peak; Highest Volume in 76 Years Puts '55 Net at $34,155,898," *NYT*, p. 41, February 16, 1956.

36. "Von Cramm Weds Barbara Hutton," *NYT*, p. 17, November 9, 1955.

37. Pierre Burton, *The Dionne Years: A Thirties Melodrama* (New York: W.W. Norton, 1977), pp. 209–211.

38. "Winston Guest Sues to Revoke Trust," *NYT*, p. 29, August 13, 1954.

39. "Mrs. F.E. Guest, Society Leader," *NYT*, p. 39, October 8, 1959.

40. "Wealthiest Americans Listed," *NYT*, October 28, 1957.

41. "Old Aldrich Estate Sold for $400,000," *NYT*, part VIII, p. 1, August 19, 1956.

42. Woolworth booklet, "100th Anniversary," p. 31.

43. "N.L.R.B. Is Upheld on Payroll Data," *NYT*, p. 46, December 11, 1956.

44. Woolworth booklet, "100th Anniversary," p. 31.

45. "Arts Center Gets Gift," *NYT*, p. 28, June 1, 1959.

46. "Lincoln Center Gets $100,000 Gift," *NYT*, p. 28, June 1, 1959.

47. "Anchorage, Alaska Store Planned," *NYT*, p. 30, May 2, 1959.

48. Woolworth booklet, "100th Anniversary," p. 52.

Chapter 15

1. Detroit Public Library, Burton Historical Collection; S.S. Kresge file.

2. "The Woolworth Lunch Counter," *Greensboro News & Record*, p. 1, February 2, 1960.

3. Only photo (taken by Jack Moebes) of first four black sit-in students walking away from Woolworth Store in Greensboro, N.C., on February 1, 1960. *Greensboro News & Record*, February 2, 1960, p. 1.

4. "White Students Act," *NYT*, p. 12, February 5, 1960.

5. "Clan Tries to Halt Negroes' Protest," *NYT*, p. 20, February 6, 1960.

6. "Negro Protests Lead to Store Closings," *NYT*, p. 35, February 7, 1960.

7. "Integration Armistice," *NYT*, p. 14, February 8, 1960.

8. "Negroes' Sitdown Hits 2 More Cities," *NYT*, p. 16, February 9, 1960.

9. "Local Customs," *NYT*, p. 22, February 13, 1960.

10. "A Negro Sitdown Ends in Fist Fight," *NYT*, p. 18, February 16, 1960.

11. William L. O'Neill, *Coming Apart: An Informal History of America in the 1960s* (Chicago: Quadrangle Books, 1971), p. 158.

12. "Johnson Assures Civil Rights Test; Accused of Trick," *NYT*, p. 1, February 16, 1960.

13. "Powell Defends His Use of Frank,"*NYT*, p. 15, March 3, 1960.

14. "Sitdown Staged at Counter Here," *NYT*, p. 1, April 3, 1960.

15. "Meany and Reuther Support Chain-Store Boycotts," *NYT*, p. 38, April 20, 1960.

16. "3 Arlington Stores End Racial Policies," *NYT*, p. 33, June 23, 1960; "Sit-In Victories End Where They Began," *NYT*, p. 1, July 26, 1960.

17. "Chain Stores Report," *NYT*, p. 21, October 21, 1960.

18. "Goal for Woolworth Sales at $1 Billion for This Year," Woolworth booklet, "100th Anniversary," p. 7.

19. "Jill St. John Weds Lance Reventlow," *NYT*, p. 19, March 25, 1960.

20. "Reventlow's Dream Cars Fail," *NYT*, part V, p. 1, July 3, 1960.

21. "Jill St.John Sues Reventlow," *NYT*, p. 19, July 12, 1962.

22. "Woolworth Donahue Marries Mrs. J.C. Church," *NYT*, p. 36, November 4, 1962.

23. "Hutton Divorce Disclosed," *NYT*, p. 42, February 8, 1962.

24. "F.W. Woolworth," *NYT*, p. 38, February 26, 1962.

25. Woolworth booklet, "100th Anniversary," p. 31.

26. *Ibid.*, p. 32.

27. "Woolworth Center of Music Is Dedicated," *NYT*, p. 4, May 3, 1964.

28. Detroit Public Library, Arts and Entertainment Dept.

29. "Vietnamese Prince Weds Miss Hutton," *NYT*, p. 10, April 8, 1964.

30. "Barbara Hutton Given High Laotian Honor, *NYT*, p. 87, November 8, 1964.

31. "Lance Reventlow Marries on Coast," *NYT*, p. 42, November 9, 1964.

32. "Woolworth Is Expanding Department Store Division," *NYT*, p. 49, November 6, 1964.

Chapter 16

1. "Worth Mart Post Filled," *NYT*, p. 44, January 21, 1965.

2. "Woolworth Sets Earnings Record," *NYT*, p. 37, February 26, 1965.

3. "Barbara Hutton in Hospital," *NYT*, p. 19, February 10, 1965.

4. "A Granddaughter of Woolworth Dies," *NYT*, p. 39, May 16, 1965.

5. "Art Sale Begins at Woolworth," *NYT*, p. 32, May 8, 1965.

6. "Woolworth Returning to 14th Street After 7 Years," *NYT*, p. 72, October 27, 1965.

7. "Malroux on a Tour of "New Versailles," *NYT*, p. 18, June 19, 1965.

8. "$114,000 Hutton Theft Seen," *NYT*, p. 2, January 6, 1966.

9. "James P. Donahue Found Dead; Heir to Woolworth Fortune, 51," *NYT*, p. 47, December 8, 1966.

10. "Death of Donahue Attributed to Alcohol and Barbiturates," *NYT*, p. 50, December 14, 1966.

11. John P. Nichols, *The Skyline Queen and the Merchant Prince* (New York: Trident, 1973), p. 129.

12. "Profit Mark Set by Woolworth," *NYT*, p. 45, February 11, 1966.

13. "Woolworth Agrees to Purchase Gateway Sporting Goods Co.," *NYT*, p. 61, June 29, 1966.

14. "Next at Woolworth: Franchises," *NYT*, pp. 49, 57– 58, July 27, 1966.

15. Woolworth booklet, "100th Anniversary," p. 33.

16. *Ibid.*

17. "Woolworth to Expand in Harlem," *NYT*, part VIII, p. 56, November 5, 1967.

18. *W* magazine, September 1999.

19. "Winston Guest to Sell $500,000 in Antiques at Auction Tomorrow," *NYT*, p. 41, December 1, 1967.

20. *NYT*, p. 84, December 3, 1967.

21. Woolworth booklet, "100th Anniversary," p. 33.

22. "Barbara Hutton, 56, Seeks Divorce from 7th Husband," NYT, p. 83, May 11, 1969.

23. "Brooklyn Store Firebombed," *NYT*, p. 43, July 1, 1969.

24. "Woolworth Store is Razed by Flames in Puerto Rico," *NYT*, p. 68, September 21, 1969.

25. "Three Bombs Exploded in Doorways Here," *NYT*, p. 39, December 22, 1969.

26. "Puerto Rican Group Describes Bombings," *NYT*, p. 4, February 13, 1970.

27. "Woolworth Changes the Guard," *NYT*, p. 93, December 11, 1969.

28. "British Holders Hit Woolworth," *NYT*, p. 4, March 7, 1970.

29. "9 Fire Devices Damage Goods in Woolworth's on Times Sq.," *NYT*, p. 33, June 7, 1970.

30. "Fire Bombs in 3 Woolworths," *NYT*, p. 47, July 1, 1970.

31. "Robbery of 2 Woolworth Managers," *NYT*, p. 1, September 13, 1970.

32. "Woolworth Set to Open Its Largest Store," *NYT*, p. 57, September 11, 1970.

33. "Wind-Swept City Beset by Blazes," *NYT*, p. 74, February 3, 1971.

34. "F. W. Woolworth Sees Sales Rise," *NYT*, p. 59, May 20, 1971.

35. "Notes on People," *NYT*, p. 35, June 17, 1971.

36. "Mrs. Jessie Donahue Dies; Woolworth's Daughter, 82," *NYT*, p. 50, November 19, 1971.

37. "Woolworth Sees Sales Rise," *NYT*, p. 27, July 8, 1972.

Chapter 17

1. Woolworth booklet, "100th Anniversary," p. 33.

2. "Woolworth Told to Cut Meal Costs," *NYT*, pp. 1 and 12, April 26, 1972.

3. "Woolworth Donahue, 59, Heir to Chain Store Fortune, Dies," *NYT*, p. 46, April 6, 1972.

4. "Lance Reventlow, Barbara Hutton's Son, Killed," *NYT*, p. 40, July 26, and p. 37, July 27, 1972.

5. "Incendiary Table Tennis-Balls Set Fires in 4 Midtown Stores," *NYT*, p. 1, August 19, 1972.

6. "F.W. Woolworth," *NYT*, p. 67, March 1, 1973.

7. "Woolworth to Buy Gateway Inventory," *NYT*, p. 41, January 20, 1973.

8. FML Hist.

9. "Merchants Go Electronic," *NYT*, part III, pp. 1 and 9, October 28, 1973.

10. *NYT*, 1974 Index (Woolworth).

11. "Sales of Chain Stores Gained 12.6 percent in March," *NYT*, p. 54, April 30, 1974.

12. "President Edward F. Gibbons Resigns," *NYT*, p. 57, June 12, 1975.

13. "W.T. Grant Faced a $300 Million Loss Before Bankruptcy," *NYT*, pp. 41 and 51, January 27, 1976.

14. "Gibbons Returns to Head Woolworth," *NYT*, p. 58, July 15, 1976.

15. "Woolworth to Sell Its Credit Operation," *NYT*, p. 57, September 14, 1976.

16. "Notes on People," *NYT*, p. 55, December 2, 1976.

17. David C. Heymann, *Poor Little Rich Girl: Life and Legend of Barbara Hutton* (New York: Random House, 1983), p. 358.

18. "Notes on People," *NYT*, part III, p. 2, July 7, 1977.

19. "Notes on People," *NYT*, p. 13, July 28, 1978.

20. "Woolworth Set to Add 240 Retail Outlets," *NYT*, part IV, p. 7, March 22, 1977.

21. "Woolworth Uses Grant Stores," *NYT*, part IV p. 1, March 30, 1977.

22. "11 Rhodesians Killed in a Bomb Explosion," *NYT*, p. 8, August 7, 1977.

23. Woolworth booklet, "100th Anniversary," p. 34.

24. "Clearer Focus on Retailers' Leases," *NYT*, p. 8, March 6, 1978.

25. "Rockower Directors Support Liquidation," *NYT*, part IV, p. 4, August 3, 1979.

26. *NYT*, 1979 Index (Woolworth '78 report).

27. "Woolworth's at 100: A Tuneful Bit of Five and Dime Nostalgia," *NYT*, p. 18, February 24, 1979.

28. "British Woolworth's Troubles," *NYT*, Business Section, pp. 1 and 29, May 29, 1979.

29. "Branscan Tells Reasons for Bid," *NYT*, part IV, p. 11, May 9, 1979.

30. "Branscan Drops Its Bid for Woolworth," *NYT*, part IV, p. 1, May 30, 1979.

31. "Barbara Hutton Dies on Coast at 66," *NYT*, p. 1, May 13, 1979.

Chapter 18

1. "Woolworth Unit," *NYT*, part IV, p. 3, December 30, 1980.

2. "British Woolworth's Troubles," *NYT*, p. 27, August 30, 1980.

3. "Woolworth 1981 Income Drops," *NYT*, part IV, p. 5, March p. 3, 1982.

4. "The Retreat of the Mass Merchants," *NYT*, part III, pp. 1 and 24, February 21, 1982.

5. *Ibid.*, p. 24.

6. "A Life Renewed for 'Cathedral Of Commerce'," *NYT*, part II, p. 1, October 27, 1982.

7. "Woolworth Net Declines 46.8 percent," *NYT*, part IV, p. 5, March 11, 1982.

8. *Ibid.*

9. "The Retreat of the Mass Merchants," *NYT*, part III, p. 1, February 21, 1982.

10. "13 Woolco Stores to Close," *NYT*, p. 19, March 31, 1982.

11. "The Foot Locker Chain's Rapid Rise," *NYT*, part IV, p. 4, March 25, 1982.

12. "Woolworth Calls It Quits on Woolco," *NYT*, p. 39, September 25, 1982.

13. "Woolworth Finds Buyer for Its British Holdings," *NYT*, part IV, p. 17, October 1, 1982.

14. "Edward F. Gibbons, Chairman of Woolworth," *NYT*, p. 25, Oct. 27, 1982.

15. "Variety—And Profits—at Woolworth's," *NYT*, part III, pp. 6 and 7, February 5, 1984.

16. "F.W. Woolworth to Open Two Specialty Stores," *NYT*, part IV, p. 3, February 15, 1985.

17. "Woolworth Financial Report, 1983," *NYT*, part III, p. 4, November 24, 1985.

18. "Retailers' Sales Gains," *NYT*, part IV, p. 8, February 1, 1985.

19. "Woolworth's New Wager," *NYT*, part III, p. 8, November 24, 1985.

20. *Crain's Detroit Business*, March 17, 1987.

21. "Dart Shows Interest in Woolworth," *NYT*, part IV, pp. 1 and 17, April 5, 1988.

22. "Woolworth Profit Rises," *NYT*, part IV, p. 3, August 11, 1988.

23. "Briefs," *NYT*, part IV, p. 3, October 14, 1988.

24. "Residents Campaigning to Keep Woolworth Store in Rye," *NYT*, pp. 1 and 8, May 27, 1990.

25. "Income Slides at Woolworth," *NYT*, p. 5, May 9, 1991.

Chapter 19

1. "Woolworth Plans Up to 4,900 Stores," *NYT*, part IV, p. 4, June 21, 1991.

2. "Profit Off 58 percent at Woolworth," *NYT*, part IV, p. 4, August 8, 1991.

3. "Woolworth Reports Major 1991 Loss," *NYT*, part IV, p. 6, March 4, 1992.

4. "Woolworth Corp.," *NYT*, part IV, p. 6, March 4, 1993.

5. "Woolworth Picks New Chief for Its Variety Store Unit," *NYT*, part IV, p. 6, September 9, 1993.

6. "Woolworth Plans to Open 800 Stores This Year," *NYT*, part IV, p. 5, March 17, 1993.

7. "Fire Destroys Store in Harlem," *NYT*, part II, p. 7, September 2, 1993.

8. "Scene of Sit-In Laid to Rest by Closing of Woolworth's," *NYT*, part I, p. 8, October 16, 1993.

9. "Five and Dimes Closing by the Hundreds," *NYT*, part I, p. 8, October 16, 1993.

10. "Woolworth Corporation," *NYT*, part IV, p. 5, November 11, 1993.

11. "Wal-Mart Takes Over Canadian Woolcos," *NYT*, part I, p. 39, January 15, 1994.

12. "Suppliers Given Warning on Woolworth Shipments," *NYT*, part IV, pp. 1 and 2, April 1, 1994.

13. United States Securities & Exchange Commission litigation release #15794.

14. "Suppliers Given Warning on Woolworth Shipments," *NYT*, part IV, p. 1, April 1, 1994.

15. "Two Top Woolworth Officials Will Step Aside," *NYT*, part IV, pp. 1 and 3, April 4, 1994.

16. "Woolworth Nearly Halves Its Dividend," *NYT*, part IV, p. 5, July 14, 1994.

17. "Woolworth, for First Time, Goes Outside for a Chairman," *NYT*, part IV, pp. 1 and 6, December 13, 1994.

18. "Woolworth to Cut 2,000 Jobs in an Effort to Reduce Costs," *NYT*, part IV, p. 3, February 2, 1995.

19. "Dow Average to Replace 4 Stocks to Better Reflect the U.S. Economy," *NYT*, part IV, pp. 1 and 8, March 13, 1997.

20. *U.S. News and World Report*, July 19, 1997.

21. "Retail Pioneer Woolworth Will Close All Stores; the 117–year-old Chain, Which Includes

Two Las Vegas Locations, Bows to Competition of Larger Stores," *Las Vegas Review Journal*, July 18, 1997.

22. "First Day of Business for Venator Group," *NYT*, part IV, p. 4, June 12, 1998.

23. "Venator Is Selling Its Last Woolworth Stores," NYT, part III, p. 3, September 23, 1998.

24. "Witkoff Group Renovating Woolworth Building," *NYT*, part II, p. 8, February 24, 1999.

25. John Compton Collection.

Bibliography

Periodicals

Crain's Detroit Business
People

U.S. News & World Report
W

Newspapers

Ann Arbor News
Detroit Free Press
Detroit News
Greensboro News and Record

Las Vegas Review-Journal
New York Times
Syracuse Herald American
Toronto Daily Star

Libraries and Museums

Carnegie Public Library, Ishpeming, Michigan
    Vertical files
Detroit Public Library Burton Historical Collection
    Arts and Entertainment Collection
Flower Memorial Library, Watertown, N.Y.
    Genealogy Department
    Historical Archives Department (Scrapbooks of N. Jefferson County; Frank Woolworth's letters)
Henry Ford Centennial Library, Dearborn, Michigan
Jefferson County Historical Society Museum, Watertown, N.Y.
University of Michigan Library, Dearborn, Michigan
Waiters and Waitresses Union, Detroit headquarters
    Historical Library

Woolworth Booklets

"Above the Clouds of Old New York"
"The Cathedral of Commerce"
"Fortieth Anniversary Souvenir" (1919)
"Fiftieth Anniversary"

"60 Years of Woolworth"
"75th Anniversary"
"100th Anniversary"

Books

Adams, James Truslow. *The Epic of America.* New York: Blue Ribbon Books, 1941.
Arce, Hector. *Gary Cooper: An Intimate Biography.* New York: William Morrow, 1979.

Berton, Pierre. *The Dionne Years: A Thirties Melodrama*. New York: W.W. Norton, 1977.

Brough, James. *The Woolworths*. New York: McGraw- Hill, 1982.

Cahn, William. *A Pictorial History of American Labor*. New York: Crown, 1972.

Donaldson, Maureen, and Royce, William. *An Affair to Remember: My Life with Cary Grant*. New York: Putnam, 1989.

Duke, Pony, and Thomas, Jason. *Too Rich: The Family Secrets of Doris Duke*. New York: Harper-Collins, 1996.

Furnas, J.C. *The Americans: A Social History of the United States 1587–1914*. New York: Putnam, 1969.

Gabor, Zsa Zsa, and Wendy Leigh. *One Lifetime Is Not Enough*. New York: Delacorte, 1981.

Goodwin, Doris Kearns. *The Fitzgeralds and the Kennedys*. New York: Simon and Schuster, 1987.

Heymann, C. David. *Poor Little Rich Girl: Life and Legend of Barbara Hutton*. New York: Random House, 1983.

Higham, Charles. *The Duchess of Windsor: The Secret Life*. New York: McGraw-Hill, 1988.

Jenkins, Alan. *The Forties*. New York: Universe, 1977.

Kessler, Ronald. *The Season: Inside Palm Beach and America's Richest Society*. New York: Harper Collins, 1999.

Lacey, Robert. *Ford: The Men and the Machine*. Boston: Little, Brown,1986.

Lord, Walter. *The Good Years*. New York: Harper & Brothers, 1960.

Martin, Ralph G. *The Woman He Loved*. New York: Simon and Schuster, 1973.

Maxwell, Elsa. *R.S.V.P.: Elsa Maxwell's Own Story*. Boston: Little, Brown, 1954.

Nichols, John P. *Skyline Queen and the Merchant Prince*. New York: Trident, 1973.

O'Neill, William L. *Coming Apart: An Informal History of America in the 1960s*. New York: Quadrangle, 1971.

Thomas, Gordon, and Morgan-Witts, Max. *The Day the Bubble Burst*. New York: Doubleday, 1979.

Winkler, John Kennedy. *Five and Ten: The Fabulous Life of F.W. Woolworth*. Freeport, New York: Books for Libraries, 1940.

General References

Funk & Wagnalls Encyclopedia

Guidebook to New York City

New York Times Indexes and Obituary Listings

Wells, H.G. *The Outline Of History, Vol. II*. New York: Doubleday, 1949.

Interviews

Compton, John, manager for Woolworth stores.

Fargo, Helen, historian for Woolworth Memorial Methodist Church, Great Bend, New York.

Hawkins, Joyce, memories of shopping at Woolworth.

Loew, Floyd, Detroit union organizer in the 1930s.

Macari, Cheryl, memories of shopping at Woolworth.

Standish, Marion Coburn, Dodge social secretary.

Index